Even the Good Girls Will Cry

Even the Good Girls Will Cry

My 90s Rock Memoir

Melissa Auf der Maur

Atlantic Books
London

First published in Great Britain in 2026 by Atlantic Books, an imprint of Atlantic Books Ltd.

First published in the United States of America in 2026 by Da Capo, an imprint of Grand Central Publishing

Copyright © 2026 by Melissa Auf der Maur

The moral right of Melissa Auf der Maur to be identified as the author of this work has been asserted by her in accordance with the Copyright, Designs and Patents Act of 1988.

All rights reserved. No part of this book may be reproduced or transmitted in any form or by any means, electronic or mechanical, including photocopying, recording or by any information storage and retrieval system, without prior permission in writing from the publisher.

Every effort has been made to trace or contact all copyright-holders. The publishers will be pleased to make good any omissions or rectify any mistakes brought to their attention at the earliest opportunity.

No part of this book may be used in any manner in the learning, training or development of generative artificial intelligence technologies (including but not limited to machine learning models and large language models (LLMs)), whether by data scraping, data mining or use in any way to create or form a part of data sets or in any other way.

A CIP catalogue record for this book is available from the British Library.

Additional copyright/credits information is on page 413.

Excerpt from *Hit So Hard: A Memoir* copyright © 2017 by Patty Schemel

Print book interior design by Amy Quinn.

Hardback ISBN 978 1 80546 101 2
Export trade paperback ISBN 978 1 80546 638 3
E-book ISBN 978 1 80546 102 9

Printed and bound by CPI (UK) Ltd, Croydon CR0 4YY

10 9 8 7 6 5 4 3 2 1

Atlantic Books
An imprint of Atlantic Books Ltd
Ormond House
26–27 Boswell Street
London WC1N 3JZ

www.atlantic-books.co.uk

Product safety EU representative: Authorised Rep Compliance Ltd., Ground Floor, 71 Lower Baggot Street, Dublin, D02 P593, Ireland. www.arccompliance.com

For my daughter River, and all the girls.

The turn of a millennium rarely
happens in a lifetime.

This is a story about the decade that defined
me and my generation, 1991–2001.

I would never wish for another time
to come into my womanhood.

Contents

Introduction: Through the Looking Glass *1*

    Act I ✹ Magic

    Dreamscape #1: Even the Good Girls Will Cry *16*

Chapter 1: Dreamy Frontline Feminist *19*
Chapter 2: The Saint and the Wall. *29*
Chapter 3: The City, She Raised Me *41*
Chapter 4: Late Bloomer, Music Lover *49*
Chapter 5: Moving in New Directions *59*
Chapter 6: A Couch to Crash on, a Beer Bottle, and the Apology. *67*
Chapter 7: 1991: The Song That Changed Everything *77*

    Dreamscape #2: 3D Sound. *85*

Chapter 8: Grounding the Fairy *87*
Chapter 9: Vermont and the Satin Minidress *91*
Chapter 10: Sunburst Precision *97*
Chapter 11: Death Rears Its Head *109*
Chapter 12: One-Way Ticket to Seattle *115*

    Nick Auf der Maur Column Interlude # 1
    "Bass Guitar Indulgence Turned Out to Be a Great Investment" *125*

Act II ✱ Music

    Melissa's Dream of the '90s Playlist. *129*

Chapter 13: The Self-Destruct Tour:
Nine Inch Nails and Marilyn Manson *131*

    Live Through This Tour: 1994–1995 . . . . *144*

Chapter 14: Warrior Goddess *147*

Chapter 15: Sensory Overload *163*

    Nick Auf der Maur Column Interlude #2
    "On Tour with My Daughter, the Rock Star from Ca-Na-Da". *166*

Chapter 16: Down Under *169*

Chapter 17: Hole Goes to Therapy and Gets Unplugged *183*

Chapter 18: Engaging with Hole *189*

Chapter 19: The Abscess and the French Hospital *193*

Chapter 20: Funny Shit and the Smoking Vagina *201*

Chapter 21: Hole Is a Band; Courtney Love Is a Soap Opera *205*

Chapter 22: The Arctic Circle, Madonna, and MTV *219*

Chapter 23: The Witch of New Orleans *227*

Chapter 24: For Love and Honor *241*

Chapter 25: Rhythm-Section Sisters *243*

Act III 👁 Death

Chapter 26: Sick Nick and Music on the Rise 255

    Nick Auf der Maur Column Interlude # 3
    "Kurt Cobain Had a Shotgun, and I Had Cigarettes" 265

Chapter 27: Making *Celebrity Skin* 267

Chapter 28: My Bass and the Rise of the Digital Soul-Sucking Monster 281

    Romantic-Comedy Interlude: A Play in Three Acts,
    Starring Adam Sandler, Chris Farley, Ben Stiller, and Owen Wilson
    (with a Cameo by Jim Carrey) 286

Chapter 29: The Hollywood Hills and My Father's Halo 289

Chapter 30: Introducing: Death 297

Chapter 31: Montreal's Daughter in Mourning 303

Chapter 32: Dance with Death 317

    Dreamscape #3
    Your Emptiness Is Calling Me 322

Chapter 33: The Drummer and the Bass Player 327

    High-Fashion Interlude: Milano Fashion Week, Fall 1998 341

Chapter 34: My Drug? Crushes 343

Chapter 35: First Loves Save the Day 347

    Courtney Says Goodbye 359

Chapter 36: Out of a Hole, into a Pumpkin 363

Chapter 37: Trapped in Mythological Webs and Shadows 375

    Dear Billy 384

Chapter 38: End of an Era 389

Chapter 39: It's the End of the World as We Know It 395

Afterword: Home—Planet Earth—2024 403

Photo Credits   413
Acknowledgments   415

INTRODUCTION

Through the Looking Glass

READING, UK
AUGUST 1994

"WHERE'S MY SPRAY PAINT?!"

The flimsy door to main-stage dressing room 5 flung open as Courtney roared her demand out into the massive festival grounds. The sound of sixty-five thousand fans and distant drums floated into the mobile trailer for a moment before she slammed the door behind her. Then the inaudible vocals and muffled bass lines boomed through the thin walls again.

Inside, our band's backstage trailer was total chaos. Silk slips, fishnet stockings, satin high-heeled shoes, and brightly colored plastic baby-girl hair barrettes exploded out of open suitcases. The catering table was covered with crisps, veggie sticks, candy, and cold cuts stabbed with cigarette butts and littered with dozens of Courtney's makeup bottles and cases. A Marshall guitar amplifier lay on its back in the center of the room. It looked like it had passed out and was waiting to be revived.

Courtney Love—fearless front woman of the band Hole and my new "boss"—paced around the amp, eyeing it like prey. She was wearing only a white lace bra and black fishnet stockings with no underwear. A big messy heart had been drawn on her abdomen with a black Sharpie. She was waiting for the tool she needed to arrive so she could leave her next mark.

It was late afternoon on Friday, August 26, 1994, the first day of the Reading Festival, the United Kingdom's largest and the world's oldest existing popular-music festival. The rural takeover that is Reading is testament to the United Kingdom's leadership in summer music festivals. Multiple stages and dozens of tents and vendor villages covered the 190 acres. The warm summer air created an idyllic rural field environment for alternative-rock fans to roam freely and explore themselves and the sounds of the day. The traveling circus made up of alternative musicians was hosted in the backstage area, which looked like trailer-park chic on steroids. Over three days, two hundred bands needed to eat, drink, change outfits, shower, get drunk, do drugs, discuss their set lists, and find places to pee.

Our band, Hole, was scheduled to play midway into the lineup that day, a few slots after the Flaming Lips and the Verve and immediately before Pavement. Pavement was rising up the ranks of '90s alternative stature with their new album, *Crooked Rain, Crooked Rain*, the epitome of our scene's "fuck fame, fuck rock-star" ethos. Prior to this, Hole had been playing clubs, so the high-ranking position on the main stage of the biggest music festival in the world was about to have a major impact on the professional advancement of the band.

"Sorry, they sent a runner into town for it; just got it!"

Joe Mama-Nitzberg, Courtney's oldest friend from her teen goth years in San Francisco, burst into the trailer holding up a can of spray paint like a trophy. He was wearing a little kid's black cowboy hat, red-and-black plaid shirt, and vintage Levi jeans, ironic "I am an American" style. Joe was a quick humored, adorable, flamboyant man who beamed with love. He was here on this trip across the Atlantic to metaphorically hold Courtney's hand for her first public performance since her husband, Nirvana front man Kurt Cobain, died by suicide four months earlier at their Seattle home.

Live Through This, Hole's first album on major label Geffen Records, had been released on April 12, 1994, only a week after Kurt's suicide. The date had been scheduled months prior, but the entanglement of the album and Courtney's new status as "Kurt's widow" was so messy and the connections so blurry. Courtney's famous husband's suicide wholly overshadowed her album's release. As tragic as his death was, that obnoxious symbol of male dominance was not lost on me, even then.

Courtney put on a tattered white slip, shook the can, and knelt in front of the amp with a lit cigarette firmly locked in her mouth. Smoke was ever present around her, making her look like a smoking dragon. Joe carefully held back her messy bleached blonde hair from behind, like a dear friend would when you're vomiting into a toilet, to keep it from catching on fire.

Joe took his caretaking of Courtney in a tongue-in-cheek but serious way. He was clearly tapped into her wildness, and their bond was beautiful. Being around the two of them gave me my first glimpse into Courtney's softer, more personable, and sensitive side—one that keeps friends for life.

The spray-paint fumes filled the trailer as a giant, childlike pink heart took shape on the amp. Then Courtney sprayed a huge, dramatic X on top of it.

Patty Schemel, Hole's drummer, took a break from her warmups to film the scene with the new-dad, tourist-worthy Handycam she'd invested in to capture this trip overseas. She was wearing a dark-blue T-shirt with a five-point white star positioned directly over each nipple. Patty's quick humor and warm presence grounded the space. I'd already come to rely on this, just one week into this adventure with the band.

Eric Erlandson, Hole's cofounder and guitar player and the only male in the band, was nowhere to be seen. He'd likely found a quiet place either to make out with his new love, Hollywood starlet Drew Barrymore, or to meditate before the show.

"Fifteen minutes to showtime!" Craig Montgomery, our tour manager, popped his peppy blond-bob head into the trailer. His eyes locked on the newly improved amplifier.

"We gotta get this amp back onstage!"

With a grunt Courtney pulled herself off the amp and then off the floor with the help of Joe. She snarled and seemed pleased with her pink intervention on the classic rock-and-roll appliance.

I turned to the small mirror in the room. My familiar makeup-free, laissez-faire, freckled face was framed by frizzy, curly red hair. I didn't feel the need to adjust anything, only to apply some browny mauve matte MAC lipstick to my lips. This was my only special touch to prepare myself to play a concert in front of sixty-five thousand people. The cultural mood of the moment was a cult of not trying, of effortless happening, even when something major like this *was* happening. My outfit said it all. I was wearing my staple of any other day back home at university in Montreal—a navel-revealing 1970s vintage polyester children's T-shirt featuring an ironic cartoon of two wholesome little wide-eyed girls holding hands in the snow, a brown-suede miniskirt, and scuffed-up combat boots.

I know now how much was riding on this day, but at the time my twenty-two-year-old mind was barely contemplating the enormity of it all. This was only the seventh live rock concert that I'd ever performed in my life, and the first outside of Montreal clubs. I had joined the band only two weeks earlier and learned the set list over the course of a week's rehearsal in Seattle.

I felt like an absurd grunge Cinderella, who'd found herself with VIP access to the ball. To some back home, my joining Hole was the epitome of a dream. To others, it was the biggest sellout of our scene. I had been trained to not hunt for this, to not give a fuck about success. I was lockstep in line with the indie ethos of the early '90s to not sell out. Success was weighted with guilt and shame. It felt like our self-worth was always at stake. Very confusing times for an aspiring and struggling artist.

The tension and inner conflict were real, but at the same time my eyes had been wide open. I'd been paying attention to the signs that led me here. I didn't choose to join Hole; it chose me.

As I stood in front of the mirror, I felt calm, resting in a sense of destiny and duty. I was replacing Kristen Pfaff, the previous bass player, who'd died of a heroin overdose just ten weeks prior. There were so many layers of tragic romance, addiction, visceral creativity, success, and aspirations swarming around this clan. Kurt's and Kristen's deaths were global news. The omnipresent sense of a rock-and-roll saga of mythological proportions unfolding in real time—starring the most significant voices of my generation—was very heavy and present. Fans around the world were moved and enthralled by it all. But while I was applying my lipstick in the eye of the actual storm, the radical emotional landscape of my new band members overshadowed the major rock-history-in-the-making aspect of what I'd just stepped into. Joining a band that had just suffered two major deaths created an intensity that made me feel I had to honor both the living *and* the dead and push my own feelings and experiences to the background. All I was tuned in to was my band members' complex feelings of loss and pain and the chords and arrangements of the songs I had memorized.

I had yet to experience a significant death in my life, but I've come to understand that like all who live in the wake of death, my new band members were in shock. And that this shock and the ripple effects of the enormous double loss were in direct conflict with making and releasing an amazing, already critically acclaimed album. It would be nearly impossible for even the most well-adjusted stable adult to integrate the two, let alone a band of, for the most part, parentless drug addicts living out their tragedies in public.

A decade later, Jenessa Williams in the *Guardian* would describe Hole's performance at the Reading Festival as the beginning of a world tour of chaos and drugs. It was beyond true, the level of dysfunction and destruction that followed. Courtney was not okay. She was grieving, she had a young daughter to raise alone, and she was on drugs. On top of that, she was the most famous widow of the most famous dead rock star in the world. She was a raging, rolling tornado. But wow—did she put on an enthralling show. No one could scream like her, throw herself into the crowd like that, or look the audience directly in the eye so fearlessly. The performances were her catharsis, and we were all her witnesses.

A local stagehand stepped into the trailer with Craig to move the amp. His gaze landed on the blonde surrounded by a halo of smoke. His starstruck shock was palpable.

This kind of gawking in our band's presence would become the norm for years to come. No matter what room, airplane, or street she occupied, Courtney rarely went unnoticed. People became transfixed. I would soon learn to cancel out their voyeuristic gazes and pretend they weren't there. I'd discovered how to do this as a child growing up in the shadow of a larger-than-life father, a prominent broadcaster, journalist, and local politician who ran his life out of downtown Montreal bars. Outside gazes followed him everywhere he went, and because I was his daughter, his often public sidekick, and a frequent topic of his newspaper columns, that meant they'd followed me, too.

The love he showed me in public collapsed our private and public lives into one. From a very early age, I became accustomed to the public gaze, and I'm comfortable with that kind of love. Maybe that's how I can be getting ready to step on a stage in front of thousands and not feel even a blip of nervousness. It's unusual, I know.

As a teenager, I'd worked as a ticket girl in a punk-rock club in Montreal and as a cassette deejay in a dive bar. These places, as well as my father's scene in the bars of my youth, all had a similar energy to rock shows and festivals. Despite the rowdy voices, loud music, and celebratory atmosphere, I grew accustomed to the underlying sadness and loneliness in the people who gathered there. They seemed to flock to each other and when they came together seemed both lost and found at the same time.

I think that all of this gave me the ability to step into the fame game and not be fucked. It was the same equation, just on a larger scale. Those formative years gave me a lot of practice fitting into chaotic scenes.

My innate shyness, I know, may have come off as aloof. I was more comfortable on the sidelines as an observer, next to the heart of the action. The periphery was my happy place to be. When things got weird or chaotic in these environments, I could feel myself transported like in a psychedelic trip, having a sort of out-of-body experience as if I were floating above the chaos. I could watch it, hold it, even admire it, while keeping a distance and letting it wash over me. This is what helped me stay calm in the eye of the storm.

The drama and chaos of Courtney Love and Hole are infamous, but to me it all felt familiar. I found comfort in the chaos. My upbringing was the perfect training ground to be in a rock band and immersed in the world of Courtney. Despite how new I was to the band, I fit right in.

On this day in Reading, I was still too new to have developed a preshow ritual. Instead, I instinctively and discreetly started snapping photos with the palm-size Nikon point-and-shoot camera that always dangled from a string around my wrist. As with most show days ahead, I shot a whole roll of film, with ironic action shots of a girl doing mundane things on the road with a rock band. I documented myself at lunch in the catering tent, mouth wide open with food going into my mouth. Drew Barrymore and I hit it off quickly, both being Pisces with easy-to-spot hippie vibes, so we took cute photos of each other taking photos of each other outside in the sun.

My passion for photography had grown in tandem with my obsession with music. In high school, I had my own darkroom. The camera lens always felt like a portal of sorts to me, like "the eye of god" or a gateway to the future. Safely stored back home in my Montreal apartment were a significant number of black-and-white negatives from my last seven years of shooting and processing film. The themes and subjects were predominantly my very intimate world. Nude self-portraits, an unmade bed, dust bunnies in the corner of my bedroom, and occasionally things in the outer world that I felt the most kinship with: local rock bands and dirty Montreal alleyways.

The Nikon on my wrist was smaller than the smallest iPhone today and allowed me to document all things '90s on tour with Hole for the next five years. Between my discreet presence and my little camera, I became a fly on the wall, taking everything in.

This day in Reading would change my life forever. Despite this, I still felt like an outsider looking in from behind a wide-angle lens, like a visitor dropped into a dream.

"Everyone needs to be on the side stage in ten minutes. Preshow pee NOW!" the production manager barked.

I still wasn't feeling nervous, but I certainly didn't want to burden our big coming-out performance with me needing to pee. So I stepped outside and followed the bathroom signs along the soft grass pathways between the lined-up trailers.

I found a relatively quiet, clean bathroom stall and sat on the toilet for a moment of quiet, alone, before the gates to the unknown opened and tossed me out onto a global stage and into the public eye.

I'd always felt in close and good company with myself in intimate spaces like bathrooms and bedrooms. In high school I had spent a lot of time in my bedroom and in bathroom stalls listening to my music and Walkman to comfort myself. Being alone was a safe place for me.

Now I turned to my long-running inner dialogue.

This was meant to be.

They found me for a destined reason.

Through the David Lynch looking glass I go.

I am ready.

I am here with you.

I raised my trusted camera above my head for a bird's-eye view of me on the toilet. No turning back, I looked up into the lens.

I SEE YOU, I thought to myself.

Click.

I stepped out of the stall and took another self-portrait in the bathroom mirror.

The casualness and calm I see in these photos are mysterious to me today. So open and sweet I looked, in the bathroom alone, a young woman on the precipice of such a radical new chapter. Was I more innocent than I remember being? I do know that with these photographs, I was acknowledging the threshold I was crossing, like the ritual of bowing upon entering a Buddhist temple or communing with holy water in the entrance of a church. Except my sacred moment was with myself, in a bathroom stall with a camera looking in on me, like the holy eye of the future as my witness.

Did I really have any sense of what my future was going to look like, or did I simply hold faith in it?

I walked into that bathroom in one state of being, and when I walked out, I crossed over into another. Behind me was an individual who'd been living freely and independently in a nurturing but challenging bohemian landscape in a romantic, classic 1900s French Canadian city. Ahead of me was a bizarre global stage where I'd been officially invited to join a larger-than-life enterprise as a culture shifter. Which is not a small, intimate thing to do in the world.

I took this task very seriously because it was not about me. I had agreed to join this band as a commitment to myself, to put women on a male-dominated landscape. I was also well aware of being part of a collective unconscious effort that was trying to wake up and break a spell. Almost halfway through the last decade of the twentieth century, it felt like an ominous future lay ahead. Beyond the giant millennial number change about to occur, there was a feeling of massive momentum that had begun in our parents' radical '60s revolution and was now colliding hard with the '80s yuppie corporate hell of predatory capitalism.

My peers and I knew that trouble was around the bend. We were deeply anxious about "selling out," a.k.a. "selling our souls to the devil," yet, sadly, many were being consumed by what they feared: corporate greed, drug addiction, death, and the dark side of fame. Our voices were warning and mourning simultaneously. We were preparing to leave the naïveté and arrogance of the past century behind and waking up to the sober reality of what experiments in industrialization and capitalism would mean for humans and for our planet.

Humanity was going to pay a high price for the decadent illusion of endless progress and possibility—all while making the most of our time together through noise, emotions, and a concerted push against the bounds of expression. An innocent nihilism was flowing through us. The scarier our future felt, the hungrier and more passionate we became about staying true to the original dream and to each other. The people who rode that wave at the prime of their creative coming of age mirrored that radical transition.

Back at the trailer, the rest of the band was leaving for the stage, surrounded by a flock of various crew and helpers. I joined them and followed our tour manager toward the huge steps that led up the side of the giant open-air stage. As the sea of people came into view, I slid my camera off my wrist and handed it to my guitar tech in exchange for my bass and slung it over my left shoulder.

It took a couple of minutes for the technicians to check our instruments and mics, and then, just like that, we strolled onto the stage.

The crowd in front of us was as abstract and hypnotic as a raging ocean from my Celtic heritage. The sound of cheers and claps began to emanate from bodies squeezed together for as far as the eye could see. It was hard to distinguish the details of anyone's face or voice. They all blended together into a merged human populous.

This was an entirely different experience from the small local clubs of Montreal, where I could recognize everyone's faces and they mine. At Reading, the distance between the stage and the first row of people created what felt like a force field of protection between them and my most intimate self. It created a sense of anonymity for such an overwhelming experience.

What a juxtaposition it was in that moment, to become a public figure yet to be hiding behind a giant infrastructure. Maybe that is what fame is? To be exposed and anonymous at the same time.

It was a wild feeling, to be sure.

On the enormous stage, I took my spot eight feet to the right of the fearless widow, who stepped up to the mic center stage, with her guitar draped across the front of her body and the cigarette still dangling from her mouth. The crowd erupted in a cheer.

"Oh, yeah, I'm so goddamn brave," she drawled casually into the mic by way of introduction. She took another drag off her cigarette. "Yeah, sure. Let's just pretend . . . it didn't happen." She raised her left hand in a stop signal. "Let's just pretend. Is that what you're doing, pretending it didn't happen? Great. Well, I'm *not*."

I have heard it described before that watching Courtney back then was like watching a car crash. It summoned shock and awe and confusion around how to react to this person who embodied so many impossibly unrelatable traits. Even with the cavernous gulf between me and the crowd, the calm the audience exuded when she confronted them was eerie. Courtney was, and still is, an unpredictable anomaly. The world was just getting to know her then.

She tossed her cigarette to the ground and, without missing a beat, gestured in my direction.

"That's Melissa—fucking last name is French—Eau de . . . Melissa, what is it?"

"Auf der Maur," I said into the mic, hearing my voice carry out over a field to more than sixty-five thousand sets of ears for the first time. "'On the Wall' in German."

"Auf der Maur, 'Off the Wall' in German, fucking French . . . ," Courtney repeated, incorrectly, and then kicked right into the opening chords of "Plump":

He shakes his death rattle
Spittle on his bib
I don't do the dishes
I put them in the crib

I played the songs that day. Sang backups, and didn't make a mistake. I had officially arrived on the wild side of my life. No matter how alien it was, or how familiar parts of it felt, I had no doubt I was supposed to be there. As dangerous as the days ahead would be, I accepted my call to duty.

That performance at Reading was the beginning of my portal into the abyss. It's almost a cosmic joke that the band's name is Hole. As I let myself fall into a deep valley of death and drugs, I was held steady on one side by my left arm on the rosewood fretboard of my Sunburst Precision bass, while my right arm locked into the beat of Patty's bass-drum foot. My trusted self, captured by my camera in the bathroom, continued to watch it all from a disembodied perspective up above.

There was no way of knowing what would happen next, what impact these dark forces and characters would have on me, yet I felt eerily calm and perhaps overly confident that I would be protected. My silent, inner dialogue continued onstage. I promised myself that I would be okay and would eventually reunite with my former life on the other side. My self-preservation instinct, developed throughout my childhood, kicked in beautifully.

I could feel the burn of all the eyes in the audience watching us onstage. As I played for them and fused with them, I also felt the distant gaze of the feminist historians from the future, who would look back at this time and witness these young women stepping out of the shadows and the pain and into ourselves and the light.

It was our time—a time of messy humanity, tragedy in slow motion, and raw music made by romantic broken poets for a world that did not yet know where it was heading. On that stage I became one with it all. I belonged with everyone in that sea of humanity, giving myself over to that moment with them and to the movement into our unknown collective future.

ACT I
MAGIC

Dreamscape #1

Even the Good Girls Will Cry

Autumn 1991, Montreal

Even the good girls will cry.

Even the good girls will cry.

The figure perched upon my chest whispers this chant into my ear. It startles me awake from a deep sleep.

It's after midnight, and the streetlight cuts through the slatted blinds in the big bay window of my parlor bedroom facing Saint-Dominique Street. The visitor's identity is in silhouette. Long, full hair frames a backlit face too dark for me to make out the details.

Its face hovers just inches from my right ear. Its weight presses all of me into the bed, even my ankles and feet.

Fear for my life escalates, speeding up my heart and breath. My insides throb.

Am I awake, or am I asleep? I wonder. Is this a wild dream—or something else?

I try to lift a single finger, trying to assess my power of self-defense. My finger is like dead weight. I am stuck here, against my will.

Even the good girls will cry.

Is this a warning? From where? From when?

Terror helps me receive the message and take it in. I'm hoping that if I don't resist, it will stop. I submit.

At once, the figure lifts and disappears. Instant relief comes over me, but simultaneously, a new form appears. A lanky, long-haired, androgynous figure now stands at the foot of my bed. It is nude or draped in light fabric, long limbed, and graceful. Both frightening and beautiful.

It slowly raises its right hand, waving a middle "fuck you" finger in slow motion, from right to left.

The vision is powerful and terrifying. Its helper set the tone with its whisper, but this figure is the real star of this show.

As it gracefully waves its middle finger, I sense a tinge of playfulness.

It just wants to be seen, and to be taken seriously, I think. To know that a good person accepts it, loves it, and is not afraid of it.

I fill myself with all the love and power I have for my favorite things, music and friends. I take the deepest breath I can and manage to raise my right hand off the bed for a short moment. Palm facing forward. In peace.

"I see you," I declare in my mind, an innocent yet direct gesture.

Just like that, the figure evaporates into dust from its head down to the ground. All that is left is the streetlight glow, and me alone in my bed.

I understand my call. To believe in the unseen, to never doubt its presence, or it will knock on my door again. I must believe and listen to the other side. It does not ring true with anything I ever heard from my intellectual parents who raised me on the here and now, or anything I've read about before. Nonetheless, it changes me forever and opens me up to a new way of seeing.

CHAPTER 1

Dreamy Frontline Feminist

I AM A PRODUCT OF A ONE-NIGHT STAND BETWEEN TWO RADICALLY BEAUTIful and adventurous souls, who in their fearless independence came together for a romantic weekend. Some of the closest people in my life have called me a "hippie" in an accusatory kind of way, or judged me for my overuse of "cosmic" words, but I want to be straight with you from the top: I truly feel that every soul has a trajectory, or calling, in each lifetime, and that I found my perfect moment to drop into this world through these two parents.

Linda Gaboriau, 1969. Photo by Guy Borremans.

My mother, Linda Gaboriau, was a frontline feminist of her generation, an effortless pioneer of second-wave feminism. She wasn't so much an activist with picket signs; it was more that her life was an act of feminism. She was born Linda Marie Johnson in 1942 in Boston and grew up in the comfortable suburb of Westwood, Massachusetts. As a teenager she dreamed of becoming a ballerina and starred as the Sugar Plum Fairy in a local production of *The Nutcracker*. But her reserved demeanor and dark looks—almond eyes, big lips, and long, straight brown hair—set her apart from her peers. By all accounts she never fit in at the local public high school, where she was called "Chink Eyes" and "N**** Lips." She found a mentor in her French teacher, who helped her discover a natural talent and passion for language. On an exchange year in Germany, she learned the language, and although she did not love Germany, she fell in love with Europe. This planted the seed for her to eventually leave the United States.

Given her opposition to the Vietnam War and racial inequality, and the overall disconnect she felt from America and her suburban upbringing, she couldn't wait to escape her surroundings. She rebelled beautifully against her conservative, middle-class family. As her father would later say to me, "The only thing your mother spared us was a nose ring!" After high school she attended Western College for Women in Ohio for a year, with the hope of transferring to Wellesley College. Disenchanted by the college experience and looking to further discover herself, she returned to Boston to audit night classes at Harvard University and landed work as a research assistant at Harvard's sister school, Radcliffe College. She was randomly placed in a job supporting a study at the Radcliffe Institute for Independent Study titled "The Changing Feminine Role." This chance placement would throw her straight into the women's revolution and change her life forever.

My mother was lucky to arrive during the center's infancy and to meet and witness the development of five of its earliest fellows: poets Anne Sexton and Maxine Kumin, writer and labor activist Tillie Olsen, sculptor Mariana Pineda, and painter Barbara Swan. Each woman was there on a fellowship with a "room of one's own"—a term coined by Virginia Woolf in 1929 to represent women's need to claim the space and the freedom to tell their own stories. It is a concept that my mother, to this day, cites as essential for every woman.

Inspired by her time at the institute, my mother—Mum, never Mom—returned to Germany for a year to study German literature in Heidelberg. During that time, she researched the best language departments and settled on McGill University, with a focus on French literature. She arrived in Montreal in September 1963 on a student visa to complete her BA at McGill and never left.

Canada has long been a more progressive nation than the United States, and specifically the city of Montreal, where the counterculture was raging. It was just what my mother's appetite was hungry for. In the early 1960s, the Quebec Independence movement was on the rise, and the French-versus-English language-rights debates were seductive to her, offering a fiery framework for the women's liberation movement that she now felt a part of.

During her early years in the city, Mum forged her way into the world of French Canadian, and in particular Quebecois, cultural journalism and activism. At the age of twenty-five, she married Montreal artist Pierre Gaboriau, a painter in the city's hip art scene. The son of acclaimed Quebecois political cartoonist Robert LaPalme, Pierre chose Gaboriau as his nom de plume—to avoid being overshadowed by his father. When they married, he was working on a large-scale stained-glass installation in Montreal's new Metro stations as the city prepared to host EXPO '67, the World's Fair, helping to transform the old city into a modern city. My mother and Pierre had a small, traditional wedding at the Episcopal church in Westwood, Massachusetts, attended by my confused Boston grandparents and Mum's younger brother, Mark. Their union sealed her break from suburban Boston. They moved into his bohemian triplex in Montreal. Half of the bottom floor was his studio, and half of the top floor was the storage area for his materials. Mum covered some of the shelves in the storage area with burlap to block off an area for a desk and a dresser. It was a room of her own.

All she has told me of their time together was that he was mentally volatile and left his motorcycle parts in the bathtub. Though the marriage lasted less than two years, Mum kept Pierre's non de plume last name. She got

what she wanted, a new name and identity: Linda Gaboriau. The transformation was complete. I still legally hold the name of a man I never met: Melissa Tara Gaboriau Auf der Maur. (You try being an American police officer pulling me over for speeding and having to pronounce that!)

With her ear for language, exotic looks, and French last name, Mum easily passed as a genuine Quebecoise beauty. Meeting her today, you would never imagine she had suburban American roots. As a child I instinctively respected the uprooting and transformation she had undergone. Her rejection of her childhood home was confusing to me, though, because of how loving and how comforting I found my "normal" grandparents in Massachusetts to be.

My grandfather George D. Johnson loved me with a warmth and stability I never felt from any other man in my childhood. The only conflict I ever witnessed between him and Mum was at the dinner table when politics came

---

George D. Johnson, 1943. (*left*)
George D. Johnson and Evelyn Reeves, 1934. (*right*)

up. "I would give my right arm to punch JFK in the nose!" he would shout as they debated the social services his "bleeding-heart liberal" daughter would defend. Despite their different political outlooks, they had a beautiful relationship. "I'm proud of your mother. She is strong and independent," he'd often tell me, revealing his unconditional love and support of her wild ways.

In contrast to her suburban 1950s family, Mum had a beatnik style, feminine but practical, effortless and au naturel. She wore knee-high socks with dark velvet A-frame skirts or "culotte" knickers and big bell-sleeved velvet waistcoats, hand-me-downs from her wicked Victorian grandmother, Violet. I remember an autumnal-colored plaid woolen coat she wore when she wrapped her arms around me to keep me warm in the impossibly cold Montreal winters.

Mum was gorgeous—not an angelic, frilly flower-child beauty, but a stoic, dark one, with almond eyes, olive skin, long brown hair parted in the middle, and no makeup. Her high, wide cheekbones and voluptuous lips were out-of-this-world dramatic. Born to English and "Black Irish" ancestors, she looked eastern European, with touches of First Nations and Sophia Loren, as opposed to me, her traditional-looking Irish daughter born on St. Patrick's Day, no less. Mum was the black sheep, not me. She was the spitting image of her paternal grandmother, born in Boise, Idaho, to a father who was a mess officer in the US Army, stationed in various First Nation reservations in Idaho and Alaska. How my great-grandmother and my mother were both born with the type of exotic characteristics traditionally associated with the Native women of this land is still a mystery. When I did 23andMe genetic testing, primarily to confirm my mother's suspicions about her "non-WASP" looks and spirit, I learned I have 1 percent Mongolian (associated with Native people) and 3 percent Ashkenazi Jewish in my DNA.

By contrast, I was a fair-skinned, freckle-faced redhead, a late bloomer who came into my beauty later in life, not until my mid- to late twenties. In certain dramatic black-and-white high-contrast photos of me, do we look similar? Something I can only wish for. Our almond-shaped eyes, of a particular shade of green, hazel, and gold; soft-shaped, undefined upper lips; and small feet are really our only shared traits.

When the summer came and we rode bikes through our neighborhood, Mum in her sports shorts and a tank top with no bra, male gazes followed us. I remember an old man at the bus stop who reached out to grab her ass in front of Cinema L'Amour, a porno movie theater only two blocks from our family house. Until that point in my life, I'd only ever seen her calm and cool in public, yet now I watched as she hopped off her bike, stopped traffic,

exploded, and scolded the perv at the top of her lungs, cursing in French, and swatted him right back.

I'd witnessed from a very young age how men behaved around my mother, and I'd studied the gorgeous professional black-and-white framed portraits of her that hung on the walls of our apartment. She was a muse to art photographers of the time in Montreal. In one, she stands nude in the same pose as the subject of Botticelli's *Birth of Venus* in a crevice of a stony

---

Linda Gaboriau, 1969. Photo by Guy Borremans.

oceanside cliff, waves crashing below her. In another, also nude, she emerges from the rusted carcass of a car in a junkyard, long brown hair blowing in the wind and wrapping around her serious face. A third shows her gliding nude through a dense forest like a wild animal, possessed by a call to the camera or to the man behind it.

These images told me who my mother was: a fearless adventurer whom no one could own or stop but only attempt to capture for a moment in a single frame. She was also not someone I could ever truly claim to be mine. She was unobtainable, otherworldly, a person unto herself, without evidence of needing anyone else.

As a journalist, Mum wrote mostly for French-language counterculture journals and produced her own English radio documentaries for the Canadian Broadcasting Company (CBC), through which she became a prominent personality. Her uniquely slow and seductive voice—a bit of a "New England meets Old World" accent—made her memorable to listeners and to those she interviewed. Her reel-to-reel tape deck lived on our living-room floor throughout my childhood, and I would admire the big puffy green headphones she'd wear while splicing and editing her own radio shows. It was satisfying to put those on my own ears and block out the rest of the world. I learned how to plug them into our home stereo receiver and play selections from her extensive record collection.

We would spend hours in our living room, listening to music and gazing at the album covers, like storybooks. As I sat on her lap, she would point at the men on the album covers and tell me stories about each of them. I vividly remember the Rolling Stones' *Between the Buttons* album, featuring a beautiful, soft-focus color photo of the five band members lined up in their rain jackets in the British countryside. Her lovely fingers with long, sculpted fingernails pointed at Mick Jagger. "This is the cute one that all the women throw themselves at . . . ," she explained, "and this is the troubled one that died drowning in a pool." Her finger paused on Brian Jones peering out from below a heavy brow and long fringed blond bangs. He was the only one smiling, a trickster's smile that captivated me. *How could he have died? Who found him?* I wondered every time I looked at that album cover.

I was raised on Mum's record collection and her admiration for the men in the bands. She was my gateway for discovering the contemporary music of one's generation as a calling, and for my desire to be *in* the band, not a woman *with* a man in the band.

The point in my mother's career that's most closely linked to my own destiny, and which makes me most proud, is that she became the first female rock disc jockey on Montreal's English airwaves. CHOM-FM is still the only local classic-rock station in Montreal. Between 1969 and 1974 she interviewed all the big names of the era, from Frank Zappa and Ken Kesey to the Band and Leonard Cohen. She was romantically linked to more than a few of them. By the way she spoke about her friendship with Zappa, I could tell there was something special about their connection. It inspired me to investigate deeper. I put my favorite album of his on constant rotation, *Cruising with Ruben & the Jets*, Zappa's reverently satirical take on the 1950s. Many hours of my youth were clocked staring at his greaser portrait on the back of the album cover.

Mum did not have a man to take care of her, nor did she want one. She wanted to do it all, to be a mother and have a blossoming career in cultural journalism when women were still on the fringe of such careers. "I wanted to be a mother, but no man was going to define who I am, so I decided to not marry and to do it alone," she would say. Another key phrase my friends and I heard from her many times as we were growing up was "I wanted to climb Kilimanjaro, and motherhood was not going to stop me." That one along with "A woman must have a room of her own" and "A woman needs to be able to drive away from a bad situation" were her mantras. I'm grateful she indoctrinated us in this way. Women of my generation owe so many of our liberties to the fearlessness of her generation.

By the time I was two, I had not yet met my father, but my mother and I had already taken a yearlong international adventure. We started with visiting friends in Paris. Then we lived for a while in a finely crafted and gilded circus caravan in a gay playwright's field in Hay-on-Wye, Wales, with Norma, one of my two unofficial godmothers, whom my mother had met at McGill. This was followed by time living in a British Postal Van that the two of them bought to travel to Morocco. We then drove it down through Spain and all the way to Marrakech, camping along the way. I slept in the front seat, and the two of them slept in the short back cabin with their feet hanging out of the open door. They feasted on hash-stewed prunes throughout the trip.

Our final stop was Kenya, Africa, this time without Norma. To get to the remote village, we had to fly to Nairobi, take an eight-hour taxi drive to Mombasa, and then ride in a tiny van to a town near the Tana River where we visited anthropologist Katherine Homewood, who was studying mangabey monkeys under the guidance of Louis Leakey. Once there, we slept on hammocks and lived in a hut in a banana grove that attracted the mangabeys, baboons, and elephants at night. Mum once had to protect me from a little vervet monkey that had fallen in love with her and become fiercely jealous of me, her baby in her arms.

My mother did get to climb partway up Kilimanjaro in a Land Rover and also sat on an alligator that she thought was a log. I have a treasured photo of me celebrating my second birthday in that village, surrounded by local children. In the sea of Kenyan children, I look white as a ghost wearing a straw hat and a striped caftan Mum picked up for me in Morocco.

Our worldwide trip came to a halt with my second bout with malaria, resulting in a flight to London and a nearly two-week stay at the Hospital for Tropical Diseases. That's when Mum decided it was time to bring me home.

I was proud of these global adventures, and growing into my teen and young adult years, I shared the tales freely. My mother's choices became my lifelong badges of nomadic, bohemian honor. Being given the world at such a young age set me up for life as a nomad on the road with a rock band and for an identity as someone on the hunt for adventure. The question I did not find myself asking until much later, when I was a mother myself, is what it did *not* set me up for. This is the confusion that burns brightly in me now, but in my coming of age as a young woman, it spun only desire, adventure, and poetry.

CHAPTER 2

The Saint and the Wall

My parents orbited around in the same Montreal cultural scene, my mother more on the Francophone side and my father on the downtown Anglophone side, where he was admired and even revered. Nick Auf der Maur had enough charm and flair to make him a friend to all. In his first adult incarnation—while Mum was immersed in early feminism at the Radcliffe Institute in the United States—he was a beatnik poet in Montreal who carried a pet rock and recited poetry for beer. He was proud to have been arrested

---

Nick Auf der Maur, 1969.

three times: He was arrested once during the October Crisis, triggered by the actions of separatist Front de libération du Québec members who kidnapped the British trade commissioner and the provincial minister of labor, prompting Canadian prime minister Pierre Trudeau to declare the War Measures Act; and once for reciting poetry nude on a street corner with a copy of Lawrence Ferlinghetti's *Coney Island of the Mind* in one hand and a glass of gin in the other. The third time was for being kicked out of a bar after getting into a brawl with Jack Kerouac, whom Nick was hosting on his trip to Montreal. He admired Kerouac as a writer until he started spewing racist and anti-Semitic conspiracies. That's where my father drew the line, never afraid to call people out on injustice against the underdog.

His strong opinions, always laced with humor, quickly got his stories into print and led to his next career as an acclaimed journalist and political rabble-rouser. My parents' work and interests were in such proximity that both of their first published articles were reviews of the same Frank Zappa show in Montreal, hers in the French-language paper and his in the English-language one. Shortly after that, she helped found a French counterculture monthly called *Mainmise* (Takeover). Around the same time, my father and a group of like-minded journalists founded the left-wing journal the *Last Post*. Their circles were small, overlapping, and tight.

If my mother's upbringing was distinctly and unfortunately American, my father's was definitively more Old World. My paternal grandmother, Theresia Scholastika Auf der Maur (née Schaelin), was reportedly not too happy to leave her Swiss Alpine village of Sachseln on a one-way boat trip to Quebec in 1929 at the behest of her prospector husband, Severin Josef Auf der Maur. Upon reaching Montreal, they became superintendents in a tenement building in the city's immigrant neighborhood, where they lived a life of poverty like many other recent arrivals from Europe. That neighborhood, Le Plateau–Mont-Royal, would be where my bohemian mother would choose to raise me fifty years later. It was a dynamic, eclectic place to grow up, with its vibrant and hardworking immigrant family-run specialty food stores—the Jewish bakery, the Polish fish market, the Greek vegetable store, the French cheese shop.

My grandmother was the family's main "breadwinner"—literally, as she worked at a bakery—while she managed the building and raised the couple's four children. My father, Nick, was born in 1942, twelve years younger than his oldest sister. He was the baby. The Chosen One. My grandmother claimed her family members were direct descendants of Swiss patron saint Niklaus von Flüe, a fifteenth-century paragon of virtue who lived the life of a hermit and fasted in a hut on a riverbank until his death. The message came to her, while pregnant with my father, that this child was the reincarnation of Saint Niklaus. She named her fourth child Niklaus, and he became the embodiment of his mother's spiritual devotion and connection to the home she'd left behind.

The Swiss Alps remained ever present in my larger-than-life, eccentric Auf der Maur family. Crumpled Xeroxes of Alpine photos were handed to me at every holiday dinner. My grandmother yodeled at all those meals while stashing leftovers in her purse. When I was twelve, my grandmother and aunt Thais brought my father and me on a Swiss Alps pilgrimage to "live like Heidi." We hiked above the clouds to visit my great-uncle during his summer farm duties. In his off-the-grid cabin he communicated with the cows with a gigantic Alpenhorn. He walked us through his daily chores and showed me how to churn butter. My father and I slept alongside my aunt and grandmother, already into her eighties, in our clothes in the hayloft above the cows, whose heat kept us warm in the chilly night. It was the most rustic experience my urban father and I ever shared.

While my father's maternal side zealously claimed a saint as one of their own, his paternal side carried the weight of an ancient lineage. The history, not legend, is that our family came from one of the three founding cantons of Switzerland. The wall that my family built to stand up to the Austro-Hungarian Empire, and lived within, created the country as we know it today. In Swiss German, "Auf der Maur" translates to "On the Wall." Remnants of that stone wall still stand today in my grandfather's town of Schwyz in the canton of Schwyz in the country of Schwiiz. The Swiss are typically so nationalistic that it says a lot that my grandfather, the radical adventurer, broke away from such a pure-blooded, historic family line.

While my grandmother worked, my grandfather lived out the dream of exploration that had brought the family to Canada: hunting for rare minerals in the mountains of Quebec. Grandpa Auf der Maur, an engineer and prospector, had acquired a parcel of remote wilderness in Charlevoix County where he built a small base cabin, began to dig, and set up his own hydroelectric energy source from the river outside the lodging to run the lights. For most of my father's preschool years, he lived with his father in this off-the-grid cabin at the Auf der Maur "mining camp" in rural Quebec. Fantastic black-and-white photos of the cabin survive, protected in our messy family archives.

Otherwise, their time spent in the mining camp remains a bit of a mystery, as this chapter of the story involved only my grandfather (who spoke little English), my father (who spoke no Swiss German), and a transient cast of wayward miners and prospectors, some from as far away as Russia,

---

Severin Joseph Auf der Maur with investor and dogs, 1945.

Europe, and Texas. Nick was used as a child assistant to drill for diamonds. "Any day now" was his father's mantra. Family stories from this time include a tale of finding a baby bear after the mother bear had been shot. After my grandfather skinned the mother bear for her hide, my father cared for the cub and slept alongside it on the mother's hide in their cabin until it was old enough to return to the wild and fend for itself. It's a story that I'd think is almost too fantastical to be true, except the photos exist to prove it.

The conflict between his transcendental maternal line and the earthly history of his paternal line seems to have created an intense internal tension within my father. After all, walls are built to keep things out and saints are created to transcend. That dichotomy may have produced the fiery, passionate man he became but also may have been what drove him to drink. By his midtwenties, my father—Nick, never Dad—was leading the entirely modern, urban, decadent life of a "boulevardier." Striding through town in his casual linen suit and fedora, chain-smoking his Gitanes French *sans filtre* cigarettes, he looked ready to step into a Fellini film or Parisian writers salon, as he elegantly pursued his daily drinking habit.

He soon became practiced in the man-on-the-street style of journalism. His notoriety soon resulted in his hosting his own ahead-of-its-time television show on the CBC, cleverly titled *QuelQue Show*. In each episode he and his sidekick, Les Nirenberg, would stand on the busiest corner of the city and ask passersby, "What is on your mind?" They turned citizens' opinions on everything from the latest snow-removal debacle to elections and birth control into entertainment.

The wildly original show captured the cultural transition and moment in Montreal history from 1969 to 1973 through the words of its people. In many ways Montreal was going through the same cultural revolution of any major city in North America in the 1960s: long hair, peace protests, racial equality, and citizens questioning the government, the 1950s dream, and "the man." At the same time, in the wake of "the Quiet Revolution" of the 1960s, the Quebec Independence movement was being born. Both my parents became very passionate about and involved with the growing Quebec separatist movement. They shared a passion to fight for the underdog, which forged their identities in this time and place. The province was reclaiming its French (and Latin) roots and rejecting the British puritanical rule that had taken over much of North America, a struggle that I was not intellectually in tune with in my youth, but that subconsciously informed my understanding of the social history of the city that made me.

My father's newspaper columns and the success of the TV show made him a trusted and fearless household name in Montreal. Inspired by what he was hearing as a man-on-the-street journalist, he decided to run for local office as an independent in 1974 and won his first city-council seat. He spent the rest of his life in politics and journalism, reporting and fighting for the people of Montreal. A true friend to all, he kept his number listed in the phone book, inviting calls at all hours of the day and night. The cast of characters who reached out to him to be heard or to vent their concerns was vast: everyone from the nuns at the convent in his jurisdiction who wanted a correction to their garbage-collection schedule to the businessman who was struggling to get a permit to expand his business, from the homeless who had no way out of a bad cycle and the gangster trying to get out of trouble to the inmate who was seeking support from people outside (which led my father to commission wall-mounted wood cutouts of Donald Duck and his three nephews from the prison shop, which hang on my own walls today). True to his reputation as a "man of the people," he had a genuine and gorgeous talent for connecting with every person he encountered and for sharing their stories with others.

In his early thirties, just as his career was coming into strong focus, Nick received a big surprise. Two years earlier he had met my mother at the launch party for *Mainmise* at the Discothèque Pamplemousse. They exchanged numbers and went on a few dates. Determined to have a child on her own, Mum had stopped using birth control and was being, in her words, "selective" about whom she slept with.

During the summer of 1971 she persuaded my father to join her for the weekend at a friend's country cottage that resulted in my conception. Nine months later, on March 17, 1972, she walked herself a few blocks to the closest hospital, alone, to give birth to me. A massive snowstorm had shut down

Montreal that day, making the streets impassable, with no cars or taxis in sight. People were skiing in the streets. Thirty years later, for my mother's sixtieth birthday, I depicted that solo walk in a watercolor painting that she keeps framed and hanging in her office, our first day together immortalized in my childlike painting style.

When I was born, we lived in a basement apartment in downtown Montreal. There was no one for us to come home to, no family to help, only random young babysitters whose names and stories we do not know today. My mother wanted to do it all herself, to be a mother and to have a career in journalism. Despite her bohemian lifestyle, I was not breastfed. It doesn't appear to have been the result of leftover 1950s industrial-age damage, but more the result of her decision to be a single mother working full-time. It made her unavailable to offer me that. I have never asked her if she considered the emotional or physical impacts this would have on a child. When I was two, she took a job at the Canada Council of the Arts that required her to work in Ottawa every week for a few days at a time. A series of young women took care of me in Montreal when she worked and commuted to Ontario. What might she have been thinking? Perhaps that counterculture acts and intellectual strength were more important than traditional, domestic home environments at a time of revolution. After all, my birth had been a personal-political act, not one born from love.

Mum's fierce independence was part of her determination to be a single mother and also of her desire to initially keep me a secret from my father, her one-night-stand ladies' man. In 1973, when I was one year old, she chose to inform him of my existence. The toddlers at my day care mostly had two parents present, and it finally sank in for Mum that it was just a matter of time before I started asking, "Who's my father?" She felt she owed it to me to be able to give an honest answer.

They were both working as freelance journalists at the CBC when my mother called Nick to a meeting in an eighteenth-floor boardroom one day. He assumed they'd be discussing a news story. Instead, she told him, "I have your daughter. I don't want anything from you. I just want to be able to tell her who her father is if she asks."

A child with no strings attached was a priceless gift to an eternal bachelor. Right there and then, at a conference table, Mum changed Nick's life. He was shocked to hear the news—and fell in love with her on the spot.

My father recounted this part of the story to me as a simple and believable narrative, sweet and honorable on both sides. Mum was independent and didn't need anything from a man but wanted to be able to tell her daughter the truth about her father. Nick was responsive and joined our family in a modern kind of way.

Soon after, Mum and I took off for our yearlong trip overseas. Not long after we returned, Nick moved into the apartment next door to us, and his commitment to be a presence in my life, and the courting of Mum to be his wife, began.

Nick's choice to move into our apartment building made him a consistent physical presence. I vividly remember how, on my fourth birthday—the first I spent with him—my mother sent me to go see him next door. The apartments were connected by a rickety back balcony, which offered access to each apartment via its back kitchen door. I navigated the elaborate back balcony, made my way through his kitchen, and walked down the long hallway into the bright front living room. It was sparsely furnished, but in the center of the room was a cozy old armchair, and on it sat a cute little teddy bear.

"Happy Birthday, Melissa," Nick said from the other side of the room, with his mischievous mustached grin and a giggle. I reached for the teddy bear and looked into its glassy, strangely human brown eyes. My little-girl instinct was to name the bear after this man with a big walrus grin popping out from underneath a bushy mustache.

"I will call him Nicholas," I said.

It's hard to know what came first for a child at that moment, whether giving the bear his name was a genuine response to my father's affection, or a response to his need to be part of my life. Either way, Nicholas the Bear has since accompanied me on tours around the world and now lives in my

bedroom in Hudson, New York. I love that bear, just as I instantly loved the new gift-giving man in Mum's and my lives.

One year later, Nick proposed to my mother, and a traditional wedding was held in an old church followed by a reception in a French bistro. Amazing black-and-white photos of the day depict a classic 1970s wedding, with my father's gregarious friends in wide-collared suits and velvet bow ties and my mother's bohemian girlfriends with flowing floor-length dresses and long hair. My milquetoast Boston family mingled with my eccentric Auf der Maur side, coming together around a gorgeous bride and groom, both thirty-five years old, who looked deeply in love.

I was the five-year-old flower girl and ring bearer, and I remember the sunny, joyful day fondly. I was as much part of the ceremony as they were.

Nick and Melissa Auf der Maur with Terry Mosher, the best man, on their wedding day, 1977.

This inspired my own wedding to my husband, Tony, when our daughter, River, turned five. For River's fifth birthday celebration and our ten-year union milestone, we chose to be married as a family.

My mother liked to remind me that I always referred to her wedding ceremony with Nick as "our wedding." I believed we were getting married as a family. But my mother's one-night-stand instincts about Nick proved to be correct. His lifestyle of drinking at the bar until dawn did not change after marriage, and my mother, left at home with all the childcare responsibilities, quickly grew tired of this arrangement. It had become clear that Nick was a bachelor who happened to newly, and only briefly, be a husband and a public figure who happened to be a father. I remember watching him trail waitress's behinds throughout a restaurant or breasts bopping down the street. I would look away and pretend it didn't happen.

The marriage lasted for just over a year. Their relationship came and went so fast, it is hard to remember my feelings about it, but I can only imagine it was confusing to the little girl who had spent her formative infant years alone with her mother, traveled the world with her, then returned home to be introduced to a nice man next door who she was told was her father, who then married her mother but left almost as fast as he arrived. It is safe to say that I must've grown adaptable to various versions of home life.

Many in my alternative-rock world would say I have a great pedigree: a fearless feminist mother and a politically independent, storytelling local-hero father. What made them different made me different, too, and I was proud of it. It was the '70s after all, and the circle of freelance and progressive families we were a part of included many nontraditional family structures and separated parents. But whenever I stepped outside our little bubble, I could see how unique we were, that we were ahead of the times and part of breaking old models that didn't seem to be working anymore. I am still benefiting from my mother's bravery to wear her adventures on her cool hand-me-down velvet sleeves.

Both of my parents separated from their families to forge their own iconoclastic paths. As their daughter, I became a natural extension of both of

Linda Gaboriau, Nick Auf der Maur, and friends, 1977.

their interests, personalities, and accomplishments. Even at a young age, I understood and admired the profound transformations they'd gone through to become themselves. That was incredibly inspiring for me, and also incredibly daunting. *They are so cool; how will I ever be as cool as them?* I often thought.

I had a lot to live up to. Not in terms of financial or academic accomplishments; that wasn't what they valued. Nobody in their orbits cared about money. They had cheap, affordable rents, and they didn't covet material possessions. They valued finding purpose in their lives, freedom of expression, and deep exploration of the self, and they raised me that way, too.

Growing up, I always had a quiet fear that I didn't truly have a choice about who I would become. It could seem that the hand I was dealt was divine and remarkable, a 1970s fairy tale involving counterculture dreamers who fearlessly broke all the norms, but they cast big shadows under which to grow. My path felt predestined for me as the product of two extraordinary people, and not something I could easily break away from. But my city, the one they devoted themselves to, I knew she carried the answers I needed to find my own purpose. I believed she would take care of me and show me the way.

CHAPTER 3

The City, She Raised Me

I can't tell the story of my early life without including Montreal. The city—radical, romantic, poetic, and imbued with joie de vivre—was an omnipresent character in my parents' histories and also in my upbringing. She was like my parents' best friend who became almost a third parent to me, stepping in to raise me when my other two parents were preoccupied or swept up in the politics and culture of the times.

In the shadow of the great romances between my parents and their city, I developed my own love affair with Montreal in the 1980s and '90s, falling for her ornate nineteenth-century architecture, her tree-lined streets, the

---

Montreal rooftop scape, 1994.

omnipresent churches and parks of every shape and size, and the ubiquitous Old World shops. The eclectic alleyways that existed parallel to all the main arteries offered a patchwork infrastructure that hosted multicultural, multidisciplinary happenings. They seduced me then and still do now. The liveliness of the people in the streets, marketplaces, busy restaurants and bars, public transport, and parks was as entertaining to a young girl like me as the plays, nightlife, and contemporary dance performed inside the buildings in this city of art.

Extreme weather plays a major role in teaching Montrealers how to live. The winters are almost uninhabitable, with months when up to seven feet of snowbanks line the sidewalks and temperatures drop to the –20s Celsius (below 0 Fahrenheit). It toughens you up for tundra-style living and sends you into the cozy, tight, closed corners of bars, theaters, apartments, and restaurants to be entertained. Beauty's Delicatessen was where my mother's friends worked as waitresses for breakfast; Santropol was the place for hippie triple-decker sandwiches for lunch; 14 Prince-Arthur was for Vietnamese pho for dinner. I ate at all these cozy, affordable spots as a child and still do now as an adult with a child. In many ways, Montreal has stayed fixed somewhere between 1942 and 1982, which is very rare for a North American city and makes me love her even more.

The intensely cold Montreal winters thaw out into long, dirty, muddy springs, which in turn explode into totally balmy and action-filled summers. "The summers are hot as Mexico, and winters as cold as Moscow," my father often said. In the summer, many streets turn into pedestrian roads to host every kind of artisanal festival imaginable: puppet festivals, mural-painting festivals, modern-dance festivals, and local community parades and street fairs. These kinds of outdoor activities happen throughout most neighborhoods and are counterbalanced by international festivals such as the Montreal Jazz Festival, one of the largest in the world. The International Fireworks Competition, the Just for Laughs Comedy Fest, and the Formula-1 Grand Prix car race also take over parts of the city for weeks at a time. This all leads into a gorgeous autumn, when the many trees and parks slowly shade from red to gold, like a slow-motion hangover after the wild summer.

Melissa Auf der Maur, class photo, 1979.

The smell of "back-to-school" autumn air still signals my favorite time of year. It is why I could never live anywhere but the Northeast of North America, and it is also because I *loved* my school. The city I love taught me many things that couldn't be learned in school, but my remarkable, quintessential Montreal school gave me the foundation for all I am today.

FACE (Fine Arts Core Education) was founded in 1975 with a bold commitment to art and the belief that making art the primary focus of children's education would ensure happier and more open-minded people. My mother and a few of her progressive, radical friends came on early as founding families. I started in grade 1 and didn't leave the building until high school graduation.

I believe my life in arts, culture, and creative communities is proof that a bold 1970s experiment worked. Our days were filled with music, visual art and performance, and teachers I trusted and loved. Madame Simone Bannon, my elementary homeroom and French teacher, looked like a nouvelle vague film star with her red hair, pencil skirt, tiny cardigan sweaters, and delicate button-down shirts. She was so warm that I quickly recovered from my deep humiliation for being caught giving her my mother's family-heirloom ivory-rose cameo as a Christmas present in first grade. She was full of grace.

Music was an essential part of the curriculum, and in school band I chose trumpet out of all the instrument options. I held the first-trumpet seat from fourth grade to eighth grade and was the only girl in the section. I took my role very seriously, which planted a seed for being the only girl in a boys' world several more times to follow. My favorite class in middle school was choir, with Mr. Ewan Edwards, a Welshman to whom I dedicated my first solo album many years later. He, like everyone's dream of the life-changing role a teacher can play in a child's life, introduced me to the power of music. His teachings transformed me on a cellular level and connected me to my soul's purpose.

The ability to shepherd wild middle school children into ambitious music students is a sacred kind of talent. Mr. Edwards illustrated the essence of what I understand music to be: bringing order to chaos. The puzzle and equation of music is in collecting and connecting groupings of infinite options of musical notes, words, rhythms, and combinations to build a crafted, poetic universe that means something both to the creator and to those who receive it. It's an awesome experience for all involved.

Mr. Edwards had Monty Python looks: a long face, salt-and-pepper poofy '70s hair, and big square spectacles. A classical yet comical character in wide polyester slacks and suede Wallabee shoes, he had a flamboyant UK-style humor that made him so likable.

"Can I go to the bathroom?" a student would ask in front of the class.

"I don't know—*can* you?" Mr. Edwards would reply, reminding us of proper English. "But you *may* go to the bathroom."

I studied with Mr. Edwards from third grade through ninth. He shared his diverse repertoire with us, from the Beatles' "Eleanor Rigby" to Canadian Indigenous music. I still have a copy of one of those scores. We were taught sight-reading for the traditional compositions, but for the Indigenous piece, symbols of natural elements and animals were used instead of music notes. This kind of curriculum encouraged us to think out of the box, learning both to read music like a typical Western student and also to see it through another lens. My choir class convinced me that music *was* the most powerful universe out there—and it sure beat history and geography.

When I was fourteen, we performed the *Mozart Requiem* with the Montreal Symphony Orchestra. It was our first public performance beyond our school auditorium and took place at Place Des Arts (the equivalent of Lincoln Center in New York). Mozart's last piece, which he was composing when he died at thirty-five, was commissioned by an Austrian count to honor the anniversary of his wife's death. Requiems are used for church services for the peaceful repose of the dead, asking an all-powerful God to accept a human soul into heaven. This particular requiem is considered the "blockbuster" of all requiems—officially and historically the biggest hit of all time to celebrate the dead. The grandiosity and intensity of this piece, written in Latin and in the key of D minor—which would become my most beloved key of all time—consist of the most intense melodies and rhythms I had ever heard, let alone participated in performing.

This concert was a significant gateway into a new world for me: the unifying power of music. I came out the other side of those months of rehearsals a changed person. It was illuminating to transcend beyond myself, into a giant shared sonic experience. It felt like visiting the cosmos. A few years later when I found myself in the rapture of playing rock music to big crowds, I realized it started for me with this concert in Montreal, but as a teenager I just felt the overwhelming rush of the power of things bigger than me.

Mr. Edwards consistently urged me to step out of my comfort zone. "With a little more confidence, you would have this, Melissa," he told me once after a private audition for an upcoming vocal solo. I never wanted a solo; I was debilitatingly shy and was happiest being part of the group. But Mr. Edwards asked for more. I never did get a solo, but the words of confidence he gave me that day have stuck with me over the years.

By contrast, my choir mate Rufus, who came from a family of folk-music legacy, was always the first to have his hand up for a solo.

"Rufus, we are not Broadway! Not so LOUD!" Mr. Edwards would shout. Rufus got all the solos during his time at FACE but was asked to keep the showboating at home.

Rufus Wainwright: my first "love" and a soul brother for certain. We met as perfectly androgynous twelve-year-olds, just before he was to discover he was a man and I was a woman. Me, a tomboy, and he, femme, we became fast friends during his one year at FACE when he was in grade 6 and I was in grade 7. We met for the first time in the big downtown Montreal schoolyard at recess when the new boy made friends with me and my gang of nice girlfriends and we instantly welcomed him into our circle.

Rufus lived with his single mother, Kate, and sister, Martha, on the west side of downtown, not far from my father's bachelor home. As we got to know each other, visiting each other's family homes after school and on weekends, it was clear that we came from similarly bohemian broken families. He was the son of iconic American folk singer Loudon Wainwright III and Kate McGarrigle, who was part of the celebrated Canadian sister folk duo the McGarrigle Sisters. His family was of the musical variety, while mine was of the cultural and political, yet the environments felt the same, expressive and a little messy.

Even back then, Rufus was charismatic and poetic and talented, with an incredible cackle of a laugh. We were at the age when birthday parties started turning into later and more complex affairs. No longer devoted to just cake and Pin the Tail on the Donkey, they turned into lengthy hangouts in living rooms, listening to music into the evening. Spin the Bottle was just around the corner, but not quite yet. The most memorable moment Rufus and I shared that year was the time we said "I love you" to each other while staring deeply into each other's eyes and shared a little peck of a kiss lying on our backs on a living-room wood floor at a friend's late-night party. It was so simple and innocent, not sexualized or romanticized. Just two seeking souls coming into their own and looking for love late in the evening.

Shortly after that, things began to change when we discovered we both had a major crush on the same boy at school: Zébulon Perron.

Now this boy was nothing less than a poetic French James Dean and equally as handsome, mysterious, and magical. I mean, just gorgeous and cool, which is very hard for a boy in seventh grade to pull off. He had black hair perfectly coiffed in a Morrissey swoosh, pale porcelain skin, big green eyes, and a set of big ruby-red lips that formed a lovely and generous smile. His style was amazing and effortless, somehow blending 1940s Paris with 1980s downtown Montreal kid. So chic, he wore these classic french cotton blue-and-white striped sailor shirts with a wide boatneck collar called St. James boat shirts. I wore them too, but they looked better on him.

Zébulon lived with his single mother and little brother in a basement apartment at the dead end of a sweet short street, ironically named Napoleon Street. It was eight blocks away from my family, also in Le Plateau–Mont-Royal. I was always trying to find reasons to be on Zébulon's quiet residential block, hoping for a glimpse of him. I would sit on my friend's stoop on his route to the Metro station or ride double with my friend on my bike around the block over and over, in hopes of catching a glimpse.

In all our years together at FACE, I barely had the courage to speak to Zébulon. Our most significant encounter was when we all discovered he was the object of both mine and Rufus's desire. It came to a head at Rufus's thirteenth birthday party that year. As always in the home of Rufus, there were piano playing and family singing, followed by cake at a big dining-room table. That's where the truth came out for all.

Zébulon sat down at the table. Following the magnetic pull to be near him, I reached for the chair next to him and was about to sit there when Rufus jumped in.

"I am sitting here, Melissa!" he announced with his usual bravado, as he slid into the coveted spot.

Thanks to my extreme shyness and pale complexion, this was the kind of social disaster that always resulted in me blushing beet red with embarrassment. It was revealed: I was a girl who liked boys, and Rufus was a boy who liked boys. Both of us were contending for the same prize.

When the party came to an end and the other guests had left, Rufus and I confessed our mutual crush. It was a revelation that the love we had stated for each other on the living-room floor earlier that year was *not* the same kind as our love for Zébulon.

My two first loves of my youth say a lot to me now. One was a gay friend for life, and the other I never got to kiss or even have much of a conversation with. The seeds were being planted for me to become a queen of unrequited love as a way to avoid romantic relationships, a role that would take me a long time and a lot of world travels to break.

CHAPTER 4

Late Bloomer, Music Lover

I AM THIRTEEN YEARS OLD, STILL WITHOUT ANY BREASTS OR MY PERIOD, clearly destined to be the latest bloomer in my friend group. My curly red hair is always fuzzy. It's never possible to make it into any cool style other than a ponytail or braids, or to use a headband to keep it from framing my face in a chaotic mess. I don't like it, but I don't blame or loathe myself for it. I just really don't know what to do with it, since it's not consistent with my increasing awareness of '80s fashion styles.

So, this year I decide to cut my hair short in the back and on the sides, to allow a curly flop to fall over my left eye. I've been inspired by the Tears for Fears front men, whose album *The Hurting* holds my tortured soul. I walk around Montreal with puffy earphones and a cassette Walkman attached to a belt that cinches my oversize green army pants, which taper silly tight at my ankles. I'm occasionally mistaken for a boy, but that doesn't bother me because all my heroes are romantic, mysterious British men who sing words that deeply comfort me and find me where I am. Their androgynous voices and their lyrics of dreams and longing, placed on top of melodies and textures, burrow into and cradle my lonely heart. These musicians feel like my best friends.

I am not happy at home. My mother is deep into her new life with my stepfather, Hervé, a handsome and gentle Frenchman. My three-year-old half brother, Yves, is central to their love and daily lives. For most of my first decade I more or less had my mother to myself, and the interruption was extremely painful. In addition, there is the incredibly disrupt-full cohabitation with my two teenage French stepbrothers (who came along with *lots* of emotional baggage associated with my stepfather's "two weeks on/two weeks off" custody agreement with his ex-wife).

These are horrid early-teen years at home. Turns out that teenage boys can be really cruel, especially when influenced by an angry parent/ex-wife. One day their Brigitte Bardot–esque French mother showed up at the door, blew cigarette smoke in my face, and called me the "little witch, Melissa." That set the tone for the new reality that awaited me.

Our blended family was cemented by the purchase and renovation of a beautiful old stone triplex town house overlooking Parc Jeanne-Mance and Mount Royal, just down the block from our apartment. All in all a glorious family home permanently holds one, overwhelming, haunting memory: When I was about twelve, my schoolmate, good friend, and ground-floor neighbor was violently raped in the basement of our house. I was alone upstairs watching TV, and she was alone downstairs in the rental apartment where she lived with her mother. Most days we rode public transportation home together, but that day I had a dentist appointment after school, leaving her to travel home alone. She had been followed home from school by a serial rapist who knocked at her door and threatened to kill her new kitten if she didn't let him in. As most days, our parents were at work when we'd get home. She let him in. By the time I came home from the dentist to my empty home, I didn't think to check in on her. But once her mother came home from work, she ran upstairs to find me. "Our apartment has been robbed! Where is my daughter?" she exploded in a panic, looking for her daughter. Shortly after, my mother and stepfather got home from work, and I watched from the upstairs living-room window while the adults frantically ran in and out of the downstairs apartment. "Stay upstairs, Melissa!" I read the muted scream from my mother's lips as she looked up in terror from the front yard, as the other mother fell to her knees, howling like a dying animal. The frightening scene of these terrorized mothers from above burned in my cellular memory.

After a full search of the house, my stepfather found her tied up in the basement. A true horror that took place under my family's roof while I was upstairs alone. Spared. I was spared. My friend didn't show up to school for weeks to come, but besides that evidence of trauma, the event was never discussed again. My childlike interpretation was that it could've been me, I was lucky, but I was on guard from that moment on, assuming that every girl would be raped. "Survivor's guilt" may also have lingered, warping my ideas around sexual abuse. To this day, I still rarely walk on city streets alone.

These unhappy situations fueled my early adolescent hunt for melancholic music that spoke for me. The British men who ruled the emerging sounds of '80s New Wave at the time—the Smiths, the Cure, Tears for Fears, the Psychedelic Furs, Depeche Mode, Echo and the Bunnymen—were everything I could've hoped for.

Youth culture of the '80s saved my soul, I have no doubt. Thank the goddesses for '80s pop culture, and for my friends during that decade, who were the greatest remedy for all hard things at home.

By that time my parents had figured out a good routine for joint custody, and I would happily spend weekends at Nick's house, always with a friend, if not a couple of them. We all agreed that Nick's house was the least grown-up of all our homes and he was the most fun of all the parents. There were no real rules; we could eat whatever we wanted and watch all the TV we felt like, go to bed late, and laugh a lot. He'd pick up me and a friend after school on Fridays, and as we hopped in a cab to head to happy hour, I'd ask, "Where are we going?"

"Crazy. Wanna come?" he'd reply without fail.

We'd wind up at a local bar, where he'd drink with his friends while my friend and I sipped on Shirley Temples and played video games with the roll of quarters Nick would get for us from the bartender.

One sunny, warm Friday afternoon we were walking through downtown doing our usual rounds, saying hello to friends in restaurants and bars. We'd just stopped into the grocery store to pick up some food he would cook for dinner when he lit up his next cigarette.

Nick was a chain-smoker. He smoked as we walked down the street. He smoked at the bars. He smoked between meals, all the time. I don't know what came over me, because I was usually a well-behaved and certainly not precocious or obnoxious child. Maybe I'd just learned in school that smoking could kill you. I grabbed his cigarettes out of his breast pocket of his blazer and dangled the pack in front of his eyes, almost taunting him, before dropping them into the sewer gutter on the corner.

Nick got mad. *Very* mad, which was uncommon. I'd seen him explode in hot political debates with other people, but never with me before.

"Melissa, don't do that again," he said in the sternest voice he'd ever used with me. "*Never* do that. Those are mine."

"But cigarettes can kill you," I insisted.

He blew it off. That's when I realized this topic was out-of-bounds. Whatever I saw in him that day was unusual but real, and it scared me. I didn't mention his cigarettes again, but he would bring up the topic every year when he'd try to give up smoking and drinking for Lent. He'd more or less spend the whole month grumpy and in bed. I never understood why he was doing it, since he was neither religious nor having a good experience with it. But it was an indication, the only one I saw, that he was conscious that his constant smoking and drinking could be having a negative impact on him.

One of my most regular companions on those Friday afternoons and for regular sleepovers at Nick's was Alice Rosenbaum. Alice was my best friend in all things music and youth culture. She was a head taller than the rest of us, very slender, with long dark hair. Alice oozed a natural melancholic style and had great taste and a deep passion for music. We had met in elementary school and remained best friends through high school, but our middle school years and our growing obsession with music during that time were what bound us together for life.

Alice's parents met as mods in Brighton Beach, England, and in my opinion, they were the coolest parents of all. Her mother was a social worker and her father a documentary filmmaker, and their house was filled with music that featured moody guitar textures and cool beats. They had better fashion sense than most of the adults I knew, with their black turtlenecks and cool leather lace-up shoes. Even their snacks were better: Jaffa Cakes and Flake bars, sent from the grandparents in London.

Through Alice and her family, I fell in love with the United Kingdom, and all its music and youth culture. At her house I became familiar with the UK music mags *NME*, *Melody Maker*, and *Smash Hits*. We devoured them all, giving ourselves a thorough pop and rock education. The Rosenbaum household felt exotic and otherworldly, with an air of mystery and escapism that I now identify as melancholy and I must confess may be my natural disposition.

Alice's parents divorced during middle school, and she and her sister moved to London for a year to live with Martin, who got a job at the BBC. This move to England was not acceptable for our tight friendship, so to protect us from total heartbreak our parents agreed to send me to visit her for a few weeks during the summers that bookended her year abroad. That first

---

Melissa Auf der Maur and Alice Rosenbaum in London, 1986. Photo by Martin Rosenbaum.

summer in London made a big impact on me. It also added serious credibility to my wardrobe when I returned with Dr. Martens and an oversize yellow smiley-face T-shirt.

Those years with Alice entirely shaped the music fan in me. Middle school kids today have the internet and a whole world right at their fingertips to occupy them, but in the '80s we had only TV to watch, books to read, and purchased hard-copy music to listen to. And for many of us, music was everything.

We listened to the McGill University college-radio station, CKUT, and began to attend underground all-ages shows in Montreal school gyms. For a while we followed a cool band of teenagers who called themselves the Gruesomes. Inspired by obscure mid-'60s garage-rock-band records, they wore matching black turtlenecks, Beatles boots, and bowl haircuts and seduced us with their humor, their cool-looking girlfriends, and their "snotty" punk musical style. Their breakout album, *Tyrants of Teen Trash*, was followed by *Gruesomania!* that reflected their rising popularity in the underground and college-radio music scene in Canada.

But the love Alice and I had for the boys in bands was totally eclipsed by our love for Blondie. I still believe Debbie Harry is arguably the most beautiful and effortless, sexy punk pop star that ever lived. What a gift she was to young girls like us. We knew every song on every Blondie album and studied each of her outfits.

Thanks to her music-fan parents, Alice had a knack for researching her favorite artists and discovering all she could about them. In the preinternet era, this wasn't easy. There wasn't a Women in Music section in libraries or a formal establishment on the planet (there barely is even now!), so we had to learn all we could for ourselves. And we did. By 1980 Blondie had peaked, so we had the benefit of being able to dig through all the used books and magazine racks at the cool music shops in Montreal. We rented the Blondie VHS of all her videos and borrowed another VHS deck to dub it so we could watch it over and over, and then—jackpot!—we came across *Making Tracks*, an entire *book* devoted to Blondie. It was part tour diary, part band memoir, and we devoured every page.

The foundation of our music obsession started with the New Wave UK scene, took a deep dive into all the classic 1960s and 1970s NYC scene—with Blondie, the Velvet Underground, Richard Hell and the Voidoids, the Ramones, and of course Andy Warhol's Factory—and included a growing attunement to the local underground Montreal scene. Our love of the cool stuff was also complemented by a healthy dose of the best of the mainstream pop culture of the day.

The biggest hitmakers that we made time for were Cyndi Lauper and Michael Jackson, with Prince and Madonna trailing further behind. I loved the Go-Gos' album *Beauty and the Beat*, especially the song "Our Lips Are Sealed," and was thrilled by the all-girl-band aspect, but something about the beauty parlor, bath towels, and facials on the album cover artwork did not resonate with me. As a daughter of an all-natural mother, those women's beauty routines—even if ironic—were lost on me.

In 1984, when we were twelve, Alice and I left school early one day with a note of permission from my mother saying we needed to skip class for me to participate in a Cyndi Lauper look-alike contest at the mall. This was one of the benefits of going to a wacky art school: the children were always empowered to express themselves, and no questions were asked.

"Girls Just Want to Have Fun" was one of the biggest hits on the radio, still a year into its release. Alice spray-painted my hair until it was neon orange and crusty. Then she helped me pin it up on one side. I wore a puffy skirt that I had hand-dyed a blotchy moss green and a baggy neon sweater, draped random necklaces around my neck, stacked plastic gummy bracelets up each wrist, and pulled fishnet half gloves onto my little hands.

When we arrived at the biggest mall in Montreal, we quickly realized I was the only prepubescent contestant. Onstage, I was flanked by tall, breasted, cool 1980s women. Their cleavage, fishnet-clad long sexy legs, and actual womanhood were intimidating. Cyndi's three biggest hits were played for us to simultaneously dance and lip-synch in a chorus line. I knew every word and used my hands to emulate Cyndi's signature move, Lauper's shout-out to "jazz hands." An audience gathered around the stage and up on the balconies in the atrium.

The startling thing to me, even now, is that a painfully shy child who was terrified of even speaking in front of a class went out of her way to dress up and lip-synch onstage in a giant downtown mall just for the experience, not even for the prize. That says something, something that runs deep in the intuition and drive of a twelve-year-old girl who likely wasn't aware of it herself yet. I struggled with a lisp at that age, enough of an impediment that my mother had me seeing a special orthodontist and taking after-school acting classes to improve my speech. The lisp perhaps explains my delight at lip-synching. Hiding behind someone else's voice was empowering.

When it was time for awards, I came in third for being "cute," while other more convincing young women won first and second places. They won tickets to Cyndi's upcoming concert. I got a poster. Fortunately, my father had friends in high places in Montreal, including concert promoters, so we had already secured four front-row seats for the concert.

During those middle school summers, Alice and I had nothing but time to burn with each other, following our noses for all the good culture of the day. Not as easily as kids have it today, with access to everything at their fingertips. We had to work for it, earn it, and we wore that effort like a badge of honor. Over the years this would add up to something. We had yet to discover what that something was, but I can give you a hint now: music-fandom credibility. We were developing the real-deal devotion, what every band should hope for.

We prided ourselves in knowing details about our favorite bands and would ask the adults at the music shops questions like, "Can we special order the Smiths' UK seven-inch single for *Panic*?" We knew our shit. I imagine all those nerdy older men working these shops who watched us regulars grow up over the years must've found us inspiring, like I do now when I see young people obsessing over music. It must've given them hope for the future generation of music lovers.

Over summers and weekends throughout our middle school years, Alice and I developed various side projects. We formed our own rap group, inspired by the Beastie Boys and the Velvet Underground combined, and called ourselves the "Wild Bananas of Cool." My rapper name was "Mulse, Eh?" I was the "scratcher," and my companion was "Alice R." We'd rap over anything, recorded on boom-box tape decks. Our most fleshed-out hit was called "Sniffin' Sister," about Alice's little sister Claire, who suffered from asthma and bad allergies her whole childhood.

We also created our own radio station, R-A-M (for Radio Alice & Melissa), on those same tape decks. We homed in on radio personalities, something that both of my parents actually were, and would blab away in our high little-girl voices about our favorite after-school snacks and the weather and play our favorite songs.

In case you're wondering? Alice has safely preserved *all* those cassettes.

The only interruptions to my time with Alice during these coming-of-age summers were the couple weeks of riding camp my mother arranged for me between the ages of twelve and fifteen. My oldest childhood friend, Rachel Goldman, had a great, outdoorsy horse-enthusiast father who found a very off-the-beaten-path, affordable riding camp for us: Poverty Hill Stables.

True to its name, the camp had us living in the basement of an old house that belonged to a salt-of-the-earth horse-breeding family. Riding horses was a life-changing and -defining experience for a young small person who did not feel particularly empowered. To learn how to interact with noble, giant creatures that could crush you or throw you off in a heartbeat was my first experience with a true superpower. Feeling safe with them in their stalls, mounting them, learning their language, and eventually galloping were electrifying. It felt like riding lightning. I had never felt so alive in body and spirit.

One of those summers also marked my first experience with psychedelics. Trusting the older girls, I placed the purple paper acid tab on my tongue, and my universe expanded. What followed was a wonderfully weird evening of hallucinatory "tracers" while communing with a baby doll whose eyes opened and closed. Of course, there's always a danger with psychedelics, but it could be argued there was a benefit for me being exposed at such a young age. I believe an injection of the world beyond the norm at that time gave me advanced warning of the demented side of life to come. Life is a trip.

In 1985, at the lucky age of thirteen, Alice and I went to our first concert without a real parent, chaperoned only by Paul, Alice's super-cool, young, and possibly stoned uncle. He brought us to see the Cure. Earlier that year, I'd purchased their *Head on the Door* album with my own money on a trip to Paris with my father. I was working various jobs those days, entirely motivated by my desire to buy new music. I worked as a newspaper delivery girl (my father wrote for the paper!) and as a squash-club laundry girl (my father's friend owned the club!). Despite the family connections, these were tough jobs, involving freezing winter morning-paper delivery runs and other people's sweaty towels and gym socks, so my money was hard earned.

The *Head on the Door* show was when I discovered where I belonged. Standing with Alice on the floor of the arena, with the masses dressed in all black, was the shit.

Melissa Auf der Maur and Patches, 1985. Photo by Mark D. Goldman.

CHAPTER 5

Moving in New Directions

"Hey, Oscar Mayer, does your father make sausages?"

The voice came from the desk behind me at the top of math period. Turning around, I looked directly into the soles of a large pair of leather biker boots with metal plates on the shins.

The boy attached to the boots, in a frayed flannel shirt underneath a long trench coat, was a duplicate of John Bender, Judd Nelson's character in *The Breakfast Club*. This guy was additionally stylized with multiple silver earrings and massive skull rings ordaining his knuckles. I recognized him to be in the year above me.

I blushed at this intimidating character's offensive question. He was deliberately making fun of my complex last name, which was already a touchy subject for me. Living with an unpronounceable name is not easy, especially in my earlier years as a shy girl with a lisp.

"No. He's a journalist and politician," I replied quietly and in earnest.

"I know who Nick Auf der Maur is. My dad and I read his columns all the time. He's cool."

With that compliment, the mood lightened. "I'm Alex," he said, as he stuck his hand out with great confidence to meet mine.

"Melissa." I reached over the back of my chair.

Somewhere along the way, some radical educators decided to coordinate with FACE and started a special program for "independently motivated teens" within the massive five-story historic building that housed our school. This new creation, MIND (which stood for Moving in New Directions), occupied a small single-floor wing of the bigger school and became known as "the alternative high school" in Montreal. In 1986 I'd made the decision on my own to move onto the "special" floor in our big school and scheduled the interview process myself. Students at MIND were placed at their level of aptitude, not with their grade, and my ease with math put me in a class with older students.

At MIND you were either a brilliant nerd, a cool alternative punk, a weirdo, or all three. As Alex and I became friends, I discovered we were both attracted to strange, dark, and alternative things. One day after school, he invited me to join him at his after-school happy-hour joint, a windowless club on Stanley Street downtown where we sat in a dark corner and ordered dollar beers. Club Thunderdome, located above a strip club, was the hub of all things goth in 1980s Montreal. It would become the site of my first obsession with the IRL music-club scene and remain so throughout high school.

I was only fourteen, but there was no scrutiny in Montreal. Everyone was allowed to have a good time. My friend Rachel from the riding camp, who'd survived LSD with me, was the most adventurous of all my friends, so I roped her into exploring this new portal with me.

The line outside the door extended down Stanley Street when Rachel and I arrived on a Friday night. We handed the bouncer the fake IDs I had made with the laminator at the job where I worked doing other people's laundry. He barely glanced at the date and name I had faked to turn me into eighteen-year-old "Melissa Johnson" to hide my family name, which was well known in the downtown Montreal bar scene.

Passing by a brightly lit poster of naked women, we headed up the narrow, dark staircase. As we entered the bar, I caught the familiar smell of cigarettes and beer from my childhood. Bartenders were outfitted in black leather, piercings, and plenty of black tattoos. They looked like fictional characters from the postapocalyptic sci-fi movies I hadn't yet seen. Music was blasting at top volume, which limited communication.

This club had put a lot of effort into transforming the bar into otherworldly scenes, which was part of its allure. Working with set designers and builders, they had created a vessel of fantasy for their escapist clients. This season was a wannabe H. R. Giger "sex machine meets spaceship" theme. Giger, a Swiss fantasy-genre artist, was best known as the visionary sci-fi set designer for Ridley Scott's 1979 movie *Alien*, which became the primary reference for all sci-fi ever made. But most important, Giger was recognized for his airbrush style of paintings that morphed women's bodies and machines. He called this art style "biomechanical"—with Debbie Harry as a muse, he created her album art for her debut solo effort. It could have been creepy looking for some, but for me it created strange tingling, sensual feelings in my still very young, coming-into-her-own body.

As I walked down the hall with Rachel, I was the picture of a young teen of the time, still with no breasts, wearing cutoff jean shorts, dyed green Converse high tops, and an oversize long-sleeved black T-shirt covered in pancake-size happy faces. Happy faces were the symbol of the rave movement, representing the drug Ecstasy that the scene was built on. It was the quintessential opposite to the goth symbols of the ancient Egyptian ankh, the Latin Cross and the Pentagram, but both movements' visceral release onto the dance floor with heavy beats made them sister movements of the time.

People were dancing inside cages on podiums in the middle of the room. I was intrigued by the over-the-top hair, accessories, and clothes that made them stand out as "outsiders" in the broader world. It was fascinating to a girl trying to find a language of her own to share the complex new feelings emerging inside of her.

Sipping on a two-dollar black-label Labatt's beer, I took in the pulsing, intriguing sounds and visuals. I watched how women with breasts and sex appeal used their bodies to express themselves and how the men in leather watched them, admired them, occasionally danced with them, and touched them with their hands and mouths.

There was a holy element to these outings for me, a newfound ritual. And the music—the music was enough to hold me. The magical Brit songs that I'd listened to alone in my bedroom, songs that had comforted me when I cried in a bathroom stall at school, took on new meaning here in a room filled with strangers who loved them too. We all wanted to be held in by someone else's pain, hopes, and fantasies. Sharing the heavy beats, the creamy synths, and melancholic melodies with these beautiful freaks felt like a revelation. Even now, these songs still bring me back to a deep place, a collective consciousness of gothic romance and longing.

Meanwhile, my inner world outside the club was also beginning to take shape. The 1980s were a beautiful time of pre-self-surveillance, before everyone had a phone in their pocket and documenting all that you eat and feel became the norm. There was still a sense of freedom and anonymity that nurtured an abundance of sacred, private self-discovery and exploration. In the absence of cameras at the club, or on the streets documenting every move, I found myself curious about documenting people, ideas, moods, and scenes. A strong desire to capture what I was seeing in myself and the world around me began to grow.

My deepening feelings about the world of music and its people felt intoxicating. I wanted to capture it all. I had kept a personal diary since the age of ten to attempt to explain what I felt, but words were not sufficient. I wanted to translate these thoughts into other forms, and my instinct was to try it out through photography.

Inspired by big photo books on my mother's bookshelves, I borrowed her 35mm Minolta camera and started bringing it around with me on my daily routine. Having a camera in hand gives a shy young person a sense of agency or power around her surroundings. I had a say in what I saw and gave attention to.

I would photograph moments at school, like Alice and me reflected in the girls' bathroom mirror during recess, and accidental still lifes on the street, like a mannequin torso poking out of a garbage can. Some of these moments were more existential teen in nature, like a meditation on crumbling brick or a rusting pipe in an alleyway.

Taking a moment alone to witness the world decaying felt natural and satisfying to me.

I also loved the patient, quiet mystery of waiting for photos to be processed. I began to look at music imagery on albums and in magazines in a new way, wondering who took those photographs and who chose them to photograph that band, thinking maybe one day I could do that too. It was my first notion of a viable profession that could connect me with the things I loved.

By high school I had access to my own darkroom, located in a small closet in my high school art classroom. Few others were using it during my time there, and I was more or less in charge of it. I was given a fast lesson in black-and-white film processing and printing and picked it up quickly. I loved locking myself into the darkroom closet to protect me and my private photo project from others and unwanted light.

The alchemy of chemicals that brought images on film and paper to life was nothing less than magical to me. The room was still and quiet, illuminated by only a dim red lightbulb, and felt so safe. Womblike, really. Watching an image come into being in a darkroom tray is something I recommend for all to experience, although good luck finding a darkroom in the twenty-first century!

My first major project was to photograph each student in the school for our end-of-year, student-made fanzine yearbook. It gave me a purpose and a connection to each person, without needing to be a showboat. I could continue to make that shy, shrouded-with-mystery persona I was cultivating work for me. Hiding behind a lens was a great comfort.

As I was growing into full-on teendom, my father's career was at its peak. His popular newspaper column was in print three days a week, on Mondays, Wednesdays, and Fridays. Most English Montrealers would start their day chuckling with Nick at the breakfast table. He was prolific, never short on tales to tell, most of them typed or handwritten at his favorite bar. He wrote concise stories with a start, a middle, and an end, always with an underlying moral message. Humor was key to his storytelling. When nothing much was happening in politics, downtown city drama, or our father-daughter adventures (which were a popular recurrence) that week, he would tell delightfully

lazy stories like about how silly it is to wrap potatoes in tin foil or his preference for strawberries over the coveted all-too-delicate raspberry. Sometimes he'd pull from his Swiss heritage and write about his eccentric mother who still pined for the Alps and her Swiss saints.

In addition to his column in the *Gazette*, he was also doing spots on radio. He'd roll in as a regular, and often late, guest at the morning show. His ranting and passion almost always inspired laughs. I witnessed that he was a total joy for others to be in the presence of. Montreal in the 1980s was his heyday, and we were all lucky to be witness to his love affair with the city.

His political career took shape after he was elected to city council as an independent in 1974, followed by the publication of his only book, *The Billion-Dollar Game*. It chronicled his singlehanded challenge of the municipal government's spending and corruption in the lead-up to Montreal's 1976 Olympic Games. He became an international expert on the issue. By the

---

Melissa and Nick Auf der Maur, 1982.

mid-'80s he held his steady position as downtown Montreal city councillor, representing the central district where the French, English, university, museum, business, and mainstream cultural lives of Montreal all intersected.

In 1986 Nick was reelected as downtown city councilor as an independent, after leaving the "Municipal Action Group" party he founded in 1982. He appeared to have no qualms about his growing and controversial reputation for founding, leaving, and switching political parties.

"It's the parties that change, not me that changes," he would say. I would often accompany him on his campaign trail, sometimes knocking door-to-door or joining him at his campaign headquarters on election night. Waiting late into the night for the polls to call in with their vote counts was something that I found quite nerve-racking.

One election night, while he laughed off his nerves as we waited for results, I asked him, "Nick, why do you do this?" I was feeling nervous and protective of my father, should he lose this round.

"Because I don't trust those assholes to do a good job," he replied, without a trace of humor.

No matter how entertaining or outrageous he seemed to some, his heart was thoroughly in the right place. I believe Montreal is a better city for having had him. I know that others agree with me. His longtime title of "unofficial mayor of Montreal" is well deserved.

Meanwhile, back at the Thunderdome . . . I had my first encounter with a penis.

It was with Alex, who had introduced me to the club. I had looked up to him and trusted him, but crossing into kissing and sexual intimacy was all new to me. Alex definitely knew more about sex than I did.

This was my first overnight with a boy. I was supposed to stay at Rachel's that night, so I was covered in that way. We stumbled into his parents' house late one night after the club closed, not really knowing what was expected of such a clandestine effort. We began to kiss on the couch and fumble around with our hands. Next thing I knew I was holding a hard penis in my hand for the first time. It was soft and then wet, not a bad experience, even a bit thrilling but also very awkward. I left at the crack of dawn. I could never look at Alex the same way again.

In addition to the goth and sexuality gateway, my other lasting impression of Alex was that he seemed to have a much clearer perspective on my father's depth of character than I did. He came by Nick's house with me once after school and stopped in front of a picture frame in my father's office.

"What's the story with this?" he asked.

The frame in question held a newspaper clipping with a large close-up of my thirteen-year-old face holding a card. The headline read, "Birthday Card Was Shamrock Summit's First Document." Negotiations at the US-Canada breakthrough summit on free trade and acid rain on St. Patrick's Day 1985 were kicked off by agreeing to a young girl's birthday card. The card was signed by my father's old friend then Canadian prime minister Brian Mulroney and then US president Ronald Reagan.

My birthday card, headline news. My father put them up to it. It was funny, he thought, and made them look human.

Alex chuckled.

"It was my father's idea," I said. "He just wanted a good story."

I was revealing that I knew how the press works. It was an ironic coming-of-age connection between me and the icon of the Reagan era that my generation would soon rebel against in the form of alternative-rock music, with its nonconformity and anticorporate ethos.

CHAPTER 6

A Couch to Crash on, a Beer Bottle, and the Apology

JULY 1991

> Starts out like magic, some sick religion
> That ain't no vulture, that's a fucking pigeon
> She's got vultures in her hair
> And blood and feathers, they are everywhere
> You want retreat, filthy and deep
> A dead moon, a drunken seed
> Baby, there is a room full of death
>   and whores and truth
> And I am waiting in that room
> And I am sorry I did that for you
> It's all whores, it's all pain
> It's all disease, man, it's all the same
>
> —"Burn Black," by Hole

IN 1991, I WAS LIVING AT THE "GRUNGE ESTATES," THE TONGUE-IN-CHEEK nickname for a sixplex apartment complex at 3711 St-Dominique Street. It was a quintessential Montreal apartment building down a mini half-block street, all occupied by arty and grungy university students. Grunge Estates had been named by one of the founders of *VICE* magazine (he who shall not be named) who attended the same university and also had an apartment in this complex.

Like the classic Montreal family-size apartments I grew up in, these buildings were the signature architectural feature of Le Plateau Montreal neighborhood, mostly turn-of-the-last-century brick or stone buildings, much like the famed NYC brownstones. Their most recognizable feature was their exterior wrought-iron staircases, which were designed to maximize space and save money from heating stairwells in freezing winters. I felt very at home in this neighborhood I grew up in, but most other students who rented here were visiting from the rest of English Canada or the United States.

Our apartment had Old World charm, with hardwood floors, high ceilings, and lovely wood and plaster moldings and trim around all the doors, windows, and ceiling light fixtures. In all of these layouts, as you entered the front hallway a tiny room gave way to a front balcony. Next to that was a big double-parlor living room, and down the hallway toward the back of the building was the central dining room. The main bedroom was usually situated off the dining room, and the hall continued back with an old-timey bathroom off to one side.

The kitchen was always at the back, usually with a large balcony adorned with planters. A tiny room was often in the back-back, traditionally used for storage, canning, or a grandparent. In our case it was always the male roommate who rented that room, which was just big enough for a single bed and tiny desk, for about $150 a month. To have the big double front parlor as my bedroom, I paid about $50 more a month than whoever my female roommate was at the time. She would take the smaller room off the central living room.

I loved my room. With its high ceiling and elaborate plaster moldings, it was bathed in loads of sunlight. It had a front part of the parlor and a back part, divided by an ornate archway. I moved the orientation around from time to time, but one section was always my bed and clothes section and the other my music, art, and hanging-out section. I painted all the trim gold and had a lot of kitschy '70s faux-velvet tapestries and cheap plastic gold candelabras, as well as mirrors and framed Renaissance paintings, counterbalanced by some rusty metal object I carried home from an alleyway.

This bedroom held me during the most significant developmental years of my life, when music began to explode inside me and into the hearts of my peers around the world. From that room, I joined a visceral generational movement. That room was also where I began to explore my photography, primarily intimate self-portraits of both my body and the tiny details of the room, like a vintage cigar box or a crack in the mirror.

The big windows looked out on the main drag, with a perfect view of Le Bifteque St Laurent, the dive bar that guided my path as a cassette deejay turned photography student turned world-famous bass player. It held me through my exploration of hosting traveling bands on our couch, but not my bed. The occasional visitor who cared to talk magic and music into the late nights might get to make out with me, but usually nothing too sexual. It wasn't in my realm of desire.

July 11, 1991, was my night off from my job at the legendary punk club Les Foufounes Électriques, but I was hanging around the club as usual. The direct translation of the French "Les Foufounes Électriques" into English is "The Electric Buttocks." The venue was Montreal's answer to CBGB, the New York club that many have deemed the birthplace of US punk. Founded in 1983 by a group of quintessentially Quebecois performance artists who loved the spectacle of live body painting, Foufounes began in a one-room apartment. Eventually, it took over half the city block and single-handedly nurtured the punk youth-culture scene in Montreal. Between 1990 and 1994 I saw almost every seminal band of the time there: Sonic Youth, Helmet, Jesus Lizard, Nirvana, Mudhoney, Ice-T, Hole, and the Smashing Pumpkins, among many others.

That night a band named Hole from Los Angeles was booked to open for Buffalo Tom, an alternative male rock band based in Boston. Hole's first album, *Pretty on the Inside*, would be released soon, but they were still virtually unknown. This was one of their first shows on the East Coast.

The band took to the stage in front of a sparse crowd of intermittently attentive people, most of whom were there to see Buffalo Tom. As cool as the aloof crowd was, though, when Courtney Love stepped into the lights, they suddenly took notice.

Courtney was rocking her signature look at the time: a tattered vintage baby-doll dress, patent-leather baby-doll shoes, and a black-and-white

Rickenbacker guitar that she screeched, scratched, and flung around more than she played. Like a spoken-word poet, she growled lyrics of the new feminist order. Taking the power of abuse in her own hands, in her songs she reclaimed words like "slut":

> *Slutkiss girls*
> *Won't you promise her smack?*
> *Is she pretty on the inside?*
> *Is she pretty from the back?*

and "whore," which was central to the catchiest lyrics on *Pretty on the Inside*'s opening track:

> *When I was a teenage whore*
> *My mother asked me, she said, "Baby, what for?*
> *I give you plenty, why do you want more?*
> *Baby, why are you a teenage whore?"*

That night I experienced the visceral shock of Hole at its very beginning, three years before I'd become a member of the band. From my first encounter, I saw this Courtney Love creature was fearless, if not also terrifying. As I'd later witness firsthand, she was truly a unique force of nature. But that night I watched with detachment and curiosity, as if I were witnessing an exorcism in a ceremonial ritual, or a wild animal in attack mode at a zoo. Despite her outrageous gestures, Courtney's performance seemed real and authentic, like she was pulling all the darkness from her personal life—you can't fake that pain.

As foils to this smeared-red-lipstick and bleached-blonde commander, the band behind her was a stoic trio. Each member had long hair parted in the middle that hid what I now know were somewhat shy and awkward faces.

The only man onstage was the tall, lanky guitarist, who played through many pedals and seemed to be almost conducted by Courtney's movements and energy. He reacted and improvised to her moods and verbal commands.

The Amazonian drummer had dyed bright-orange curly hair and played repetitive, primitive, rolling tom beats, while the attractive bass player—a slight and statuesque woman wearing wide-legged glitter pants and a button-down black-satin blouse—held her cool and tamed the wild mess effortlessly.

Jill Emery, the bassist who left Hole in 1992 and later went on to play in Mazzy Star from 1993 to 1996, was to me the most intriguing, or at least most relatable, person on the stage. I identified with her stoicism and her unfazed air, a personality trait that in my own life had made me a magnet for volatile women. I think those women saw me as an open-minded and polite friend, with a "free-to-be" philosophy inherited from my bohemian parents and a generally high tolerance for "crazy." Standing up there with Courtney and grounding her, Jill somehow made me realize that I was meant to play bass—and, shockingly, I would fill her exact position in the band a few years later.

That night, I noticed a man standing on the side of the stage who seemed to be Hole's roadie. I thought he was cute, with his edgy confidence, James Dean looks, and throwback auto-mechanic look with his greased-back black hair. He was cool and irresistible.

In those days, among my scene at least, it was common to offer a couch to sleep on to complete strangers traveling in a van through your hometown. That summer I had one roommate, Aileen, who was an acting student from Edmonton, Alberta, and we often had touring bands stay at our house.

Despite my generally introverted personality, I could be very direct when I wanted to be. After Hole's performance, I approached the roadie as he disassembled gear at the side of the stage. He introduced himself as Cali, and before many other words were exchanged, I simply asked, "Do you guys need a place to stay tonight?"

"Sure, that would be great," he replied. I smiled, and we agreed that we'd leave together when the band was ready.

A few minutes later, I was on my way to the club's dirty bathroom when the ferocious lead singer stopped me and asked, "Were you the babe talking to our roadie?"

"Yes," I said.

"Fuck him. We're all sexually frustrated." She grinned.

I responded with a cool and collected nod, perhaps a smile, slightly removed, as if I were still watching her performance onstage. Inside I felt a little tingle of excitement and intimidation.

Those were the first words I exchanged with Courtney Love.

Back at the bar, I announced my hosting plan to my friends. "What?!" my roommate Aileen shrieked. "That crazy bitch Courtney Love is not staying in my house!"

I'd never heard of Courtney until that night, but Aileen was apparently aware of her acting career. She went on to tell us all about how Courtney had starred with Joe Strummer from the Clash in 1987's *Straight to Hell*, a parody of spaghetti westerns about a desert town full of coffee-addicted killers. Alex Cox, who wrote and directed the film, had written the role of Velma, the unhinged pregnant woman, specifically for Courtney.

"She's a psychopath," Aileen said, "and she's not staying in my house."

It wasn't worth starting a drama with my roommate, so I went and found Cali, the cute roadie, and uninvited the band.

Exactly twelve days later, on July 23, 1991, Aileen, her boyfriend Bruce (who'd recently moved in with us), and I decided to step out into the muggy Montreal streets for "Loonie Tuesdays" night at Foufounes, a dollar special to see a live band for cheap every Tuesday night. The club had many offerings to serve the diverse underground culture of our city—industrial dance nights, punk nights, Francophone and Canadian prog-rock concerts—but the only themed nights I was interested in were the Anglophone alternative-rock-band lineups.

The three of us were dressed appropriately for the era: leather shoelaces tied tight around our necks, bicycle chains worn as bracelets, jean shorts with black leggings underneath, weathered combat boots or Vans, and secondhand faded T-shirts with random logos of forgotten industrial companies. When we arrived at Foufounes that night in the summer of 1991, I reminded my housemates of the Sub Pop logo on the flier for tonight's show. I'd never heard of the band the Smashing Pumpkins, but I figured that the Seattle label that had released Nirvana's first album, *Bleach*, as well as albums by Mudhoney, Soundgarden, and other great bands we loved must be on to something.

It was a quiet weeknight at the club. We each had a mug of local microbrewery beer on the patio before the show began. After downing our drinks, we stepped out onto the nearly empty club floor with about twenty other people as the band hit the stage.

I took note of the band members as they checked their levels. I was fascinated to see a woman on bass with long, straight platinum-blonde hair and a very pretty Japanese man on guitar. Their presence onstage, like that of the women in Hole, instantly set the Pumpkins apart from the all-white, male rock bands who played Foufounes every other night of the week.

When the music kicked in, I noticed that the drummer played faster and was more obviously competent than most. And at center stage was the cherubic lead singer and guitarist, a very tall man with wispy curls that framed his face and fell to his shoulders, in a paisley-patterned button-down polyester shirt and a pair of tight dark-purple jeans. He was one of the most serious, intensely dramatic, sincerely emotive lead singers and guitarists I'd ever seen. As the band played on, I became more and more alert to the front man's impressive guitar technique and sophisticated songwriting. This was rare at the time, at least in the live-music world that I'd been immersed in. Most bands were very expressive but played more basic punk or experimental rhythms and styles, not as refined as this. I supposed some might have described it as "slick."

I'm not sure which came first: my decided love for the band or my new roommate Bruce's hatred for them.

"Who do these guys think they are? They aren't playing an arena . . ." Bruce began mumbling his dislike and then started catcalling, eventually yelling during a transition between songs, "Drop the fucking attitude, man!!!"

The bandleader, to whom Bruce's comment was directed, had been gazing down at his guitar and the many pedals at his feet. Coolly, he lifted his head and said, "I'm just tuning my fucking guitar, asshole."

That was when the beer bottle went flying out of Bruce's hand and smashed dead center onto the lead singer's guitar.

Absolute silence and stillness followed. I thought that Bruce had just ended one of the best rock shows I'd ever witnessed. I'd been elated, as if I'd found a new part of me, suspended in deep discovery, before this strange and violent exchange interrupted it.

The lead singer leaped off the stage toward the crowd, hands outstretched in front of him, reaching for Bruce's neck. The two crashed into one another and rolled on the ground at my feet until one of Foufounes' signature giant skinhead bouncers broke it up. Bruce got back on his feet, having been dwarfed, but not hurt, by the very tall singer. He mumbled to himself about the "fucking asshole wannabe rock star." Then he and Aileen left the building while the crowd's attention turned back to the band.

I was horrified by Bruce's rudeness and figured the show was over. Yet the singer got back up onstage, straightened out his shirt with radiant pride, and slung his left-handed guitar over his shoulder, with a calm he'd radiated just before the encounter with Bruce.

"PUNK IS DEAD! PUNK IS DEAD!" he screamed in the mic with drama, then politely concluded, "We've got one more for you, Montreal."

"I Am One" opened with a tribal drumbeat and a hypnotic, rumbling bass line, then a glassy guitar swell that swept into the full band. This song and the band's commitment to it broke me open and sent me soaring into a new universe. The simplest yet most powerful rhythmic bass line thundered through me. It was the best thing I'd ever heard. Soon I'd learn to play it at home alone in my bedroom, and it would guide me into my future in rock.

The sound of the Smashing Pumpkins was, for me, real-life magic. I'd been deprived of all the glamour and intensity of '70s metal and progressive-rock bands. During my painful teen years in the '80s, the melancholic, melodic New Wave comfort of the Smiths and the Cure was everything to me. But the sounds I heard that night in 1991 were brand-new, a revelation. They overwhelmed me with their power, excitement, and possibility.

After that last explosive song, having proved a point, the band ended their set and quickly began to pack up and move their gear off the stage.

They clearly didn't feel welcome to stick around Foufounes after an ass like Bruce had thrown a beer bottle at them.

I'll never know what moved me, a relatively reserved nineteen-year-old girl of few words, to do what I did next. I do know it had nothing to do with manners and everything to do with what I'd discovered in that moment as my newfound musical calling. I headed to the side of the stage, walked right up to the lead singer, and said, "On behalf of Montreal, Canada, I apologize, and I promise to follow your band from here 'til the end of time."

His smile was very warm, revealing the coolest set of teeth I'd ever seen: his two front teeth sloped back, while his incisors stuck out. He was sweet and grateful, and we introduced ourselves: he was Billy Corgan, and I, forevermore, became known as "Melissa from Montreal."

Billy's voice was high for a man of his stature; he had a pronounced nasally American accent, which I now know to be from Chicago. He told me that the band was heading out of town right after the show so there was no time to hang out, but in this fast exchange with the band packing up around him, we exchanged addresses and agreed to be pen pals.

I left Foufounes on a natural high, with the Smashing Pumpkins' vinyl single "Tristessa" in my hand. Later that week I bought the *Gish* cassette at Sam the Record Man, our now long-gone Canadian record-store chain. The Pumpkins' first album, *Gish*, was soon on endless rotation on my stereo, dominating my bedroom during the days and my deejay booth at night.

That first encounter with Billy was a turning point for me—musically, personally, and cosmically. We didn't lose contact—which, in a world before emails, cell phones, and social media was no small feat and proof of a sacred connection. His music made a profound impact on me that night, but I would never have believed it then if you'd told me that one day, Billy would have more influence on my life than anyone other than my parents.

CHAPTER 7

1991: The Song That Changed Everything

IN THE SUMMER OF 1991, I HAD JUST COMPLETED MY LAST YEAR AT DAWSON College prior to heading into my first year at Montreal's Concordia University. I'd started at Dawson in the Photography Department, but photo classes at Dawson were lame and angled entirely for a career in commercial photography. In the first week of classes we were given an exercise to photograph a refrigerator in a studio, and I quickly realized that such a focus was not going to lead me to the life I'd envisioned as a fine-art photographer.

I immediately transferred to the general Creative Arts Department as a holding pattern in preparation for my next stop, a *real* bachelor of fine arts at Concordia University. Thanks to the love I had for my alternative schools, I took education very seriously.

The man responsible for the artistic nude photos of my mother lining our apartment walls, Guy Borremans, became my photography mentor in high school and helped me learn the tricks of printing in the darkroom. He also helped me compile my portfolio for college applications. My first body of work, slipped into plastic sleeves bound in a black leather binder, consisted of a selection of black-and-white finely printed photographs with a good balance of live music concerts, decrepit Montreal alleyways, body parts, and moody still lifes.

Behind the camera my shy eye was protected by the shield of the lens. The results were naturally a bit goth, romantic, and melancholic in essence. Not

Sunshade self-portraits, 1993.

too long after, my music-loving hands would find the bass, which became my sword. This shy girl began to finally feel equipped to take on the outside world.

As the 1980s came to an end, the fucking incredible influx of American alternative bands was picking up and blowing our teen minds. In late 1990, Jane's Addiction came through Montreal for *Ritual de lo Habitual*, their follow-up album to the gorgeous *Nothing's Shocking*. The following summer they would headline and launch the legendary '90s traveling music festival known as Lollapalooza, but at this point they were just coming into their power. They'd never played Montreal before. My friends and I were lucky to get to see them at the Rialto, a historic ornate old theater that was larger than the usual punk clubs and refreshing with all its beauty and class.

That night, in the elegant lobby, I ran into a solid group of familiar faces that I saw at most shows. We gravitated like a pack up the stairs to get seats in the balcony. As we filled the front row with a divine view of the stage, a fistful of magic mushrooms got handed down the line. I chewed up my portion, holding back my gag reflex. Despite my love of that natural altered state, I despise the taste. It was worth it.

L7 was an all-female hard-rock band from LA whose album *Smell the Magic* had just been released. They were on tour with Jane's Addiction as the opening slot. It was amazing to see tattooed, crusty, fearless babes with heavy guitars and drums holding their own as they warmed up the stage for the legends in the making. As the L7 set ended, the mushrooms began to kick in. By the time Jane's took the stage, front man Perry Farrell's Witchiepoo high-pitched vocalizations, over swirling guitar textures and thunderous rolling drums and bass, were amplified by the psychedelics. I felt a part of something very very very powerful and real.

Jane's were the West Coast crest of the alternative-music wave, in perfect harmony with the Pixies from Boston. A wave of gigantic musicality and strong individuality permeated the alternative scene. No two bands sounded or looked the same. It felt like a well of infinite individuality had sprung forth from the underground and we were all being empowered by that. The concert solidified my connection with my peers, and the visceral power of the new decade clicked in for me.

The most significant evolution for me at this time, beyond witnessing these incredible bands, was the real-life education I got with my first legit *cool* jobs. I had two jobs to support myself and pay for college: a rock-club ticket girl and an even more serious career as a cassette deejay.

The deejay gig started in 1990 at Bar Le Bifteck (Bar Beef Steak), a former Portuguese steakhouse turned dive bar on St. Laurent Boulevard. Le Bifteck, which still exists today, is in Le Plateau–Mont-Royal, a turn-of-the-century immigrant-family business quarter that had merged with bohemians like my mother. My generation, with its own counterculture scene, was moving in now, creating a glorious tapestry of eccentricity.

My deejay booth at Le Bifteck was built into what used to be the kitchen of the Portuguese steakhouse. Strip it of all appliances, put a foosball table in, and turn the former pantry into a makeshift deejay booth, and there you have it. The gear was a set of double tape decks stacked on top of each other and a little stereo sound mixer.

I was lucky to get the deejay gig from Jonathan Cummins, an older and established rock musician from the band the Doughboys, who were Montreal local heroes. Cummins and I had seen each other at shows around town, talked about music a bunch, and ran in the same circle that frequented Le Bifteck several nights a week. He'd had the idea to bring late-night rock music to the steakhouse and was their first cassette deejay.

One night he asked me to cover a shift for him. I think he thought it'd be cool to invite a girl into a then all-boys deejay club. And so, at eighteen my first job in music began beautifully.

My nightly ritual consisted of walking down the little lane that connected my apartment to the bar. It was a straight shot only one block long, and I had a perfect view from my bedroom window to my second home, the bar. My shift started at nine, and the sun would just be setting to the northwest of the cityscape.

On warm summer Montreal nights, the city is magical. The dirty sidewalks were flooded with golden pink light. I would often head in an hour or so early before my shift, while the bar was still empty, to play a game of pool with the old-man crowd who spoke little English or French, which was common among many of the shop owners and my neighbors. My pool game got very strong, and I could hold the table down all night with my mixtapes on auto-reverse.

The night owls would start to filter in around nine and hunker down until three. Perched on a wooden stool against the back wall, I was in charge of setting the mood. The emergency back door was right next to my deejay station, and on hot summer nights they'd leave it open to support a little breeze circulating from the front to the back of the bar.

By contrast, my other job as a ticket girl at Foufounes was in the sex-club district, just down the hill from Le Plateau–Mont Royal, next to the Gay Village. This area was laced with strip clubs, prostitutes, porno theaters, and an abundance of squatters.

My girlfriend Rachel was also drawn to the excitement of nightlife, and once we became regulars at Foufounes, the staff noticed us. The job as a sometimes ticket girl was offered to me by a nice older Francophone bar manager. I must have seemed like a trustworthy non-fuck-up to him, and the gig seemed like an easy way to see shows for free.

During the sweltering summer of 1991 I spent most nights working at either Le Bifteck or Foufounes. One evening when I wasn't working and there wasn't a show on, I went down to Foufounes alone anyway to see if anyone was around. When a club of that size is empty on a weeknight, it's hard not to feel haunted by that emptiness, to think wistfully of the crowds that have stood there before and will soon again. I've always found a strange comfort in the particular atmosphere of a forgotten industrial factory, alleyway, or, in this case, a big rock club on an off night.

I was standing on the second-floor balcony, which looked out over the empty stage and dance floor, by the oversize deejay booth. As I walked down the hallway to the bathroom, a guitar riff jumped out of the club speakers, joined by an epic drum fill that quickly gave way to a rumbling bass line and dropped into a simple reverb guitar lick. It was a song I'd never heard before, and it captured my attention instantly.

Then a man's silky yet raspy voice came in, mumbling something mystical and sad.

She's over-bored and self-assured,
Oh no, I know a dirty word.
Hello, Hello, Hello, how low? . . .

I locked myself in the bathroom stall as the revelatory verses continued to flood in through the sound system. The lead singer—he was speaking to me. The song exploded into the most beautiful and familiar rage and caught me, entirely. I stayed in the stall and let it wrap itself around me. An ethereal chill shuddered through the lonely teen in me—the girl who, just a few years earlier, would hide in the high school bathroom stalls to listen to her favorite Smiths song to comfort her and blot out any care she had about being late for class.

The fog from the club's smoke machine was crawling down the hallway when I emerged from the bathroom. The song was over, but I was on a mission to find out what had just moved me so deeply.

I didn't know the deejay who was locked in the booth, a giant cage filled with gear, but that didn't stop me.

"Who was that?!" I screamed over the next song, amplifying the question by pointing to my ears, shrugging my shoulders, and lifting up my hands. "Who?!"

The deejay held up a twelve-inch vinyl record and opened the cage door to let me in. He handed me the record. I had recognized the blond waif of a guitar player on the cover, but it took a moment to register that it was the same guy I knew from black-and-white photos of him in his band. The album's bright-blue glossy cover and the slick professional photo of the band were a stark contrast to the other images I'd seen of this band, and the sound I'd just heard was something completely new.

The cover conveyed their change, and I was clearly ready for them: Nirvana and "Smells Like Teen Spirit."

"They sent us an advance copy of their new single!" the deejay yelled. "They are putting out a new record on a major label!"

I went straight up to Foufounes' upstairs office to track down my friend Paget Williams. He was the promoter who often booked bands at the club.

He confirmed that he'd heard the advance copy of the single and was going to book the band on their next tour.

"I need to hear that full album," I said.

He had an advance cassette at his home, and the next day I went there to copy it with a tape-to-tape player, my sacred tool for all my deejaying and music sharing. In the days that followed, I reached out to my closest friends about "the album that will change everything." I hosted one-on-one listening sessions in my apartment, directly across the street from Le Bifteck. I'd point my lucky friend to the listening corner of my room and tell them to sit still and listen to *Nevermind* top to bottom without speaking, without breaks. Then we'd cross the street to have a beer at my home away from home, Le Bifteck, to discuss.

"What do you think is going to happen to our scene now that this has arrived?" I'd ask, waiting for them to match my conviction that everything we knew about our world was about to blow open. It was not as clear to most of the others as it was to me, but many have since told me that they've never forgotten that session and claim I was the first to open their eyes to what was to come.

Riding the momentum of the underground, this band was clearly going to be the breakout and give our alt-rock tribe a new power over the airwaves and outside of our little clubs, college-radio stations, and local social circles. We were being called to arms, in the form of guitar riffs, haunting melodies, and existential lyrics, about who we were as a collective. The experience was exciting but also confusing, in a "buckle up and get ready!" kind of way.

During my cassette-deejay shifts that week I did nothing but play *Nevermind* in full, on a loop. I was known not to take requests, but now I wouldn't even change the album. Everyone in the bar was obliged to bathe in the sounds of the future.

I was ready.

Dreamscape #2

3D Sound

I find myself among a large group of strangers, walking together along a dirt path toward a modern-day pyramid in the distance. We are surrounded by a sandy desert landscape and bewildered to find ourselves in the middle of nowhere.

"What is this place? How did we get here?" I ask.

I follow the crowd into a large triangular hall. We move into the middle of the space as a pack and gather under the impressive triangular ceiling. The shape and location are reminiscent of ancient Egypt, but this is a modern structure. It has an intricate truss system that seems to defy gravity or standard engineering. The high-tech metal is shiny and new, with ornate delicate engravings throughout. From previous dreams I recognize scriptures and symbols that are not from this time. They look either ancient or futuristic.

Barry "Tinker" Thomas, my music friend, appears to my left.

"Do you know what we're doing here?" I ask. Tinker loves explaining things about frequencies coming out of vintage amplifiers or distortion pedals. He will know why we are here.

"Three-Dimensional Sound: a new invention and way to experience music," he explains. "They've selected Kyuss and the Smashing Pumpkins to demonstrate it for us. The sound will enter through our skin, into our blood, and follow our heartbeats. The music will become us, and we will become it."

I understand at once. This is a gift from another world, designed to transform humans. We are a test audience. Possibly it's created by an alien race or as a gift from the spirit world. Or could it be from the future?

This otherworldly revelation cracks the seam between awake and asleep. My earthly self, lying in my bed, becomes aware that I am receiving a message in my dream.

"The show is about to begin," Tinker says.

I wake up. My calling is clear.

Music.

To maximize my human experience, I am meant to connect with others through the power of sound. This is my duty. I have to pass it on.

CHAPTER 8

Grounding the Fairy

IN 1991, AT THE AGE OF NINETEEN, I STARTED TO RECEIVE OTHERWORLDLY messages in dreams like this one about 3D sound, with visions of mystical communal rituals, set in postapocalyptic desert landscapes, featuring a language of ancient symbols that held us mere humans in thrall to the power of sound. "The hauntings"—that's what I came to call them. Their messages felt like commands and crescendoed into a revelation that music was my purpose in this lifetime.

Music felt like magic to me, and it also connected me to people. And because the people I encountered in the music world were larger-than-life—from my childhood choir teacher all the way up to the musicians in the wild rock bands I worshipped and eventually played bass in—they fulfilled my deep craving to feel complete.

In music, I found the meaning I was searching for.

But that took time. At first, any intrigue I may have felt around these extreme dreams—week in and week out, abstract and mundane dreams *within* dreams, with the occasional sci-fi cinema-like narratives ranging from apocalyptic landscapes with female warrior tribes to an androgynous shadow threatening me from the end of my bed—was overpowered by fear. The dreams were not something I had tried to summon, and I had no context for understanding them. There was nothing in my waking everyday hours that resembled ghost stories or otherworldly pursuits. My parents were intellectual atheists, fired up by the politics and cultural shifts of their day. They never spoke about spirituality. I was raised on the here and the now. The only signs of magic or mysticism I was exposed to came from my father's Swiss mother—who claimed he was the reincarnation of the Swiss patron saint and always referred, with a childlike giggle, to the guardian angels she saw resting on my shoulders. I was no Ouija-board player, or mystical researcher, whatsoever. Never heard of tarot cards. After accidentally watching *The Shining* at a twelve-year-old's sleepover party, I was terrified of scary movies and never watched them, preferring *Star Wars* and *ET*, both of which my father loved.

I had, however, when I was about twelve, developed a "fortune-teller" ritual in middle school, where I was convinced I could read my friends' fortunes in Smarties (Canada's M&Ms). My system was simple. They shook the box of Smarties, asked a question in their minds, and with eyes closed put three in the palms of their hands. I deciphered an answer based on colors. Green was envy; yellow was friendship; brown, trouble; blue, tears; and red was either rage or love, depending on the colors around it. But otherwise I didn't think about magic, ghosts, the power of dreams, or any spooky things beyond gross men who flashed in the park or masturbated in cinemas next to me and my friends.

When these dreams began, they were deeply disturbing. I shyly asked around the bar whether anyone knew anything about interpreting dreams. I got a recommendation for a girl who came in from time to time wearing a lot of black. We met for coffee one afternoon, and I described a specific series of stressful dreams that had just occurred.

For a few nights in a row, I would "wake up" within a dream, in my bedroom, thinking I was awake, but then quickly assess things were not quite right in my apartment. For example, there would be whispering in the walls, a giant knife on my nightstand, or a strange voice down the hall speaking a language I did not know. I would then wake myself up, or at least think I did, only for it to happen again. After some time, I'd be waking up within the dream dozens of times. When I'd finally wake up for real, in a sweat, I'd be anxious and unable to trust if I was *really* awake. I'd pinch myself, hoping it was real.

"What sign are you?" she asked.

"Pisces," I said.

"Well, that explains it," she confirmed.

I read my weekly horoscope in the local paper and had flipped through a few zodiac books in high school, where I'd learned that the star sign of Pisces is the last sign of the zodiac, and the most common traits of Pisces were *dreamy, intuitive, artistic, empathic, moody, psychic, healers*. So, I understood that those born under the sign of the two fishes had the tendency to attract or be attracted to psychic phenomena.

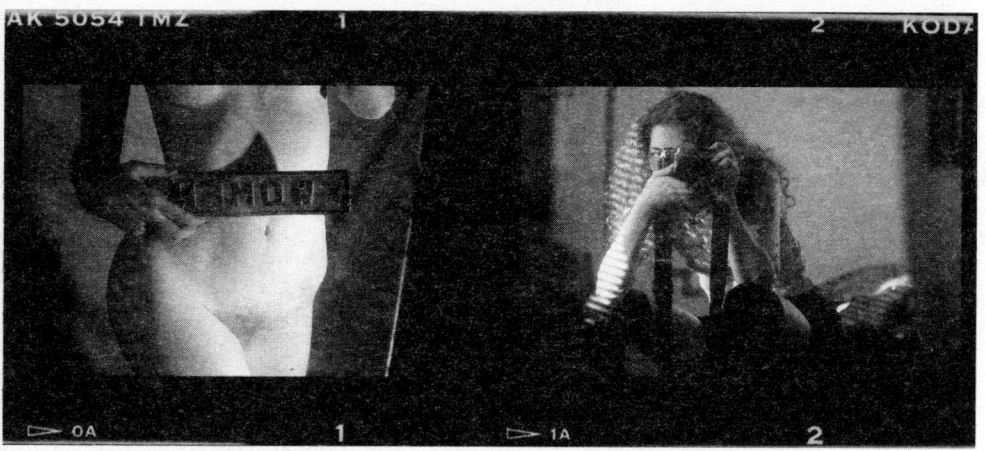

Later I would learn that Pisces represents the end of the life cycle, connecting the material world to the afterlife and divine. The sign is symbolized by two fish tied to each other's tails, one swimming upstream and the other downstream. This duality would come to define me even more than the narratives and details of my mortal life. I have always been torn between the mortal and the ethereal sides of myself. How to live on both sides? This inner conflict has always defined me. And I was beginning to believe it defined my generation.

But all this was an abstract concept for me then, and intimidating.

From her self-taught studies in dream analysis, this girl understood waking up within a dream to be a way of the subconscious catching your

---

"Female-gaze" self-portraits, 1993.

attention. Her theory was that once you were aware of the fact that you were *dreaming*, you would pay closer attention to whatever message it had for you. This kind of incessant waking up, in her opinion, meant an important message was coming my way.

What was my subconscious trying to tell me? What even *was* my subconscious? I had just begun university and had decided to explore mystical topics in classes like Buddhism, Psychic Phenomenon, and the philosophy class On Death and Dying. At the library, I'd pick up an extra book or two like Carl Jung's *Man and His Symbols* and texts on astrology.

This was a very quiet, inner solo journey at the time. I wasn't sure what it all meant, or how to even articulate the abstract concepts and feelings I was experiencing. A veil was being lifted, to reveal parts of myself previously unknown. The nomad in me was feeling ready to explore.

CHAPTER 9

Vermont and the Satin Minidress

NOVEMBER 1991

IN NOVEMBER 1991, JUST FOUR MONTHS AFTER THE BEER BOTTLE AND THE apology, Billy and I reconnected in Burlington, Vermont. The Smashing Pumpkins were picking up a stronger fan base after *Gish*'s release, which had landed them a spot on a mega alternative-rock bill as an opening act for the Red Hot Chili Peppers' US tour. Pearl Jam, a band that had never interested me much, was booked in the middle slot. They were coming up as the leaders of the exploding Seattle scene.

I hitched a ride from Montreal to Burlington to see Billy's opening set, which was the only set I cared about. He was the person who would change the sound of the future—or at least my future, I believed.

The show was held in the Burlington Memorial Auditorium, a glorified school gymnasium with a capacity of only twenty-five hundred. The Pumpkins took the stage in the half-full room. Just as I had seen them do in front of a tiny crowd of twenty on a Tuesday night in Montreal, they gave it their full romantic rock explosion, filling the room with an ocean of rhythm, textures, and Billy's visceral and particular style of singing and screaming. I drank it all in as if it were medicine.

I was well versed at this point in how shows worked and knew to look for the sight line of the backstage opening door if you wanted to find a member of a band. After their set, I strategically headed toward the front of the room, off to the side of the audience, to find the sight line. I'd been standing there for a few minutes, keeping watch on the backstage doorway, when Billy's tall, cherublike silhouette emerged from backstage. As I'd hoped, he had come to take a look at Pearl Jam from the side of the stage.

I was leaning casually up against the bleachers, with my eyes focused on him, when miraculously he looked up. Our eyes connected. I waved at him stoically and watched his face turn from a blank glaze to an expression of recognition.

"Melissa! Melissa! From Montreal!" I saw his mouth through the loud music. He directed me to come down and join him backstage. As I walked over, my heart elated, he hurried me past the security guard.

"She's with me," he said with ease.

Once we were out of the noise, he greeted me with enthusiasm. "What are you doing here?!"

"I came to see *you*. I've been listening to your record so much. I had to see you play again. It's only an hour drive!"

He led me past some locker rooms to his band's tiny changing room, where he introduced me to James Iha (the guitarist) and Jimmy Chamberlin (the drummer). They offered friendly hellos, then resumed chatting with others who were drinking beer with them in the room.

The changing room felt like all the other backstage Montreal rock scenes I had been in: friendly, intimate, relaxed. The group was sharing lively stories about their time on the road when one of them said, "Remember when we were on tour in Europe and it was Billy's birthday?"

Without missing a beat, I looked at Billy and asked, "When is your birthday?"

"March 17th, St. Patrick's Day."

"So is mine," I said.

Our eyes locked, and my understanding of who he was expanded instantly, as if a part of him existed inside of me.

"And, I know, I know you '*don't want feelings*' and you're '*going crazy— mother fucking crazy*' . . . ," I was quick to reply, quoting a hidden track on their album Gish.

"Wow. You are the first person to quote a song of mine." He beamed a big smile, with adoring eyes for the girl who may have just well been the biggest fan of his band on the planet at that time.

We locked into each other for the rest of the evening. When the show was over and everyone was loading out, we headed to a local college bar. For the rest of the evening, we huddled together in the corner by the pool table. We shared a single beer. We talked about life, our parents, and our passion for music and exchanged our mystical beliefs.

He nearly cried on my shoulder when recounting his recent heartbreak with his ex Courtney Love, who'd left him for Kurt Cobain earlier that month. He was clearly still in love with her and also felt very competitive with Kurt. I couldn't tell if ambition or love fueled that competitive streak. I assumed both.

Billy and I were very comfortable together and effortlessly affectionate. I decided to miss my ride back to Montreal and stay the night with him. We walked to the economy motel from the bar. The autumn night was brisk, and the excitement of getting to know my musical inspiration personally felt like the most important thing I could be doing at that moment. Pure bliss.

It was very late when we walked into the dark motel room. We got right into bed. Our physical connection was tender and sweet, much more emotional and spiritual than visceral. As we settled into each other's arms, Billy's bandmate pounded on the door.

"Hey, asshole. Let me in. Come on, I don't want to sleep in the van!"

Billy ignored him, and after a little bit the bandmate gave up and moved on. We stayed up all night in each other's arms, kissing, caressing, and looking endlessly into each other's eyes. Time lapsed, and we moved into a meditative state of mutual immersion.

"I am you and you are me," he said.

It was a romantic dream come true for a girl like me who longed not for climax, but more for the desire to sustain the moment of discovery and allow emotions and words to turn into rhapsody—"soul fucking," a good term for it that I learned later.

When morning came, I headed for the cheap Greyhound bus back home. Billy and I parted without making future plans but knowing entirely well that we'd see each other again.

I left Burlington feeling high and in love with Billy's soul, essence, and everything about him—but mostly with an energized drive to play music. That night together strengthened my commitment to learn an instrument and create music, so I could meet him in his realm of music and magic making.

But first, there was San Francisco.

Just a month later, in December, when I was still nineteen, I took off the winter semester. I'd decided it was time to see parts of the United States and to hunt for the alternative-music scene happening across the nation. There was a concert at the Cow Palace in San Francisco that no one in their right mind would want to miss. So, I bought a one-way Greyhound bus ticket to San Francisco where a friend had told me about a possible squat.

The plan was to make my way up to Seattle and Vancouver after San Fran on an independent '90s-woman road tour with a couple of girls I knew from the bar. I look back at this now, and I think, what an insane thing that was for a nineteen-year-old to do for Christmas and New Year's Eve! To get a one-way ticket to a city she'd never been to, with a girl she met at a bar, to hopefully find a squat to stay at, to try to see a show she didn't have tickets to, nor could she afford. But my commitment to be on the front lines of rock history in the making eclipsed any logic that might have existed at the time.

We boarded the bus in Montreal and woke up on Christmas Day in San Francisco. They had lost our duffel bags, but we happily went to see Flipper, a local infamous punk band, play in the same clothes we had worn to ride across the entire country. I guess that's why they called us kids grunge.

My San Fran leg of the trip was with one of the two girls. She was very savvy, a bit older than I was, and a promising indie-rock band manager who knew how to talk the talk. The New Year's Eve celebration concert at the Cow Palace was the primary reason for our trip. The Red Hot Chili Peppers were headlining, but it wasn't the headliners we cared about. It wasn't even the middle act, Pearl Jam.

It was all about the opening band, Nirvana.

Nevermind, their major-label debut and breakout hit album, had been released just that past September, and their overnight success was happening in real time. We knew this band would make rock history, and we wanted to be witnesses. Because this kind of big-ticket touring bill is booked six to nine months out, when Nirvana was booked as the Chili Peppers' opening act, no one could have imagined how big this little band from Seattle would be by New Year's Eve. Nirvana's opening set was in front of a half-filled arena, but man did that crowd explode when the "Smells Like Teen Spirit" guitar riff came through the PA. It felt very important for rock fanatics like us to be there.

My friend and I didn't have tickets to the sold-out concert, so we talked ourselves into the show *and* backstage. The story we used, which was true, was that we were from Montreal and our friend was a friend of Nirvana's drummer, Dave Grohl. Even though our names were not on the list, my female partner in crime, the industry pro, explained that our friend had called Dave in advance.

"Yes, we're certain, we should be on the Nirvana guest list," she said, with such conviction she almost convinced *me*. "There must be some mistake. Please go backstage and ask the tour manager right away. We came all the way from Montreal. Our friend is an old friend of the drummer. He'd be upset if he knew we couldn't get in." Her confidence and persistence got us into the show, with backstage VIP passes no less. When I say I had no money, I really mean I had *no* money. I'd saved up my entire bar-jobs savings and was traveling with $300 for an entire month. At first we shared a couch with a music-manager friend, but I then found a squat in the Mission District thanks to a hippie poet named Leif.

Earlier on the day of the concert, we'd window-shopped on Haight Ashbury. Although it was 1991, the neighborhood felt still frozen in the 1960s and '70s. In a small vintage clothing store, I fell in love with a 1970s satin minidress. It was red and black, with a curved white flower-petal collar and a low-cut neckline. This dress was exactly what I wanted to wear to the show that night, but it cost $30. That was enough to cover a week's worth of burritos and black tea, which was my San Francisco diet.

Backstage that night at the show was exciting, surrounded by the who's who of the time. I recognized the band Alice in Chains hanging around the backstage bar and the eccentric actor Crispin Glover. My travel companion and I scoped out all the cute guys backstage. The energy in the whole room shifted when Nirvana's lead singer emerged from their dressing room.

I wasn't attracted to junkies, so I wasn't one to romanticize Kurt Cobain, but there was no denying his iconic spirit. On his arm was Courtney Love, the original "crazy bitch" from my failed couch offer that past summer, a.k.a. the girl who had broken Billy's heart. Between then and now, she had landed the cutest guy in the biggest alternative band ever. Soon after that night, the couple became world news. Kissing on the cover of *Sassy* magazine, they were the new "it" couple of our time.

But what eclipsed everything in that moment? Courtney was fucking wearing *my* dress, the black-and-red satin minidress I'd coveted earlier that day.

The subtle encounters I was having with the woman who would change my life forever seemed to be premonitions of some fundamental things to come. I would go on to join a band led by a very powerful woman with a terrible reputation who would give me a lot of dresses, because she would always have more dresses than I. Immortalized in her own lyrics, from one of her biggest future hit songs, she wanted to be ". . . the girl with the most cake." She became that, but in time it would prove to come at a very steep price.

CHAPTER 10

Sunburst Precision

DEEP WINTER 1992

AFTER SUCH CLOSE CONTACT WITH THE AMERICAN MUSIC SCENE, MY INSPIration burned even brighter. That following year I stayed focused on my photography studies and simultaneously made the alt-music scene my full-time social occupation. My friends and I hung out every night until dawn at Le Bifteck drinking local beer, playing pool, and listening to all the new releases, loud. Unless a show was playing at one of the music venues, that is, in which case we could be found there instead.

There was an intensity in all of us, an emotional heaviness, but we carried it with such irreverence and fun. We didn't take ourselves too seriously, and we weren't obsessed with success. We just wanted to connect and have a good time while creating something meaningful in our lives.

I'd found a gang of slightly older male rock mentors in Derrick Beckles, Barry "Tinker" Thomas, Jonathan Cummins, and a handful of their friends who'd moved from Toronto together to work and study in Montreal. They were all tall and dressed in ripped denim, leather, and plaid. Tinker and Jonathan had waist-long, straight blond hair under backward baseball caps. Beckles, the tallest, had shoulder-length dreadlocks. I'd been transitioning out of my high school social group of friends and stepping out on my own into the late-night rock scene, and soon these guys were accompanying me to every alt-rock show that came through town. None of them ever made a pass at me, or treated me with anything but the loyalty-and respect I saw them offer each other. I think they were curious about my independence and my genuine interest in all they knew and loved about music.

There was no internet to learn from in 1992, no books about the underground scene to consult as references. Everything had to be passed down by word of mouth. I taught myself to keep up with my bar friends' language and soon committed to memory a virtual encyclopedia of the tiny details and insider knowledge they possessed about bands, gear, music styles, record labels, and producers. Some of the things I learned: tube amps are always better than transistor amps; the band Fugazi from Washington, DC, was the most politically active and ethical band around—they had a record label called Dischord, and every band on that label matched their credibility; Danzig, a dark and bluesy crooner I couldn't help but love (even though my cool friends made fun of him for having big muscles and making accessible songs), had been in a punk band from New Jersey called the Misfits (not to mention Samhain!) that they all loved way more than his solo stuff. Beckles, Tinker, and Jonathan offered me endless knowledge that I still carry with me today.

This year of hunger for all things music helped steer me toward the bass. Between the wondrous role models around—Kim Deal from the Pixies, D'arcy Wretzky from the Pumpkins, Kim Gordon of Sonic Youth, and Jill being "the most relatable" member of Hole—the bass seemed inviting. I suspect now that the more subconscious appeal was the rumbling feeling and the space it kept in a song. Regardless of gender, the bass player was never too flashy or a showoff, and that was far more my style than the other roles in most bands.

That winter, with my twenty-first birthday on the horizon, I knew exactly what I wanted: my first bass. And my bar friends were there to help, taking me to a few secondhand music shops to help me select a sunburst-colored Squire Precision bass with a rosewood fretboard, made in Japan. The autumnal colors appealed to me, as did the classic glossy finish exposing the natural wood grain in various places of the body. It was a romantic object that matched my own red hair.

We located the bass with my name on it at York Music, a downtown shop just a couple blocks from my father's favorite haunts. The proximity to Nick's stomping grounds made it easy to loop him into my plan.

I didn't ask for much from my parents; they both lived on very little money. But this bass was $700, and I needed a wad of cash from a bigger bank account than mine. Nick was thrilled to oblige and bought me the Sunburst Squire Precision on the spot. Then he handed me $20 for the cab ride home.

When I wasn't studying at school, working at the bars, or taking black-and-white photos of found objects and my body parts and developing them in the darkroom at school, I was now holed up in my bedroom, learning new bass lines. I'd always felt a sense of purpose, but playing my bass helped me understand what I loved and longed to do. My fingers just needed to catch up.

I quickly taught myself "I Am One," my favorite Smashing Pumpkins song. The bass line was simple enough. This was followed by "Black Top" from Helmet's *Strap It On*. Helmet had a heavy and atypical brand of metal, with distorted guitars and intensely monotonous yet complex rhythms. I'd seen them play at Foufounes earlier that year, where their long-limbed drummer, John Stanier, had blown me away. Well over six feet tall, he towered over his drum set, his arms stretching way over his head before crashing down with as much force as possible. His syncopated rhythms played math games in my mind. John was the first drummer to really make me think about the rhythm section as a force. I could play those Helmet riffs for hours. It felt powerful, efficient, and driving, like a large mammal's heart skipping beats. I had long sought this deep sense of connection. I discovered a new bliss in playing the same riff in a loop, like falling into a self-soothing bass zone.

One late night that winter, after "last call" at Le Bifteck, my rock-boy mentors invited me to jam in their basement practice space in the alleyway behind the bar. For the first time, I plugged into an Ampeg SVT bass amplifier, nicknamed the "fridge" because of its size. These gorgeous, huge amps, covered in silver and blue sparkling cloth, were originally made for accordions before becoming popular for basses in rock bands. The volume of the notes that emanated from them even when my fingers were only lightly touching the strings was overwhelming. I'd played alone at home and in school bands and choirs, but this was the first time I was properly plugged in, and it changed my perception of what it was like to command sound.

My mentors were wonderfully enthusiastic and supportive. Alex MacSween, a drummer, also played for modern-dance troupes, and Jonathan Cummins was a singer–guitar player from the band the Doughboys and my fellow deejay at Le Bifteck. That first night in the basement, we began to improvise—Alex leading off with a heavy beat, followed by a Jonathan guitar riff, and then me finding my way in. The exhilaration I felt in jamming with them, keeping up with them, watching and following Jonathan's hands on the fretboard to help myself locate the right place on my own guitar neck, was the most pleasurable game I'd ever played. I was such an amateur, but I got away with it. As I've long maintained, bass is easy if you just feel the beat. I surprised myself that night. I'd never played rock music with others before, but I was ready to step into the collective effort, and these guys seemed to enjoy bringing me along on their ride.

We soon convened whenever we could to jam in the basement, where nights evaporated into early mornings. Playing made time disappear, offering a threshold into another world. Sometimes we'd head to the basement after last call, or we'd skip the bar altogether. "Are you in the mood?" one of us would ask, and we'd end up in the jam space. I loved the feeling of doing something with deeper meaning than just drinking and talking.

After a few months, we decided to form a band. Jonathan was in between tours with the Doughboys, so we became his "fake" band on the side. One night we were playing in the space while Barry "Tinker" Thomas was hanging out with us and tinkering with his piles of gear that he kept stored there. We decided that night to name ourselves after him. Thus, Tinker the band was born.

Tinker smiled a proud and shy grin as we made him our musical mascot, and then he plugged my bass into a Super Fuzz guitar pedal, a coveted '60s-era distortion pedal that he had just repaired.

Distortion was a revelation for me. I'd heard it on all the guitars of the era, a signature of all bands I loved, but to *play* it with my own hands and through a bass, which is always heavier than a guitar, was absolutely amazing. Smooth like butter, but also crunchy like a crackling volcano. It had so much personality.

With that addition, riffs began to write themselves. We soon enlisted one of my classmates at Concordia, a recording engineer student named Howard Bilerman, who'd eventually go on to record the first albums by both Godspeed You! Black Emperor and Arcade Fire. With his help, we laid down some tracks during an overnight session in the university recording studios that we had access to during off-hours.

A few weeks later, Tinker booked our first show at a tiny hole-in-the-wall blues bar called Bar G Sharp, around the corner from my mother's house. The club was tiny, dirty, and unintimidating, a bit like having friends over to our basement jam space, with a stage on the floor at the back. As a deejay, I was used to shaping the mood in the room with music, and performing with a band didn't feel much different. My bass allowed me to jump head-first into the dreamy late-night world of music. I also had the advantage of being able to hide behind our outgoing and better-known front man, Jonathan, though I'd quickly become more comfortable in the spotlight.

Soon after the show, Jonathan went on tour in Europe with his real band, the Doughboys. Having built a little momentum around Tinker, Alex the drummer and I reconfigured the band. We invited Steve Durand, another bar regular, to join our weekly jams, which naturally led to him taking on the singer–guitar player position.

Steve and I had met a year earlier at Le Bifteck and bonded by the pool table. It was the week after the beer-bottle incident, and my obsession with the Smashing Pumpkins had kicked in hard. I was playing the whole first side of *Gish*, their first and only album at the time.

"You the deejay?" Steve approached as I was assessing my next pool shot.

I glanced up briefly and nodded and took my shot.

"Is this the Smashing Pumpkins?" He was attempting to make a conversation out of this.

"Yes," I replied, hiding my enthusiasm that someone else knew what band it was. At the same time, I felt suddenly territorial about my personal connection. A very specific experience occurred among obsessed music people back then, where you were desperate to share the enthusiasm about a particular artist or band and also felt compelled to protect this thing that felt sacred to you alone. We were all lonely and seeking to share, *and* we were also afraid of this being used or abused by someone who was not worthy of it. So, we acted weird and cagey around each other until trust was established. When I met Steve, it was like a light went on upon discovering that connection between us. At the same time, I was also wondering, *Is he really as serious as I am about this band?*

"I just saw them play in Toronto. They were fucking amazing," he said.

"I saw them play here. They blew me away," I replied.

Steve and I became fast music friends at the bar that summer. We could talk about music all night while drinking and playing pool. Like many cool

---

Melissa playing pool, Montreal, 1993.

students from Ontario, Steve had come to Montreal for university. His hometown was Ottawa, our nation's capital, a place *not* known for its cool, though it had a decent punk scene, as any political capital should. His musical roots were deep in hardcore and punk. In high school he'd been in a punk band called Anal Chinook. It was a clever name, "chinook" being the strong Canadian winter winds, and "anal" being . . . anal. I suppose it was a fart joke between the punk boys in the band.

Steve and I had an ease playing together and began to write our own original songs. I suggested we invite a childhood school friend of mine from FACE, Sanjay Mullay-Shah, who had mind-blowing talent on the electric guitar. Sanjay, a shy, striking young man with long dreadlocks, was the secret ingredient that made Tinker special. He was left-handed and played an upside-down Fender Jaguar guitar. His style was part punk Hendrix and

Tinker, Melissa Auf der Maur, Steve Durand, and Sanjay Mullay-Shah, Montreal, 1993.

part Eastern sitar, which reflected the influence of his family who had emigrated from India to Montreal in the 1970s.

Tinker recorded a demo cassette that I passed out as a calling card in New York City at the New Music Seminar (NMS) and CMJ Music Festivals that year. I was unafraid to network and handed our tape out to bands that caught my ears, in hopes of finding connections that might lead to good opening slots, an eventual tour, or even a record deal. All of Tinker lasted only a year, in which time Steve and I went through two drummers and two lead guitar players and we got involved romantically. We had an open relationship, where it was clear that the music was our priority, *not* the romance.

At the top of 1994, Tinker signed a two-single record deal with a little indie label in NYC and released two seven-inch singles. We barely had an album's worth of songs yet, but we recorded and released our strongest tracks: "Green Machine" with "Gnosis" as a B-side, and "Real a Lie" with "Saxon Princess" as a B-side. We got a good review in *Billboard*, but Tinker was not meant to last. My life was about to drastically change.

In the fall of 1993, the Smashing Pumpkins had just released *Siamese Dream*, their follow-up to *Gish*. This new album was the band's *Nevermind*, their career-defining rocket launch. They had a big hit on the radio with "Today," a remarkably uplifting song, but as always laced with melancholia: *Today is the greatest day I've ever known*—every alternative kid related to the sarcasm. *Can't live for tomorrow, tomorrow's much too long*—referring to the extreme, almost suicidal, live-in-the-present style we all shared. *I'll burn my eyes out, before I get out*—raging with the bittersweetness of our hardcore generation, as we exploded onto radio airwaves, ever more ironic for the freak kids who "didn't even try" to make it.

We will all get burned before we get out . . . Billy's poetic Pisces spirit still speaking to me. As conflicting as these success beams felt, I was over the moon that my big brother had "made it." *Can't live for tomorrow . . .*

It had been two and a half years since my clandestine meeting with Billy Corgan. When the Pumpkins announced a new tour, I was determined to open for them when they came through Montreal. The promoters of the show were my friends, and they knew the Pumpkins were my favorite band, so at the bar one night months before the show I asked one of the friendly promoter guys if Tinker could open up for them when they came to town. "Sorry, Melissa, they're touring with Swervedriver from the UK as the opening band, and haven't requested a local opener," I was told.

I wrote Billy a letter and mailed it to the address he'd handed me after the beer-bottle incident. Soon after it was "returned to sender." I decided to try another avenue. I wrote to the Virgin Records post-office box listed on the back of the Pumpkins' new CD with the blind faith that the letter would reach him.

If you were to ask me now if a fan can get in direct touch with a band through the post-office box printed on the back of a record, I would say most definitely not. Today you might have some luck with social media, but there was nothing of that kind to rely on then. It was REAL LIFE ONLY, BABY!!!! The goddesses of communication and music must have been on my side, because my letter reached him.

```
Dear Billy,

   It's Melissa! Remember me and the beer bottle
in Montreal? Guess what! I now play bass and
finally started a band!!! It would mean the world
to me if my band Tinker could open up for you in
Montreal on your Siamese Dream Tour this fall.
Would this be possible?
   I LOVE your new album, it blew me away. It
is greater than I could've ever imagined, you
continue to fill me with INSPIRATION!
   I cannot WAIT to see you play again.
                    Love, Melissa from Montreal,
     Your St Patrick's Day Pisces Sister FOREVER
                                              XO
```

As headliner, Billy and his agents had say over who the opening bands would be. After receiving my note, his team sent word to the Montreal concert promoters that "Melissa's band" would be the local act when the Pumpkins came to play their sold-out show.

My band of stoner boys could not begin to compute how I'd made this happen. This would be Tinker's fifth show ever. But to me, it all seemed obvious and predestined. Even my own wild dream about 3D sound had predicted I'd be reconnected with Billy through the power of music. I'd also been very proactive in my beliefs. I knew where I belonged and what I was supposed to do to get there.

When we showed up for sound check on performance day, Billy was waiting for me, open-armed and proud that I'd started a band. He chatted with me while I set up my gear on the side of the stage, entertaining me with stories of the band's expanded global success, MTV video rotation, songs on the

---

Smashing Pumpkins all-access pass, 1993.

radio, and being on tour nonstop for the past six months. He had married his longtime on-and-off-again sweetheart, which was a surprise to me. Last I had seen him he was crushed by Courtney leaving him for Kurt, but his wife was on tour with him, so that was that. He seemed very grown-up, and had "arrived," presenting himself much more as an official mentor at this crucial juncture of my life in music. It felt sweet and exciting, like knowing a genuine champion who had crossed over to the other side.

During our performance, Billy watched us from my side of the stage, smiling. It was the biggest crowd we'd ever played to, twenty-five hundred people at a show that sold out way in advance. The venue was packed even by the time we hit the stage early. There was crowd-surfing, and Steve, Sanjay, Alex, and I all played well. In a VHS recording of the show, taken from up in the balcony, I look incredibly calm, and I'm amazed by how casual this all seemed for me. I wasn't trying too hard. It just felt like this was where I belonged.

After I walked offstage, Billy met me in the wings and wrapped his arm around my shoulders in a big-brother kind of way.

"You're better than my bass player, and one day you will play in my band," he said into my ear. I pulled out my camera and took a self-portrait of us together to immortalize the moment.

That declaration, I realize now, revealed both his faith in me as a musician, and also a strange disconnect from his own band members. At the time, it lifted me to a new place of confidence and determination. His belief affirmed my belief in myself.

After that night I felt like I'd never need to see my mentor again to soar. But as fate would have it, Billy would soon come back into my life. He would become, as an ex-boyfriend of mine later hissed at me during a fit of jealous pique, my "spiritual fucking cowboy."

CHAPTER 11

Death Rears Its Head

APRIL 1994

"HE WAS *THE ONE*. MY HERO! THE ONLY ONE!!!!"

My overly dramatic friend practically threw himself against a brick wall downtown while sprinting toward a phone booth to call his best friend.

It was a spring afternoon in April 1994, and news of Kurt Cobain's shotgun suicide was spreading fast on our university campus. The death, already world news, was a shock to us all who had watched Kurt's trajectory from indie-rock freak to reluctant mega rock star in the past few years. To some people, like my friend, the loss was so tragic, he seemed to feel it personally.

I was sad to hear it, but there was also a realistic part of me that imagined that Kurt's life must've been a mess. Perhaps I was too grown-up for my own good, or perhaps the cynical, aloof ethos that my friends and I embodied contributed to this, but the death felt comparable to and consistent with the kind of tragedies that had occurred to my mother's heroes: John Lennon, JFK, Marvin Gaye. It was both hard for me to believe and also not a shock, at the same time.

"He was a junkie and had all those stomach issues that must've taken him down. But to blow his brains out . . . ," another friend added.

"He was the most important voice of our generation! He can't be gone. I can't imagine my life without him. How could he leave us all?" This from our super-dramatic friend again. His obsession with music was sometimes annoying, but also the reason we were close.

"Andrew," I said. I was trying to bring him back to earth and reality. Kurt was part of his fantasy life, but Kurt had also been real. "You're an idiot. This isn't about you. Just think about his wife and kid . . ."

That night, and for the weeks that followed, Le Bifteck paid homage to Kurt. We lit candles for him at the deejay booth and played his albums on a loop. But nothing could make up for this new hole and crack in the storybook of our music scene. We were all, in one way or another, building our lives around music, aspiring to rise up in the ranks of local indie bands and graduate to international touring acts. We had watched it happen for so many in the wake of Nirvana's success. Every band in every little city with a music scene could imagine becoming the next big thing. Now, we were adrift in a sense of the unknown. Had Kurt sold his soul to the devil at the crossroads, as the legend goes? Or had he paid the high price of success with his life?

Six weeks later, the sweet early-summer season began to settle in after a long, wet spring. My university classes were winding down, and I headed down to New York City for the New Music Seminar, a weeklong music-industry convention of networking and showcases. I had been to NMS before, but this was the first time I had real business to attend to. Tinker was mastering our seven-inch songs at a music studio in the city for our first release on an indie label. And as always, I was motivated to check out bands I liked, and I passed out our demo cassettes at those shows.

While there I was sitting in the lobby of the music studio, flipping through the new issue of *Rolling Stone*, when I came across a photo of Kristen Pfaff, the bass player of Hole. It was a short news story about her overdose in her Seattle apartment the month before, another tragic, sudden loss to our collective music scene.

Mike, who was acting as our music manager, glanced over at the article. "Melissa, you could be the one to replace her," he casually said.

No way, I thought to myself. His comment seemed callous, considering the level of recent tragedy in this band (first the husband, and *now* the bass player?!). I wouldn't stoop so low to think of death as an opportunity (but *who* could've possibly believed he was right?).

Kristen's death, like Kurt's, had been shocking and sad, although overdoses seemed common at the time. Heroin addiction was rampant in all of the music scenes. In Montreal two of my peers had died just in the past year, including my beloved grade school friend and former Tinker guitar player Sanjay. It seemed like a combination of generational malaise and unintentional rock glamorization that had started with the Velvet Underground, made its way through Sid and Nancy, and found its newest expression in Kurt and Courtney. The messy fun was beginning to feel bad.

But Kristen's death felt extra eerie, in that it seemed like an echo of Kurt's. Both were related to addiction, and of course both were connected to Courtney Love. Hole had released their album *Live Through This* the same week Kurt died, and their songs had been getting a lot of traction in the past few months. With Kristen's death, the album title took on an even more intense meaning.

Would the musical legacy of the '90s be forever intertwined with sadness and death?

✗

About a month later, I got a surprise call from Billy. It had now been seven months since Tinker had opened for the Pumpkins, four months since Kurt's suicide, and five weeks since Kristen's overdose. In the wake of Kurt's and Kristen's deaths, Billy had taken it upon himself to act as some kind of savior to Courtney. One of the many tasks on his list was to find his ex-girlfriend a new bass player for her band.

When I answered the call on my rotary phone, I heard his instantly recognizable nasal voice.

"It's Billy. I've got good news and great news," he began.

My heart skipped a beat when I heard his voice. Our connection existed on such a profound soul level, and my pull toward his music still very much captured my heart and imagination.

"I'm coming to town to headline Lollapalooza," he told me. "I've got a day off so we can hang out, and I'll put you on the list for the show." That was the good news.

"The even *better* news is you are going to join my friend Courtney's band," he continued.

Oh no, no fucking way am I entering that chaos storm of pain, I thought. So much drama and death surrounded the band in the wake of these two deaths. What made him think it would be a good idea for "Melissa from Montreal" to step into that?!

"I'm really excited to see you," I said. "But no thanks. I'm not interested in joining that band."

He accepted my response with a chuckle. "Well, let's meet for lunch, and we'll talk about it when I get to town," he said.

A couple of days later his large, hippie male frame emerged from a Montreal cab. We walked through my childhood neighborhood, talking about our upbringings, then wound up sitting in the grass in the park where I grew up, across from my mother's house, talking about music and our place in it.

"Are you sure you don't want to be in the biggest female band in the world?" he asked.

"No, it sounds terrible, and I don't really connect with the music," I admitted. "And then there's the shitty pain of the overdose and suicide. I don't want to be part of that insane fame." It was true. Not an ounce of me wanted to be in that band. "Besides, I like my life here." I'd begun to dig deeper into art school and photography, where there seemed to be more room for exploration and experimentation.

Billy and I parted that day on sweet terms. That afternoon became a highlight in my strange and eventually strained relationship with him. Once I crossed over onto the real playing field, things would never be the same between us. I can still feel sentimental for that innocent afternoon and the connection we had, when I was just an unknown, confident dreamer in Montreal.

The next day, I dropped a gram of magic mushrooms with Steve, my Tinker bandmate and kinda-boyfriend at the time, and headed to Lollapalooza.

If you got there early in the day, you would catch some of the smaller bands. One of my favorite bands playing that year was Girls Against Boys, from the Washington, DC, scene. They were on the side stage, which was where I always projected myself to be one day. The band members had a sexy poetry to them, and two bass players, which was rare. Their recent album, *Venus Luxure No. 1 Baby*, was out on the Chicago-based label Touch and Go Records, which released most of my favorite bands at the time: Arcwelder, the Jesus Lizard, Slint, and Brainiac. I enjoyed the Breeders from the sunny field and watched some of the Beastie Boys, whom I'd always loved. Though the music was good, the scale of it all didn't grab me. I missed the intimate experience of music in our small clubs. As our songs began to hit mainstream radio and TV waves, the scene had gotten so big. It left me feeling disenchanted.

By the time the Pumpkins hit the stage, the sun had already gone down. Billy had left "all-access" passes for me, which allowed us to watch the band from the side of the main stage. I was tripping hard and in my own universe, dancing with the cosmos. The sounds floated across the sea of people worshipping at the outdoor mega stage of the Alternative Nation. I was so far out there that I didn't even think to say good night to Billy backstage.

My favorite way to descend from a psychedelic trip is to take a long urban walk. As the mob streamed out of the festival grounds, Steve and I decided to walk all the way home.

"You sure you don't want to take Billy up on that offer?" he asked me, humbly.

"I'm sure," I said. The sun was coming up, and I felt resolved.

CHAPTER 12

One-Way Ticket to Seattle

AUGUST 1994

"Courtney Love called. Twice. She really wants you to call her back."

This was how my then roommate greeted me when I returned home late one night after work.

It seemed that Billy's "Melissa from Montreal" recommendation held a lot of weight, but when he reported back to her that the girl from Montreal had declined the opportunity to join her band, Courtney wanted me even more. She asked Billy for my phone number.

Despite the late hour, I figured I should get it over with. It was almost midnight in Montreal, and the number she left started with 206, one of the most famous city area codes at that point. Seattle. The West Coast was three hours earlier than Montreal, and I had an inkling that this wild card living in the wake of such drama would be up late by the phone.

Before I called, I looked around my double-parlor bedroom with the ornate wood trim that I'd spray-painted gold. This was the room where I'd experienced the dreams that called me to play music, where I'd learned all my first bass lines, where I'd spent the past few years learning how to use the camera by photographing myself nude from different angles. Prints I'd made in the darkroom were scattered across the floor, in mid-edit. *My life is here*, I thought. I wasn't looking for a way out, and I definitely wasn't dreaming of a life of fame bathed in death in the United States.

I dialed Courtney's number on my orange rotary phone. She answered immediately, her husky voice coming through clear on the line. After I identified myself, she got straight to the point.

"Why don't you want to be in my band? Billy said you were a great player, and I trust him. I need a bass player, the album is out, the tours are booked, and we can't find the right girl. You're the one."

"Thank you, but I'm very busy with my life," I said. "I have my own band in Montreal, I have a year left of my photo degree, and then I'm planning on doing my MFA at RISD [Rhode Island School of Design] or San Francisco Art Institute—"

"Will you just get on a plane," she interrupted, "and tell me to my face that you don't want to be in my band?"

Courtney was direct and pushy as expected, and also charming and respectful. My noncommittal sensitive-girl style started flailing a bit in the presence of this force of nature, and I felt myself begin to bend. This *was* a remarkable invite, and I realized I owed her the respect back. So, I agreed to think about it.

"My manager will call you to book your flight," she said. "Bring your bass." Then she hung up.

The next day Eric Erlandson, Hole's guitar player, called. Courtney had passed along my info, and I guess it was his turn to vet me next. He was soft-spoken on the phone, coming across as slightly shy, but direct. "I have three questions for you," he started. "What sign are you?"

"Pisces," I replied. At the time Kurt was one of the most famous Pisces in the world, and I knew my answer would land with impact.

"Do you play with a pick?"

"Yes. I don't ever play with my fingers, don't know how."

Question number three: "Are you a drug addict?"

"No," I replied, assuming I'd passed the test.

"Okay, we'll see you later this week. Oh—one last thing. Are you fucking Billy?"

"No," I said. I realized this answer might be the one that mattered most. Thus concluded my quick and slightly cold first phone call with Eric.

By this point, word had gotten around in Montreal that Hole had been calling me at Billy's recommendation. The overall response was more intense than I'd expected. Everyone wanted to chime in on the "once-in-a-lifetime opportunity" I was being offered. Even my father called me up.

"I've been thinking," he said. "You need to call that Big Pumpkin back and tell him you've reconsidered, that you'll take the job." The opportunity to join a globally famous band would allow me to see the world, he said.

No one other than me seemed to think that sticking to the life I was making for myself here was a good idea. It strikes me now, as the mother of a twelve-year-old girl, who's emotionally going on twenty-two, how everyone in my life was ignoring my gut, my clear instinct that it was not a good idea for me to join a band of grieving drug addicts. It's as if everyone in my bohemian community had all of a sudden become ultra career focused, causing the emphasis on ambition to override my good personal intuition about what was right for me. Perhaps it was because everyone around me perceived me, still only twenty-two and still in school, as very ambitious, strong, and stable.

Who are we really? Are we who people tell us we are? Are we who we came into this world to be? I love to ponder the theories of innate versus nurture. I assume we're a hybrid of both, but a twenty-two-year-old is still developing mentally and physically. Hell, I still looked like a teenager until I was twenty-six, when I lost the redhead baby fat that lined my face and body.

Over the next couple of days, I spoke to various friends at the bar about this outrageous invitation. English Montreal was a small town within a big multicultural Francophone city, and Seattle grunge music was omnipresent globally. My resistance to it began to feel strange. After a couple of messages had been left on my answering machine by some 212 NYC-based managers, I reluctantly called them back and agreed to spend a couple of days in Seattle. I avoided using or even hearing the word "audition," because that was not what I was flying there to do.

✗

I boarded a plane at the end of the week with an overnight bag, the Sunburst Precision bass, and my cassette Walkman. I planned to listen to a dubbed copy of Hole's recently released *Live Through This* album all the way to

Seattle so I could start getting familiar with the songs. It felt like the least I could do for a widow who'd insisted I come see her in person.

This was the first time I'd listened to the album with intention. It was powerful, unlike anything else out there. Courtney was clearly on track to becoming the female counterpart to Kurt and Billy. The album had what the record label heads wanted—"hits"—but, like Nirvana's and the Smashing Pumpkins' breakthrough albums, the authenticity and raw power were still there, even with slick production, catchy hooks, and candy guitars.

The first two singles, "Miss World" and "Doll Parts," were already becoming instant anthems of the time. The bass playing on the album was incredible, subtle but very sophisticated. It inspired me in a way I did not expect. And the song lyrics, the raw power and vulnerability behind them, made Courtney's story start to feel meaningful. She'd been abandoned by her husband, the king of grunge, leaving her to parent their two-year-old daughter alone. Plus, she was working through the additional guilt of her bass player then overdosing on her watch. Hole was living under a dark cloud at the same time that their accomplished album was rising up the charts.

Hole's music wasn't exactly my thing; it wasn't heavy or messy enough for me, and the simple arrangements and catchy melodies were not something I aspired to, though I could tell something special was happening, especially from a feminist perspective. These hooks were going to trick a larger audience into paying attention! That was *smart*.

> *I'm miss world, somebody kill me*
> *Kill me pills*
> *No one cares, my friends*
> *My friend*
> *I'm miss world, watch me break and watch me burn*
> *No one is listening, my friend*
> *Now I've made my bed, I'll lie in it*
> *I've made my bed, I'll die in it*

✗

Through my tiny airplane window, I watched Elliott Bay and the Port of Seattle come into view as the plane descended. I'd immersed myself in Hole's new album for the whole flight, preparing myself for the world I was about to enter. As foreign as all of this was to me, something about it also began to feel familiar, like a fairy tale I'd heard as a child, one with a tragic, yet lesson-filled, ending.

The plane came to a stop on the runway at Seattle-Tacoma International Airport, and I filed off the plane in the midst of a crowd of regular people most likely traveling for work and family. Walking through the cinematic jetway tunnel, I wondered if anyone else was heading toward the scene of a suicide and overdose. I felt quite sure that I was the only one heading into the eye of '90s-rock mythology in the making.

And then I saw them. They were standing at the bottom of the escalator waiting for me as I rode down to baggage claim, a small but striking group of women. In the middle was the unmistakable platinum blonde in a vintage slip, barefoot. To her right was a little girl cradling a stuffed animal and holding the hand of a wholesome-looking Drew Barrymore look-alike (I'd later learn this was the nanny). And to her left stood a sporty girl with red hair and a regal stature, whom I recognized from the photos as the band's drummer, Patty Schemel.

My descent down that escalator felt like it was happening in slow motion, as if my destiny was revealing itself in a fluid and one-directional motion. The pull I felt toward these women was instantaneous and overwhelming. It came in an involuntary rush of emotion. These women needed me. I had a role to play, for them and for others. Though I wasn't conscious of it at the time, that was the moment my spirit joined Hole.

"Melissa from Montreal!" Courtney said with a husky voice and big smile.

"Welcome to Seattle! How was your flight?" Patty politely asked as we walked to the carousel to grab my bass. We headed out to the parking lot and piled into a red vintage 1960s Dodge Dart. Patty drove like a pro while Courtney occupied the front seat, resting her bare feet on the dashboard while a chain of cigarettes paraded in and out of her mouth. I sat comfortably squeezed into the back seat with a bright and chatty almost two-year-old Frances Bean Cobain, who was very at ease with the nanny seated next to her.

"My name is Melissa," I explained to Frances. "I flew on an airplane from Canada to meet your mommy and her band."

Patty exited the freeway and drove us into a remarkably fancy neighborhood, the kind where the popular jock kids live in Hollywood movies, not where I imagined these two grunge idols would choose. I had never been to a neighborhood like this before. Winding roads took us past large estates that overlooked green hills with a view of Lake Washington. As we pulled up to the gate of our destination, I noticed security guards standing along a high fence. A makeshift altar had been assembled against the fence, with candles, letters, and gifts for Kurt. We passed a few teenagers who were holding vigil there and crying as we drove through the gate.

The wood-shingled garage perpendicular and to the left of the house was still wrapped in yellow security tape. Above the garage was a room that served as a greenhouse. This was the room where Kurt had died. We had all seen the single haunting photo that had been leaked to the press, an aerial zoom view that peered into the greenhouse door and showed a sliver of Kurt's arm and leg, with his one black Converse sneaker lying on the linoleum floor. I glanced to my left, but was careful not to gawk, assuming it was best to avoid even the thought of the tragedy.

Courtney's home was bright inside, with big bay windows in the large living room that looked out over hills speckled with other enormous mansions. From the outside, the house looked like an upper-class family abode. On the inside it was housing a troop of punk bohemians. The place was sparsely furnished, with velvet couches, vintage oddities, Buddhist shrines, and a lot of candles. A windup tin monkey sat on a table at the foot of the curved staircase.

Patty lived in downtown Seattle but had come to the house to help settle me in. I could already feel the comfort that existed between her and Courtney, an intimacy and trust that felt warm in a world filled with sadness. Patty clearly had spent a lot of time in that house since Kurt's death and was a source of support to the widow, the toddler, and the nanny, forming a nontraditional family unit.

She showed me to my room, which was festooned with Victorian lace and artifacts, and sat down on the bed next to me.

"Thanks for coming," she said. "It really means a lot to us. Eric and I have been auditioning bass players for weeks. Courtney hasn't come to one rehearsal or even met with any of them. Obviously, none of them have come to the house. She seems to know you're the one." Her matter-of-fact statements emphasized, *You are special, Mystery Girl, whoever you are.*

"I hope you'll consider staying," she continued. "We really need you, and you're a fellow redhead like me. And I love Canadians. They have the best humor. I grew up watching SCTV."

"Me, too," I said, my heart opening to her. "My father and I watched it every weekend." Nick taught me to love Monty Python, Benny Hill, and SCTV, and I sensed right away that Patty, an incognito natural stand-up comic, got my kind of UK/Canadian-influenced humor.

Patty's warm nature would eventually bind us together and make her my best friend in Hole. At the same time, the confusion she and the others must have felt in the wake of the double deaths had to have been immobilizing. But as is always the case for those of us called to music, the answer is always music. And this band needed a bass player for that to happen.

The house was quiet that first night. Courtney retired to her room down the hall, which she rarely left. Patty told me to help myself to the food in the fridge and that she'd pick me up in the morning and bring me to the downtown practice space, where I'd meet Eric.

Alone in my room, I wrote in my diary and quietly took photos of myself and my surroundings. The guest room overlooked the garage that was hard to ignore, considering all the pain that emanated from it and reverberated around the world. I became aware of the surreal situation I was in, planted in the eye of the storm that music fans around the world had been tuned into for the last months. My camera and diary offered tools for me to step into the future and tune into a storytelling perspective.

In the morning, I woke to a very quiet house. I ate a bowl of cereal in the kitchen alongside Frances and the nanny just before Patty came to pick me up to go meet Eric in town.

The practice space was a huge, professionally equipped rental, the likes of which I'd never seen before. There was even a technician hanging around whose only job was to tune the guitars and drums and take our lunch orders. This was what it would be like to be in a professional band with a crew and a team setting things up to make it all possible, I registered.

Eric and Patty walked me through the notes and the arrangements of the songs. Listening to *Live Through This* on the plane had paid off. The songs had hooks, and it was easy for me to tap into the part of my brain that held the melodies and rhythms and let it take over.

The magic of music memory is a mystery, even to those who've studied it for most of their lives. Once you've heard and learned a song simply by listening, it just locks into some permanent place in your brain. The melody, rhythm, and arrangement of a song are the building blocks to its architecture, and you can tap into that grid and find your way around inside. It's the road map that you and the band members follow once there is an established song to play.

Writing new music and songs is a whole other process, often called "jamming" or "improvising." That's when you reveal your creative voice to others in the room. Today I was here just to play an existing role, in songs that had already been written.

Because Patty had told me that Courtney hadn't come to meet any of the other prospective bass players, it was a pleasant surprise to everyone when she joined us in the practice space that evening. We were playing "Doll Parts," Hole's current single on MTV and on radios around the world, when she strolled into the room, walked right up to the mic, and completed the song with her intense, textural scream. It was powerful, and I thought about how cathartic it must have been for Courtney to play the songs she'd worked so hard on while Kurt was still alive.

> *I want to be the girl with the most cake*
> *I love him so much, it just turns to hate*
> *I fake it so real, I am beyond fake*
> *And someday, you will ache like I ache*
> *Someday, you will ache like I ache*

Later that night Patty drove me and Courtney back to the house. It was a gorgeous summer night, and the top of the convertible was down. I'd learned that this was Kurt's vintage car Patty was driving. Courtney did not drive, nor has she ever to this day. The radio was blasting classic-rock hits that didn't leave us much room to talk, but driving together was better than talking. It was sharing a moment of being alive in the night together.

We pulled back in through the entry gates and past the nighttime security guards. Courtney disappeared into her bedroom again, while Patty and I snacked on chips and veggie sticks at the kitchen counter. I felt at ease with her, enough to share a dream I'd had just before coming on this trip.

In this one, I'd joined a lesbian clan that was living like cave women in an apocalyptic desert landscape. We protected ourselves from beasts who were trying to attack us by telling jokes that lifted them into the air so we could escape. *Make them laugh. Make them laugh.* That was our survival chant.

"The predators were *Planet of the Apes*–style creatures, and we were fighting to survive against insane shit," I explained. I knew it sounded ludicrous, but Patty was a lesbian and this piqued her interest. I also now knew about her northwest US humor, informed by Monty Python and SCTV, the late-night Canadian sketch comedy.

"Wow! *Planet of the Apes*? That's a hilarious world to find yourself in!" She walked out of the kitchen toward the entry hallway and returned with the vintage windup toy monkey. It had been one of Kurt's prized possessions, she told me. He collected them. As she cranked the music box and the monkey began crashing its little cymbals, we giggled about the absurd idea that, upon arriving at the house, perhaps I *had* joined a lesbian monkey clan in real life.

At practice the next day I harmonized with Courtney on "Doll Parts," recalling the backup vocals on the record. She lit up. "Wow, Billy didn't tell me you could sing," she said. "We had to pay some random backup singer to sing on our album. So cool that the bass player can sing."

The ease with which I stepped right into the songs was undeniable. I could read the emotions and signals in the room, and I adapted quickly. On my third night in Seattle, Courtney called me into her room. She was nested in the center of a king-size bed overflowing with silk sheets, lace pillows, books, diaries, and ashtrays filled with cigarette butts.

"Melissa, stop playing hard to get," she began. "You have to tell me now. Will you be in my band?"

I admired how direct she was. Observing this skill would become a great lesson for me.

I paused and took time to quiet my body. I trusted my heart to know the answer. The past couple of days had revealed themselves to be a very meaningful, unexpected fork in the road of my life and one that I should heed. It wasn't Courtney's undeniable force that was pushing me; I had control over that. It was my own force calling to me from within.

"It seems so. It seems like it's meant to be."

Without skipping a beat, she said, "Well, the Reading Festival is in a week, and the tour is booked. You have to go home and pack your bags. We have a big trip ahead of us."

And with that, my fate was sealed.

I went to bed that night in a sad Seattle home that had just begun to glimmer with hope. I understood on some profound level that I was being asked to participate in a joint commitment to carve a place for women in the male-dominated landscape of rock music. Being the minority gender in the rock world seemed very significant to me now. I had not felt it before, when I was back home surrounded mostly by men. But in the presence of Hole, their songs, and their stories, I heard my call.

"Bass Guitar Indulgence Turned Out to Be a Great Investment"

Melissa came back to Montreal last weekend with the news that she got the job, and two months of touring to promote Love's latest album, Live Through This, an ironic title since it came out at the same time as Cobain's death.

Last night Melissa flew back to Seattle for a few days of rehearsal.

After all, she has to learn how to play the songs on the album they're promoting.

Then she flies to England next week, where she'll play on the main stage of the Reading Festival, the biggest annual music deal in Europe.

Then comes two months of touring all the big cities, and a spot on "Saturday Night Live."

Melissa has her head screwed on right and is going to have a great time. That's what bass guitars are for, I'm now fond of saying.

—Nick Auf der Maur, column for the Montreal Gazette,
August 17, 1994

ACT II
MUSIC

Melissa's Dream of the '90s Playlist

Melissa's Dream of the '90s Playlist ——————— OXOX
"50 Million Year Trip" — KYUSS
"Tragic Carpet Ride" — POLVO
"Bullet Proof Cupid" — GVSB
"Cranberry Sauce" — Arc Welder
"Pat's Trick" — Helium
"Motionless" — Chokebore
"Into Your Arms — The Lemonheads
"Black Sunshine" White Zombie
"Doe" — The Breeders w/ Iggy Pop!
"Black Top" — Helmet
"I, Fuzzbot" — Brainiac
!!! ———— LAST CALL ———— !!!
"Groove is in the Heart" — Deee-Lite

CHAPTER 13

The Self-Destruct Tour: Nine Inch Nails and Marilyn Manson

SEPTEMBER 1994

> The first night of the Nine Inch Nails tour, in Cleveland, there was a death threat against me. The Chief of Police came down and told me that he didn't want me to play. I'm like: "It's from a girl, it's bullshit." Besides, if someone were to shoot me on stage, what a nice footnote to rock 'n' roll history. You can't tell me not to jump into the crowd; it's so deeply rooted inside me, this sickness, this disease, this obsessiveness. The only way to get rid of it is to fucking get it out.
>
> —Courtney Love, 1994

THE SUMMER OF 1994 IS A SEASON OF MANY FIRSTS: IT'S COURTNEY'S FIRST performance since Kurt's suicide, my first performance with Hole, and my first time on the road with a rock band. It's also the first time I've been out of school since I was a child.

Our first tour begins immediately after Reading. Trent Reznor's pioneering industrial project is kicking off the American leg of "The Self-Destruct Tour," a giant world tour behind their genre-defining and explosively successful second album, *The Downward Spiral*. Hole has been booked as one of the two opening acts for Nine Inch Nails.

Whoever thinks this is a good idea, putting our fragile grunge-pop-girl band, headed by a broken widow and single mother with an addiction problem, on "The Self-Destruct Tour" with high-tech industrial-goth rockers with a growing cult following and high production values, whose most memorable chorus at the time was: *Head like a hole / Black as your soul / I'd rather die than give you control*, I never ask. I am still learning my bass parts and adjusting to my radically changed environment, with no real friends yet, and moving too fast to make any.

I guess it's the obvious juxtaposition, potential volatility, and possible headlines the pairing can generate that compel the industry puppeteers to make the call. Playing in front of sold-out big concert crowds is probably also very enticing for those in charge of getting Hole ahead.

When we were in the airport in London, heading to Ohio to start the tour, Courtney boarded the plane with a stack of American and British magazines with NIN on the cover. She had given the decision her blessing and was excited about this double bill, but between her grief for Kurt and her struggles with addiction, she wasn't exactly in a place to make the best decisions for herself. And though I'm not thrilled about being on the same bill with NIN—I find their harsh electronics alienating, grounded as I am in the "real" sound of guitars, bass, and drums—it obviously isn't my place to express an opinion, or even to have one. My perspective will eventually count with Courtney and with the band in general, but for the moment I have to assume there's a good reason for us to be here.

The tour begins with two sold-out nights at an outdoor amphitheater in Cleveland, where Reznor went to college. We land the day before the show and check into a hotel you'd imagine your grandparents feeling at home in: affordable 1980s beige furniture and drapes, reproductions of generic landscape paintings on the walls. In the two short weeks since I've joined Hole, I've begun to plant the seeds of a friendship with Patty, yet her attention is laser focused on her lust for the nanny, who accompanies us everywhere to look after two-year-old Frances. This involves Patty throwing herself into outings to the mall, watching *Barney* on television at the hotel, and seeking out anything a toddler would have fun doing on tour. And so I am alone for the most part and left to my own devices.

That first day in Cleveland, I take a walk with my camera to see the sights. Dreams of a master's in photography at RISD or the San Francisco Art Institute are still fresh in my mind as I climb a rusty industrial bridge next to the waterfront concert venue to take some self-portraits. I have a private ritual of finding a stable ledge to prop my camera on, looking through the viewfinder to get a good frame, setting the timer, rushing out into the frame, and gazing with purpose into the lens or on a focal point in the horizon. I'm taking my own picture every day, something no one else is doing at the time. Back then, these photos were called self-portraits, but I had literally gone to art school for "selfies." I'm capturing and cataloging deep feelings and messages for my future self, who will be editing, reliving, and writing about the moments captured in these photos later.

The first opening act for this tour is Marilyn Manson, an unknown Florida band that Reznor recently discovered and signed to his label, Nothing Records. These funny-looking guys dressed up in goth and gore are as brand-new and young as I was, in their early twenties. They warm up the open-air stage and audience for us with a set that almost seems like a practical joke. Or maybe it's high-concept and simply over my head. I watch a bit from the crowd. Their music feels calculated and forced, not effortless and natural like the music I gravitate toward. When I move a little closer to the stage, the ghoulishness of their makeup and outfits confuses me. The sloppy handmade Halloween-style goth-kid getup is endearing in a way, but not for me.

We go on next. This first night of the tour is intense. Our lo-fi instrumental setup—punk girl drummer, innocent redhead bass player, and practically invisible, effeminate male guitarist—feels raw and vulnerable in front of the savage audience dressed in black. We rely on the supernatural force of Courtney's performance to slay this largely male crowd.

We play a rough set full of live-wire power, but the audience doesn't instantly connect. Some boos and many shouts of "Show us your tits!" are hurled at us. I barely know my bandmates and have no way to sense what they're feeling, so I just stick to my parts.

Courtney, however, is fearless. She matches her performance to the dark energy of the night, confronting the audience with direct eye contact, foul language laced with dark humor, and that growling scream. I dare to say hers is the only one that comes close to rivaling Kurt's haunting scream that broke through most teenage misfits' bedrooms all over the world, helping them find their voices in the privacy of their own spaces.

✗

Backstage after the show, we're surrounded by a small, sweet Hole entourage. This includes our very friendly Geffen Records rep and, most memorably, Joe Mama-Nitzberg, who'll be continuing on for the front half of the American tour. He helps Courtney in simple ways, such as choosing her outfits, which are always based on what lingerie she'll wear underneath, since the dresses are often torn off by the crowds she stage dives into.

Joe's own style is a little nerdy-preppy: a button-down shirt and simple jeans, short brown hair neatly parted and combed to the side.

"This tour is going to be great!" he says in a catty voice with a sly smile, clearly trying to make sense of this night. "You've got those Florida kids dressed up in Halloween outfits screaming about serial killers, and the little big men breaking toy keyboards and hiding behind smoke machines threatening to cross over to the dark side, while on our side, we've got Courtney, a devilish woman in a slip, steeped in darkness, already living in hell!"

He jumps up on the couch and waves his hand in a come-hither gesture. "Come on, boys!" he says in a sexy, Marilyn Monroe–style voice. "I am already here in hell! I dare you to join me!"

Our small crew explodes in laughter. Courtney's boisterous laugh reveals a confidence and self-awareness when it comes to the dark side of her life. She knows who she is. And, in turn, we know who we are, where we are, and ultimately that we have a leg up on our tour mates. Despite the simplicity of our stage show, and despite being the odd girls out, our authenticity and our fearless bandleader place us in a different league than these poseur boys.

The end of the official Self-Destruct Tour bleeds perfectly into Hole's two-month mini version of it, minus the dudes and the goth. This is the kickoff of our official *Live Through This* headlining tour that, unbeknownst to any of us at this time, will grow to include more than 150 shows in fourteen countries this year, ranging from *Saturday Night Live* to Lollapalooza, from the Land Down Under to the Arctic Circle, culminating in our performance on the 1995 *MTV Music Video Awards.*

The next day we head off for New York to kick off our own tour at the Academy, as part of the CMJ music convention. We are traveling in a van, driving by day and staying in cheap hotels by night. The label has us on a budget and sharing rooms. I alternate between sharing with Patty and sharing with Courtney, depending on who has Frances and the nanny in their room each night. Patty has a bit of an old-man vibe to her lifestyle, which includes comfort food and TV, versus Courtney who is tornado meets philosopher, all of her bags turned inside out, and on constant phone calls about business and pop culture while watching TV, reading a deep book, and flipping through a trashy magazine. The only thing they both have in common is chain-smoking.

Joining us as openers for the tour is Veruca Salt, an emerging female-led power-pop group from Chicago, whose hit single "Seether" is all over MTV and the radio. In theory, they're a much more appropriate touring act for us than NIN was, a sweet counterbalance to the boys' club we began this messy cross-country tour with. They feel like a breath of poppy fresh air, and personality-wise they're more along the lines of the Montreal mini scene of girls in bands that had begun to pop up a bit as I was leaving town.

The Hole tour is sold out well in advance of our arrival in every city. This makes for a generally great mood among the bands, crew, and venues. Veruca Salt can play their instruments, sing, and write songs. It feels profound with purpose to be on the road and sharing that commitment with other women, real peers who aim for a higher bar than I had seen back home.

Veruca Salt is also a fun social escape for me, easy to hang and talk shop with—non-hard-drug users!

The Hole camp, on the other hand, is still a mystery to me. Courtney keeps mostly to herself and never shows up for sound check, arriving only for our set and even then usually late, but the bustling crowd never seems to mind. I wonder how my new band members are coping with their losses plus the pressure of the music industry's new focus on them, but it's not something anyone will talk about. Everyone just shows up and keeps the focus on the here and the now and the show that night. And so do I.

Waking up late in a random small town, heading to the venue in the afternoon to snack on whatever food is provided—mostly cold cuts, veggie sticks, and chips—while we wait for sound check becomes the usual routine. I quickly learn that if you find the local promoter or venue rep, you can get tips on where the closest thrift shop, health food restaurant, or record store is. This soon becomes standard information to get for the band prior to our arrival. I make the most of every US town we stop in by making one of those cultural anchors the center of my adventure. I also manage to get the tour manager to add a roll of color 35mm film to our backstage rider. This becomes Melissa's special request, along with Patty's pair of gym socks.

My days now begin with loading a fresh roll of film into my Nikon point-and-shoot so I can document the routine. I photograph backstage, the motel room, the cool club decor, the opening band, and, without fail, a shot of each crowd from the stage every night.

To my weekly routine I soon add locating a one-hour photo-processing shop to the mix, where I get the week's worth of film processed and grab a couple of small, puffy plastic photo albums. Editing the little photo prints and working on the pairings and selections for the albums become the new version of my photo school assignments. I often write a letter to a friend back home and add a carefully selected grouping of photos, taped together as a series or on scrap paper found in the club, usually on flyers for an upcoming show.

I'm also avidly committed to keeping a daily diary, where I log certain photos, flyers, and memorabilia. My diary, photo books, and letter writing become my creative outlets, taking the place of the beloved art classes and assignments that created structure for me since I was very young. I find it easy to make and stick with my own routine, and I find inspiration everywhere.

The tour keeps stretching and growing. We start in the Northeast, head to the Midwest, and then zigzag all the way to the North and Southwest and back again. Many of the cities feel the same to me, but some major ones come around again a month later, and I realize we're in Boston again . . .

only this time at a venue twice the size of the last one. All signs point to us growing in popularity, and momentum is building. From time to time I get my own hotel room on a day off, and it feels extravagant and fun to be able to use my mother's Bell Canada phone card to call my family and friends back home. I don't have a lot of alone time on the road, so these rare days are treasured.

On our occasional nights off, we get to explore a city's nightlife and check out other live shows. There are *so many* bands of our kind out on the road

---

Hole fans in line at First Avenue, Minneapolis, 1994.

right now. Every night is close to a guaranteed good show in any major city. All you need to do is find a copy of the local alternative weekly newspaper and check the listings. Often, we just go to the club where we're scheduled to play the next night and catch a great band. Sometimes I go alone, or with Eric, who is the only other curious one. Courtney is too famous by now to go out in public, and Patty, as I've learned by this point, is working on staying sober. Watching TV and chain-smoking back in the hotel with Frances and the nanny is a safer pastime for her than heading out to clubs.

Most of the midwestern cities morph into one big city for me, but Detroit, Minneapolis, and certain Ohio cities stick out. Those areas have strong music legacies and very cool vibes. Detroit is of course legendary for Motown, and from the moment we drive into town I'm intrigued and excited by the commanding, yet decaying, urban landscape and the edgy people everywhere. Our first time through Detroit we play in a legendary venue called St. Andrews Hall, an old church turned rock club, to a

---

Courtney Love stage diving, United States, 1994.

boisterous crowd that sings along with all our songs and is unafraid of stage diving and crowd-surfing.

By now the record label has finally provided us with a bus. We no longer sleep in motels. Instead, we live in the bus and drive to our next destination overnight. It's a much more efficient way to travel but creates even more of an isolated bubble that keeps us more or less landlocked between the clubs and the bus. Occasionally, there's a hotel nearby where we can use a shower in what's called a "day room," but often we have to use the showers backstage. They're usually disgusting, so I barely take showers. We really are keeping it real.

A giant tour bus parked out in front of a venue is easy for music fans to spot, so I begin to make daily small talk with the fans who often surround the bus before or after the show. It still feels casual and familiar, like my days of working at clubs and bars in Montreal. I talk to them as I would with any stranger I'd meet while taking their ticket or rejecting their request at my deejay booth. Really, I relate more to the fans at the shows than to my own bandmates.

Our show at the Hollywood Palladium sticks out as a real "You Have Arrived" moment. It's the biggest venue we've sold out by far and a star-studded event. After the show, there's a meet-and-greet with guests and music-industry reps in the glam upstairs-balcony section. Many familiar faces fill the space, but the star who eclipses it all for me, and the only one with whom I take a selfie with my point-and-shoot camera, is Danny DeVito. Having watched a lot of TV with my father growing up, meeting this character from the legendary show *Taxi* seems like a major big deal. I can't wait to tell Nick about it.

On December 2, we roll into Cleveland. This is where Huey Lewis and the News' hit song claims the "heart of rock and roll" is located, but in my mind, Dayton, Ohio, is the shit. Starting with the fact that Kim Deal, the bass player from the Pixies, is from there and, even better, Dayton is the home of her side project with her twin sister, Kelley, the Breeders. But more important to me, Dayton is where Brainiac, one of my new favorite emerging bands on Touch and Go Records, is also from.

I fell in love with Brainiac at the New Music Seminar in New York last summer, just prior to joining Hole, when I saw them play well after midnight at Brownies on Avenue A. They were raw, outrageously confident, and stylish in their wacky, colorful polyester suits. "They" are two blonds named John and Juan and two brunettes named Timmy Taylor and Tyler Trent, all exactly the same height. You could not be a more perfect band than Brainiac. Tyler, the drummer, is wild and has electronic drum pads for making industrial sounds, which is very rare for lo-fi rock bands in 1994. Tim, the lead singer, uses multiple mics that give his voice an overdriven sound effect, which sounds like a broken old record. The guitars and bass are dissonant, angular, and insane.

I love every part of Brainiac for their originality. After their show in New York, I did my usual "Hello, I'm Melissa from Montreal, I love your band, and here's a copy of my band Tinker's cassette demo. I'd love to play shows together one day!" That's how friends are made. With no easy way to get or stay in touch, one just relies on faith that the road will lead you back to each other again. Our scene still feels so intimate and accessible.

In Cleveland (our second time since the opening night of the NIN tour), Courtney decides she wants to seek out the goth scene that Trent Reznor told her about. She's become fairly obsessed with him since touring with NIN earlier that fall. Eric is old news, they never seem to socialize, and Patty is still trying to hide and stay sober. So Courtney and I hit the town.

It's the first time Courtney and I have ever gone out in public together or socialized outside of a music venue. Our natural curiosity and our public club personae are instantly compatible. We have no official security guards yet, but our tour manager finds us a local contact at the club to help guide us around town. We're brought to a giant nightclub, not unlike the beloved Thunderdome of my youth. Except this time we're ushered straight to the manager's quarters and never even check out the dance floor.

We find ourselves in a back-office type of space. Alongside the messy desk in the corner are an unmade bed, a tanning bed, and a shower. The men in black suits who greet us have slicked-back hair and big-toothed grins and hold drinks clanking in their hands. They're flanked by big-breasted women in revealing skin-tight outfits, stylized like from a 1980s workout shoot with a lot of makeup and teased-up big hair. We've just entered an intimate party, with a group of very intoxicated people. The behind-the-scenes scene of this club is sleazier than anything I've ever experienced back home.

"Have a seat, girls! Join us!" One of the men gestures toward the unmade bed. Immediately, we are offered drinks in plastic cups and directed toward lines of white powder on the coffee table.

I have very little experience with cocaine. It's not my kind of high, but I can dabble a bit to fit into an evening if the scene calls for it. Courtney and I each take a line. Everyone is very chatty. I begin seeing this as an interesting sociological experiment with strange people who are excited to get to know us a bit better.

While I'm thinking how ludicrous it is to actually be in conversation with these cheeseballs, one of the men starts making out with one of the women sitting across from me. More lines of coke quickly come and go.

"Yeah, I worked as a stripper too, at Jumbo's Clown Room in LA—'Crazy Bitch' was my persona," I overhear Courtney say in an attempt to bond with one of the girls.

Another girl starts taking off her clothes and turns on the shower.

"Come on, babe! Join me!" She reaches for Courtney's hand.

Courtney turns to me with wide eyes and a giant grin that immediately tells me to read between the lines.

"Melissa?" she says. "Don't we gotta go meet the rest of our band *right now*?"

We run out of there giggling. Outside the manager's office the club is bustling. The crowd and the noise in the club seem amplified, and my jaw movements are as speedy as my speeding heartbeat. I realize we are both very high. We hold hands as we weave through the crowd with determination, heading toward the bathroom.

In the privacy of the stall, I sit down to take a pee. Within moments Courtney's hand appears from under the stall wall. It's holding a pill.

"Take this to take the coke edge off," she yells over the booming music.

This marks the first and last time I ever take a pharmaceutical for recreational purposes. In what seems like just minutes later, the room begins to spin. While Courtney talks with some fans about the show, I manage to slip out of the club alone and get a cab back to the hotel and the safety of my room.

Next thing I know, I'm waking up to hotel security opening my door and Courtney standing at the end of my bed.

"Melissa! I was so worried about you! *Never disappear like that again,*" she says.

Coming to, I notice the wastebasket by the side of my bed is filled with vomit. I sit up, straight up. I'm shocked to find myself so disoriented and sick. And to feel so exposed in front of my imposing new bandleader. At the same time, I'm instinctively enraged by the idea of anyone trying to control me, telling me what I can and can't do. Let alone the person who slipped me the pill that made me vomit. This contradiction is absolutely not lost on me in the moment.

"For twenty-two years I've been trying to get away from my mother!" I shout. "Get out of my room!"

I'm shocked again when I hear this statement come out of my mouth. It's not like me to speak back to anyone like that, and I won't do it again with Courtney, not in any of our wild years that will follow. Feeling anger toward my mother is also a big surprise. I won't "officially" feel any anger toward Mum until I'm forty, a mother myself, and in deep therapy. So this is definitely out of character for me at twenty-two. But I'm probably still under the influence of whatever was in that pill.

My hotel bed is the site of an awakening: Courtney and I bonded for the first time, which led her to fuck me up, which then led to her coming to my rescue. In my vulnerable, raw state I exposed something I hadn't even known was in me. This rare night of dark exploration and drugs opens up something between me and Courtney. She unveils one of my hidden vulnerabilities: my mother. In six months, she'll use it against me when my mother visits us backstage on tour. But for the moment, it gets Courtney out of my room.

Polaroid from first photo shoot with Hole, 1994. Photo by Michael Lavine.

Live Through This Tour: 1994–1995

8/26 Reading, England Reading Festival	10/02 Atlanta, GA Masquerade	10/29 New Orleans, LA Rendon Inn
8/29 Cleveland, OH Nautica Stage	10/04 Pittsburgh, PA Metropol	10/29 New Orleans, LA Tipitina's
8/30 Cleveland, OH Nautica Stage	10/07 Boston, MA Avalon	10/31 Houston, TX Numbers
9/01 Toronto, ONT, Canada Phoenix Theater	10/08 New Haven, CT Toad's Place	11/01 Austin, TX Liberty Lunch
9/02 Clarkston, MI Pine Knob Music Theater	10/10 Rochester, NY The Horizontal Boogie Bar	11/02 Dallas, TX Deep Ellum Live
9/03 Chicago, IL UIC Pavilion	10/11 Buffalo, NY The Marquee at the Traft	11/04 El Paso, TX Metropolis
9/05 St. Paul, MN Roy Wilkins Auditorium	10/12 Montreal, QC, Canada Metropolis	11/05 Tempe, AZ Minder Binders
9/07 Milwaukee, WI Riverside Theater	10/14 Columbus, OH Newport Music Hall	11/06 Las Vegas, NV Huntridge Theater
9/11 Seattle, WA Seattle Center Arena	10/15 Detroit, MI St. Andrew's Hall	11/08 San Diego, CA SOMA
9/21 New York, NY The Academy	10/16 Cincinnati, OH Bogart's	11/09 Hollywood, CA Hollywood Palladium
9/23 Providence, RI Lupo's Heartbreak Hotel	10/18 Indianapolis, IN The Eastwood Theatre	11/11 San Francisco, CA The Fillmore
9/24 Asbury Park, NJ The Stone Pony	10/19 Louisville, KY The Brewery	11/12 Palo Alto, CA The Edge
9/26 Philadelphia, PA The Trocadero	10/21 Chicago, IL The Metro	11/14 Seattle, WA The Moore Theater
9/27 Charlottesville, VA Crossroads Concert Hall	10/22 Madison, WI Paramount Music Hall	11/15 Vancouver, BC, Canada Commodore Ballroom
9/28 Washington, D.C. WUST Music Hall	10/23 Minneapolis, MN First Avenue	11/16 Portland, OR La Luna
9/30 Virginia Beach, VA The Abyss	10/25 Columbia, MO The Blue Note	11/30 Minneapolis, MN Target Center
10/01 Blacksburg, VA Commonwealth Ballroom	10/26 St. Louis, MO Mississippi Nights	12/01 Chicago, IL UIC Pavilion

Date	Location	Venue
12/02	Cleveland, OH	Agora Theater
12/04	Boston, MA	The Orpheum Theatre
12/05	New York, NY	Madison Square Garden
12/08	San Jose, CA	San Jose Events Center
12/09	Berkeley, CA	Community Theater
12/10	Los Angeles, CA	Universal Amphitheater
12/12	San Diego, CA	San Diego Civic Theater
12/17	New York, NY	*Saturday Night Live* (TV Show)
1/13/95	Melbourne, Australia	The Palace
1/14	Sydney, Australia	Selina's
1/16	Perth, Australia	Metropolis
1/18	Adelaide, Australia	Thebarton Theatre
1/20	Auckland, New Zealand	Big Day Out
1/22	Melbourne, Australia	Big Day Out
1/24	Brisbane, Australia	The Roxy
1/26	Sydney, Australia	Big Day Out
1/29	Osaka, Japan	Club Quattro
1/30	Osaka, Japan	Club Quattro
1/31	Osaka, Japan	Liquid Room
2/02	Tokyo, Japan	Liquid Room
2/03	Tokyo, Japan	Liquid Room
2/09	Honolulu, HI	After Dark
2/14	Brooklyn, NY	MTV Unplugged
2/15	New York, NY	Roseland Ballroom
2/16	New York, NY	Roseland Ballroom
3/09	Raleigh, NC	The Ritz
3/10	Charlotte, NC	Ritz Capri Theater
3/12	Tampa, FL	USF Special Events Center
3/13	Ft. Lauderdale, FL	The Edge
3/14	Orlando, FL	The Edge
3/16	Memphis, TN	New Daisy Theatre
3/18	Albuquerque, NM	Sweeney Center
3/19	Denver, CO	Mammoth Events Center
3/21	Salt Lake City, UT	Saltair Pavilion
3/30	London, England	*Top of the Pops* (TV Show)
04/04	Toulouse, France	Le Bikini
04/05	Barcelona, Spain	Zeleste II
04/06	Madrid, Spain	Aqualung
04/08	Montpellier, France	Rockstore
04/09	Lyon, France	Le Transbordeur
04/10	Milan, Italy	City Square
04/12	Cesena, Italy	Vidia Club
04/13	Zurich, Switzerland	Rote Fabrik
04/15	Munich, Germany	Terminal Einz
04/16	Stuttgart, Germany	Longhorn
04/17	Frankfurt, Germany	Volksbildungsheim
04/19	Hamburg, Germany	Docks
04/21	Koln, Germany	Live Music Hall
04/22	Berlin, Germany	Tempodrom
04/24	Amsterdam, Netherlands	Paradiso
4/25	Brussels, Belgium	Luna Theater
4/26	London, England	Virgin Megastore
4/27	Wolverhamton, England	Civic Hall
4/29	Sheffield, England	Octagon
4/30	Manchester, England	Academy

Date	Location	Venue
5/01	Glasgow, Scotland	Barrowlands
5/02	London, England	*Later with Jools Holland* (TV Show)
5/03	Nottingham, England	Rock City
5/04	London, England	Brixton Academy
5/06	Bordeaux, France	Theatre Barbey
5/07	Rennes. France	L'Espace
5/08	Paris, France	Le Bataclan
5/09	Paris, France	*Nulle Part Ailleurs* (TV Show)
5/10	London, England	Shepherd's Bush Empire
6/17	Irvine, CA	KROQ Weenie Roast
7/04	George, WA	The Gorge
7/05	Vancouver, BC, Canada	UBC Thunderbird Stadium
7/08	Englewood, CO	Fiddler's Green Amphitheater
7/10	Bonner Springs, KS	Sandstone Amphitheater
7/11	Maryland Heights, MO	Riverport Amphitheater
7/12	Noblesville, IN	Deer Creek Amphitheater
7/14	Columbus, OH	Polaris Amphitheater
7/15	Tinley Park, IL	World Music Theater
7/18	Cincinnati, OH	Riverbend Music Center
7/19	Clarkston, MI	Pine Knob Music Theater
7/20	Clarkston, MI	Pine Knob Music Theater
7/22	Cuyahoga Falls, OH	Blossom Music Center
7/23	Barrie, ONT, Canada	Molson Park
7/25	Mansfield, MA	Great Woods Center
7/26	Hartford, CT	The Meadows Music Theater
7/28	Randall's Island, NY	Downing Stadium
7/29	Randall's Island, NY	Downing Stadium
7/30	Camden, NJ	Blockbuster/Sony Entertainment Center
7/31	Pittsburgh, PA	Starlake Amphitheater
8/03	Charles Town, WV	Charles Town Racetrack
8/05	Atlanta, GA	Lakewood Amphitheater
8/06	Raleigh, NC	Walnut Creek Amphitheater
8/09	Austin, TX	Southpark Meadows
8/10	Dallas, TX	Starplex Amphitheater
8/12	Phoenix, AZ	Desert Sky/Blockbuster Pavilion
8/14	Irvine, CA	Irvine Meadows Amphitheater
8/15	Irvine, CA	Irvine Meadows Amphitheater
8/17	Sacramento, CA	Cal Expo Amphitheater
8/18	Mountain View, CA	Shoreline Amphitheater
8/25	Reading, England	Reading Festival
8/26	Hasselt, Belgium	Pukkelpop Festival
9/03	Tuktoyatuk, Canada	Molson Ice Polar Beach Party
9/07	New York, NY	MTV Video Music Awar

CHAPTER 14

Warrior Goddess

OCTOBER 1994

It quickly becomes clear that I am on tour with a force to be reckoned with. Never before have I seen anyone possess Courtney's level of power and destruction while also revealing what it means to have survived pure hell. In less than six months, she has lost her husband and her bass player, been left a single mother, and been publicly accused of using drugs during her pregnancy. Soon she will be similarly accused of killing her husband. Her performances are full of unpredictable body movements, accusations, and screams, laced with dark humor and no small amount of drugs to take the edge off. She has very little to lose and everything to gain by being her most empowered and imposing self onstage. Audiences are captivated, night after night.

I grew up going to cutting-edge, wild rock shows, but I've seen only two performers in the punk clubs of my youth who ever came close to the kind of wild and terrifying energy Courtney can produce, and both of them were men. One was David Yow, lead vocalist for noise bands Scratch Acid and Jesus Lizard. He achieved his notoriety for playing shows completely drunk and incoherent and for taking his clothes off.

The other was GG Allin, a punk rocker known more for his notorious stage antics of self-mutilation, defecating onstage, and assaulting audience members. A self-identified extreme individualist, misanthrope, and antiauthoritarian promoting lawlessness and violence, Allin died from a heroin overdose in 1993 at thirty-six years old.

Being an audience member and witnessing both of those provocateurs had been both intimidating and confusing. It was uncomfortable to watch someone seem to fall apart at the seams. At the same time, their catharses throbbed with magnetism. You could not look away. Until Courtney, I have never seen a woman match this energy, especially not from the perspective of a band member onstage, night after night. Other than being a woman, this is what makes her stand out in the male-dominated rock landscape.

Being on tour with Hole makes me think of a time when humans were sent to battle on a public stage, like gladiators in ancient Rome. Gladiators were armed fighters who were usually slaves, criminals, or prisoners of war. Occasionally, a gladiator was allowed to fight for his freedom. Criminals who'd been sentenced to death were sometimes thrown into the arena, unarmed, to serve their sentence. Though it was a revered profession, gladiators usually fought to their deaths, and life expectancy was low. They tended to die young, and this new world I'd entered had similar tendencies.

Getting to know members of the drug-addled American youth movement of the '90s, I learned that most of them had grown up in environments of either neglect, abuse, poverty, or mental illness, or some combination of the four. The contrast with my utopian, bohemian upbringing in Montreal was stark. I hadn't needed to fight for my freedom, nor had I been beaten down into a criminal. In fact, quite the opposite. I honored my surroundings growing up, despite my natural tendency for melancholia. At the same time, my mother's rants about the social injustices of America started making more sense to me in just the first month of touring the United States. The lack of access to health care, decent education, and general dignity has turned many of the people I encounter into what feels like warriors. The ones in the music scene, like Kurt and Courtney, have become role models to many unsung heroes at home, who show up at concerts to sing along.

I come from another land, one that was established as part of the British Commonwealth and gained its independence through lengthy and diplomatic negotiations. But likely due to my mother's American roots and her passionate disdain for her homeland, the struggles of *this* land, born out of a revolution, deeply resonate with me, and I take my calling seriously.

I knew it was risky for me to join Hole. Let's not forget, my initial instinct was to say no. But here I am, taking everything in.

A typical Hole show during this time is like boarding a high-adrenaline roller coaster every night, with equal concern for the safety of Courtney, the audience, and the band members and, ultimately, our sanity. It's a bit like what I imagine going to battle in front of an audience might feel like, like gladiators on display. We never know what's going to happen next.

In October 1994, just a month into our headlining tour, we hit Chicago and its active and exciting music scene. Chicago is home to the best indie labels outside of Seattle: Touch and Go and Thrill Jockey. The Metro, where we're playing, is a legendary rock venue. Every up-and-coming band in the '90s plays here. Just a few days before our sold-out show, a new band from the United Kingdom, Oasis, played the Metro in support of their debut album, *Definitely Maybe*.

Chicago is also the Smashing Pumpkins' hometown, and the omnipresent Billy "who discovered me" looms large here. When we show up in Chicago I wonder if my "spiritual fucking cowboy" might make an appearance at our show. While my heart is curious to see the man who represented everything to me for the past three years, I also recoil from any desire to see him, knowing that I mean very little to him in comparison to Courtney. As soon as I stepped into Hole, whatever special connection I thought Billy and I had was quickly eclipsed by their massive drama-filled bond. I can't keep track of the state of their relationship from month to month.

It soon becomes clear that Billy and Courtney are back in a rough patch. Backstage, while we're getting ready for the show, I hear Courtney muttering as she applies her big red lips, *"Fucking asshole is not invited to my show—but James Iha is coming."* This answers my question.

As much as I'm a romantic, I'm also a realist, and I understand that it's important to protect my heart. To do this I know it's time to forget my childhood fantasy and let the real rock stars take the lead on this dynamic. So I do.

Backstage at the Metro is the usual mess of graffiti and band sticker–filled walls, a couple smelly couches, and bathrooms. The floors are sticky with booze from last night, and the room reeks of stale cigarette smoke. Baby Frances sits on a couch with the nanny and watches the room get ready. When the tour manager gives us our five-minute warning, I take my pre-show pee and apply my usual MAC mauve-brown lipstick before heading out to the stage.

Courtney heads over to the couch and plants a goodnight kiss on Frances's forehead.

"Night-night, baby," she says, and then to the nanny, "Get her to sleep early."

And on that note, the four of us leave the dressing room and head to the stage.

Our walk to the stage every night feels like moving in slow motion. The grubby hallway of any old club transforms into the portal of a timeless mission: to share our souls with the world. Our walks turn into more of a strut. We take deep breaths to calm our racing heartbeats before we come together in a four-person huddle. As we awkwardly hold hands for a moment, Courtney recites a prayer of her choosing for that day—either a Buddhist chant or part of the Lord's Prayer, and punctuates the end with a visceral "Hhhhh-hah!" creating an electric shock that runs through us. Then we release our hands and take our positions onstage.

Patty always walks up first to get settled behind her drum kit, followed by Eric and me to claim our opposite sides of the stage. We pick up our guitars to be ready for the main attraction to take center stage.

Courtney swaggers onto stage last. Tonight she wears a tailored black waistcoat, which she removes to reveal a black long-sleeved, very-very short minidress with a white Peter Pan collar. Someone throws a sweaty T-shirt up onto the stage, and her thigh-high black nylons, garter belt, and underwear flash the audience when she leans over to pick it up. With a wobbly high kick, she tosses the shirt under her leg and back into the crowd. Then she picks up her surf-green Fender guitar from the stand in front of the drum riser, throws her cigarette down, and gets right into it without addressing the crowd.

It's common for a band to grow accustomed to a particular opening song that warms up both the band and the audience alike, setting the tone of the night just right. Our go-to opening song is "Plump," one of my favorite tracks from *Live Through This*. With notable confidence Courtney plays the opening heavy riff perfectly, and we, the band, kick in.

The crowd, jammed in tight and thrashing around on the open floor, goes crazy. An attentive crowd is also wrapped around the room up in a balcony section. Those up above are usually the shy, the VIP, and the serious musicologists who do not want to miss a moment, as opposed to the crowd who wants to lose themselves *in* the moment.

We are about thirty shows into the tour by now, and I'm feeling comfortable on the stage. I know all my parts by heart and am beginning to be able to let go. This allows a musician to have a visceral connection to their instrument, the band, and the audience, one that transcends the mind that's keeping track of the arrangements and lets the music take on a life of its own. In this state, one literally gets carried away from reality. In my case, it means away from the shock that my radically new life now includes . . . this.

We are less than ten minutes into the show when, predictably, Courtney makes a point of introducing me to the crowd between songs.

"This is Melissa Auf der Maur from Montree-all," she drawls, pronouncing my name slowly and carefully before her speech pattern spins out all over the place, alternating between slow and fast. "She speaks some mean French and thanks to . . . um . . . someone in this town—an *ASSHOLE!*—she's here. But I'd like to thank him. He's . . . a dick."

This early introduction of me has become somewhat of a show routine. By putting the crowd's attention on the new bass player at the top of the set, Courtney sets up the dynamic for her to keep turning to me throughout the show, positioning me as a sidekick she can bounce material off of.

Courtney rarely introduces Eric and Patty by name. More likely, she refers to something Patty once did musically or chides Eric in a crazy-sister kind of way. The preferential attention I am getting makes me uncomfortable, and I feel a bit bad for the other two. But there is no controlling or questioning

Courtney's power-dynamic instincts. She has clearly set out to establish me as her Wonder Twin, the good girl to her bad girl, the virgin to her whore, the calm to her chaos. To this end she has perfectly cast a Canadian redhead as the straight woman to her crazy bitch.

Being introduced in front of hundreds or even thousands night after night knocks out any remaining shyness from my youth. I can no longer *afford* to be shy. This woman is fighting for her life onstage every night, regularly sending her arrows over to me, and I have to deflect them. I never know what the fuck is going to happen in a show, when she's going to turn to me, or what I'll be saying into a mic in response. At all moments I have to be prepared for any shocking thing to be thrown my way.

Although it is a compliment of sorts for Courtney to put such focus on me, these introductions also feel like a slow, incremental daily acid drip on my fair skin. An intricate, self-protective armor begins to form around me, a metaphysical field that I can tighten or loosen up, depending on the circumstance. I take note of this in my diary and in letters to friends back home, developing insights into human behavior and how we slowly morph and shape-shift according to our need to survive and desire to succeed. In this way, stages all over the world become both training and learning grounds for me.

I understand by now that sharing personal feelings in public is Courtney's go-to bonding style. As my father's daughter, observing and considering the intricate social tactics of complex people come naturally to me. He uses the public platform of his newspaper columns to express his love and devotion to me, so I'm used to receiving that kind of attention from someone who struggles with more intimate relationships and methods of closeness.

After we play "Jennifer's Body," a fun high-energy song that gets the crowd moving and sweating, we go straight into "Asking for It," a deceptively melodic, mellow song that opens with a descending bass line and then challenges existing conceptions about rape. This song showcases my backup vocals in the chorus and the outro. Harmonies have a way of pulling at heartstrings, and my harmonizing has quickly become one of my musical strong suits and offerings to this band. It offers a complement to

Courtney's gruff shouts, juxtaposing my choir-girl innocence against her raspy wild child.

The song ends with a gorgeous outro that we've newly extended on this tour for extra emotional impact, repeating the album title:

> *If you live through this with me*
> *I swear that I would die for you*
> *And if you live through this with me*
> *I swear that I would die for you*

I get chills repeating these words every night. These are lines Courtney had surely written for Kurt while he was still alive. And then he had left her, had failed to *live through this* with her, and now she was *begging* her band and the audience to witness her dual obsessions with pain and ambition.

Moments in the show when Courtney confronts the audience always get a little nerve-racking. Someone could throw something at the stage and hurt one of us, or they could shout out the wrong thing and piss her off. She might ignore it, or she might choose to engage. There is never any way of predicting.

Semicoherent streams of consciousness are becoming more common the deeper we get into the tour. They'll get way worse over time, eventually devolving into endless rambles of nothing.

I never play under the influence of anything, so the effects of the use and abuse of heroin are foreign to me. I have no way to assess what part of Courtney's behavior is her personality, her posturing, or the drug. As time goes on I begin to pick up on the signs of clear heroin use, such as track marks, pinned pupils, nodding off, and slurring of words. The gods of punk rock who came before us, such as the Sex Pistols, had also looked and acted like this, whether they were on drugs or not. The stumbling, the "fuck you" flipping of the bird—all of that had been painted by the punks before us.

Knowing how smart Courtney is, I can't tell what's an act and what's real debauchery. At this moment in Chicago, she's pulling it off with a decent balance. But that balance is precarious, and it's not going to sustain itself throughout the *Live Through This* tour. As the drugs get heavier, they'll start to ruin performances.

✗

Still so new in the band, I don't have much rapport with the other two members onstage yet. During a show, I have limited bandwidth beyond—in order of importance—my bass, Courtney, and the crowd. I suspect the same goes for Patty and Eric, too. In truth we really are not much of a band. We never really play off of or tune in to each other. The leader leads the whole show. Her moods, rants, and assault function as conductor. The rest of us exist in our own vortexes, trying to stay sane and stick to our commitments to get to the finish line.

By this point I've learned that Eric and Courtney were romantically involved at the band's inception. The Hole origin story is not mine to tell in detail, but in brief it says a lot about them both. They were radically different creatures. Eric was raised in a large Catholic family in the Los Angeles suburbs and was working in the accounting department of Capitol Records when he and Courtney met. She had grown up in what was, by all accounts, an unstable household led by her mother and populated with various stepfathers and siblings and had legally emancipated from her crazy parents at sixteen. In the San Francisco goth-rock scene she experimented with forming some bands. After moving to LA in 1989, she put an ad in the local music paper looking for a guitar player. The influences she listed were Neil Young and Sonic Youth. Apparently, the shy accountant who had never played in a band before was the first to reply. She arrived at his apartment with her suitcase and moved in, and they became both a couple and the founders of the band.

Eric kept them both afloat with his record-company job until Hole made their first album, *Pretty on the Inside*, for Sub Pop records, and went on tour. Like any working-dating relationship, I am sure theirs was a precarious one and that their drives for music and success took priority. What I also heard from the inner circle was that shortly after the band took off, Courtney left Eric for Billy Corgan while the bands were on tour together. That's when the pieces of Courtney's romantic history started to intersect with my history, too. I clearly remember the night in autumn 1991 when Billy practically cried on my shoulder in the Vermont bar about Courtney leaving him for Kurt.

Courtney seems to go back-to-back in her relationships, again in contrast to me. I've barely had a steady boyfriend; the notion of back-to-back ones seems absurd. How would you get to know yourself if you weren't alone, emotionally *and* physically, for long periods of time?

I have a particular phobia of getting too attached to anyone. My emotional independence is of too much importance to me. But Courtney is different in that way. And now, in her current moment of crisis as a grieving widow and single mother, there is no man or relationship for her to dive into. Just herself, her band, and the audience. We are now her partners in survival and success.

Eric tends to keep a low profile onstage, hiding behind his blond bangs and well-cultivated guitar tones. From time to time he tries to defuse the tension with silly sound effects, which turns the attention to his inherently shy self for a brief moment. As the only guy in the band, he naturally sticks out but is the least flashy of us all so in some ways seems to disappear. His guitar is his main identity, and his go-to slightly strained persona beyond that is of a goofy clown. His big, toothy smile appears from time to time and sheds a welcome light upon the moment.

"Eric, do something, come on!" Courtney taunts him tonight. "Do it. You were in Little League—go ahead . . ."

Her playful teasing manner quickly escalates to a roar. "*ERIC!!! Now you know six FUCKING YEARS, I'M SO FUCKING SICK OF YOU.*" She walks to his side of the stage and with a devilish smile gives him a kick in the butt. Eric leans over in an act of submission, welcoming the abuse and playing it off as a comedic act. Patty kicks into a drumbeat, adding a bit of a circus vaudeville-act mood to the scene, and then elevates it into the military marching beat of U2's "Sunday Bloody Sunday."

Is this deliberate comedy? Uninhibited tragedy? At this point, who can tell?

This four-person stage act continues to develop over the next year, with me serving as Courtney's sidekick, Patty punctuating the scenes with comedic drum accents, and Eric taking the abuse and wrath of his ex-girlfriend. Eventually, it will become clear to me that these acts, and these roles, are not funny at all.

It's said that band dynamics are like family dynamics, pathological and often top-down. There is always a leader. In a family, that's most often a mother or a father. If the person at the helm is destructive, unpredictable, or struggling with mental health issues, the members lower down on the totem are tempted to follow the path of least resistance to avoid conflict. This is absolutely the case with Hole. Each of the band members under Courtney struggles to find his or her place in the dysfunctional family dynamic, hoping to get out in one piece, while counting on the music and the mission to give us a reason to be there. In the meantime, subjecting ourselves to unhealthy pathologies instead of more mindful and caring ones is unfortunately the norm.

✕

Somehow, we make it through the entire Metro set without a major incident. It always feels like a success to still be in one piece, physically and emotionally, and leave the stage at the end of a set. The trick is to surrender, not to break. This is literally living life on the edge of chaos.

At the side of the stage, out of view of the audience, Courtney prepares for an encore by stripping down to her short black lace-and-satin slip. We wait for the cheers to grow to a sufficient volume to deserve our return to the stage, a silly tradition that somehow prevails even for punks. We are all riding high on adrenaline, sweating, feeling energized, and forging forces with a room of alternative kids. It is the place each of us always dreamed of being.

When she decides the timing is right, Courtney struts back onstage in her slip with a cigarette in her mouth. We follow and resume our positions.

"Hi," she says coolly. Pressing her mouth way up close against the mic, she kicks into heavy breathing, building and building with sexually suggestive deep grunts and movements before coming to a climax.

"I faked it every time, I just wanted you to know," she tells the room.

Self-portrait with Patty Schemel, 1994. (*top*)
Self-portrait with Eric Erlandson, 1994. (*bottom*)

The audience is in the palm of her sweaty, honest, and fearlessly sexy hands. Our go-to closing punk-rock anthem comes next: "Rock Star," or "Olympia," as she calls it, which is the Pacific Northwest city that inspired the song.

The crowd goes wild. Random crowd-surfers are passed along the crest of the surging mass. Bouncers at the front of the stage fight to keep the rowdiest ones from trying to get up on stage by pushing them, forcefully, back into the pit. As the song ends with heavy thrashing, Courtney gives it her all as she screams and furiously plays her guitar.

Don't you please
Make me real, come on
Make me sick, come on
Make me real, yeah yeah yeah
Do it for the kids, yeah
Well I went to school in Olympia

The last line comes out with a schoolgirl innocence to counterbalance the rage that inspires her next.

Only one person is bestowed with the honor of stage diving tonight. The final chords of "Olympia" are still ringing when, in one seamless movement, Courtney flings her guitar off and dives headfirst off the edge of the stage, surrendering herself to the waiting hands of the crowd. Propped up by her fans, her body floats and dips below the surface, riding the human waves. The band remains onstage futzing around, making noise to accompany her final effort of the night.

These few minutes of Courtney's surrender to the sea of hungry youth stretch into slow motion. A sea of hands passes her around, pulls at her clothes, grabs her body. Her exposed broad shoulders and bare back are slapped. Her hair is pulled. She is flipped over onto her back as random, anonymous hands grip and grab her soft, strong thighs. Like a rag doll in a ritual of sacrifice, her body hovers limply over the crowd.

Then her hands come to life and reach toward the stage, a subtle motion to bring her back "home."

The meatiest of the security guards carries her out of the pit, cradled in his arms. She wraps her arms around the big man's neck like a damsel being saved from a dragon, but this damsel is *not* in distress. She whispers something into his ear, gives him a kiss on the cheek, and stumbles back up onto the stage.

Now dressed in nothing but a shredded black-lace bra and bikini underwear, one leg of her nylons still clinging to her body, she strikes a pose with an ironic beauty-queen check of her hip. She saunters up to the mic and casually says, "*You fail*," suggesting the crowd has been a test audience for her this whole night.

"You do that to the guys?" Kurt, Eddie, Chris—none of them have had their flannel shirts ripped off their backs. She knows that, and now we all realize it, too. She flips the crowd a subtle bird with a cheeky smile. "I liked that fucking slip! Thanks a lot."

Night after night, Courtney's body and actions become testament to pushing the boundaries of women's liberation. Are the assaults she endures because she dares to expose her wild warrior ways? Or are they reflections of the audience's ingrained, even subconscious, attacks on women? Denim and flannel are inherently more durable than silk slips. The boys in bands are *not* being manhandled like this.

On her way off the stage Courtney knocks her mic stand to the ground, then does the same to the rest of the mics onstage. Before she exits for good she staggers around, hurling objects through space. It is a shocking display of volatile power. And also frightening and impressive in its boldness, at the same time.

Fuck you, all of you, it says.

And then she stumbles offstage, back into her life, having blown many minds with a force of womanhood that no one has seen the likes of before.

Progress. I view this as progress, even if it can also be interpreted as grotesque and rude. Courtney is waking people up to the innate failures of human instincts. She allows them to destroy their heroes, to rip her apart to get a piece of the prize.

During these moments in the show, we onstage and the engaged audience members—not the ones there to gawk at a world-famous controversial character, but the mindful ones—realize we are witnessing the exorcism of a powerful, witchy woman who is processing unfathomable loss and shock, as well as a maternal legacy of loss. Her grandmother was left in a basket on a church stoop, her mother given up for adoption at birth. Courtney was abandoned throughout her childhood and emancipated herself at sixteen. She's a third-generation motherless daughter. Where will this leave Frances? I wonder.

When Courtney loses herself in these moments onstage, we hold her. We offer her a sonic cradle to help pacify the justifiable pain of a whole life that has led her to this moment. The public is only just becoming aware of the horror that was Courtney's life. It is intense, and heavy, on a psychic level.

In these moments, I know exactly why I am here: To help create music that will hold us all. And for women to be leading this ritual for all who need it.

I am grateful that Courtney has music to bash these dark feelings around, grateful that we all do. Rock music saves lives. I have always believed that. But living with the unpredictability of how long this experiment will continue, whom Courtney might scream at, just how deep her sorrows are, and what demons she might summon next—this part isn't an easy ride.

Courtney Love applying perfume backstage, 1994.

CHAPTER 15

Sensory Overload

As the new member of Hole, who didn't play on the *Live Through This* album, I feel half in and half out of the band, a wandering visitor who's not quite sure how long she might stay. This turns out to be a good position to occupy.

I learn that I need constant retreat from the volatility of the situation, and shelter from being on constant display and receiving projections from others. During my first year in Hole, I'll be witnessed live by approximately three hundred thousand pairs of ears and eyes, and that's not counting radio listeners, angst-ridden teens seeking salvation in their bedrooms, MTV video watchers, readers of weekly reviews and interviews, other bands, the crews backstage, and the omnipresent music-industry execs, radio reps, and journalists who hold the whole charade together.

In this situation, the ears and eyes are both receiving you and then in turn projecting what they see, need, and feel from you. Even if you are just the bass player, standing to the left of the main attraction and spared a lot of the gawking, you are on that stage, giving and receiving. They're seeking something from you. Eventually, you begin to wonder what it is you must have been seeking that led you there, too.

My prolific diary keeping and letters to friends back home become my lifeline to sanity. My solo ritual of shooting photos becomes my sanctuary. I travel with a cluster of items that act as a shrine to my Montreal life and make me feel like home is close. My big brown faux-leather 1970s vintage shoulder bag carries my treasures: my camera; my Discman, to listen to the albums kept in my overstuffed CD booklet; my favorite hardcover diary that features a close-up of the face of Botticelli's *Birth of Venus* on its cover; and a big binder covered in band and city stickers. The binder is stuffed with random photos of and postcards for friends, materials to make care packages, and DIY stationery to correspond with friends back home and eventually new friends I make on the road.

I've gotten into making custom Xerox stationery, my personal version of a fanzine or homemade show poster art. I raid a pharmacy stationery section, find the copy machine, and use my own photos or cool cutouts from street posters to copy onto special paper I feed into the machine with the help of a clerk at the shop. The result is custom one-of-a-kind paperworks on which I write intensely personal messages in my oversize, hard-to-read bubble writing. Sending these messages back home, or putting them into my diary, feels like a commitment to being honest and pure of heart. This bag is with me

---

Diary on a hotel bed, 1999.

at all times—my airplane carry-on, backstage, in my bus bunk. I am never separated from it.

The personal ritual of retreat is something I learned as a lonely only child who was raised with a hippie art-school education. It became an invaluable coping mechanism for just about anything. When I'm lonely, confused, or needing to escape, I write about my feelings or take a photo of what's in front of me while listening to music. It becomes my home base in the midst of chaos.

When I was a young girl, suffering from debilitating shyness, my father said, "It's okay to be shy, Melissa. You're watching, and you'll have a lot more to say later." He empowered me as a wallflower. He saw me. And in me, maybe he saw a bit of himself.

"On Tour with My Daughter, the Rock Star from Ca-Na-Da"

SOUTH MIAMI BEACH—*We were barreling up Interstate 95 in the heavy rain toward Fort Lauderdale on Monday, caught in the mist and spray between two trucks.*

"Could you turn on the radio?" Melissa asked the driver. "The metal station, please."

A melodic guitar and cello instrumental filled the car and then a voice sang bittersweet lyrics. "That's Nirvana, Nick," Melissa said. "That's Kurt Cobain singing."

Now that my daughter is in this band, Hole, with Cobain's widow, Courtney Love, she thought maybe I should pay a little attention to it. We were heading for Fort Lauderdale for a 4 o'clock sound check of their instruments and the full truckload of electronic gear they drag around. There was a cluster of fans and groupies hanging around the stage door when we arrived at The Edge, a funky club housed in a converted 1930s sawmill.

Courtney Love didn't show up for the sound check. She's not into details and spends most of her off time during tours in her hotel room with her two-and-half-year-old daughter. Mostly she chats on the Internet.

She has a serious computer habit. She also has a personal assistant and a huge entourage.

"It's weird," Melissa commented.

"Everything gets done for you. They have this idea the artist is just there to perform so you don't get to do anything else. Never carry a bag, pay a bill, talk to an airline.

"And sometimes I find myself taking advantage of it. Ask an aide casually to do something. And it gets done immediately."

Do you feel comfortable with that, I asked her.

"No," she answered. "It's a bit soulless. I want to stay independent, be my own person."

When we went back to the club after dinner, the crowd at the stage door had grown. A young man with long blond hair walked up to Melissa and very respectfully held out his hand. Melissa took it and he stammered something like "Good luck tonight."

Soon we were surrounded by young fans, holding out CDs, notepads, paper scraps, dollar bills, anything for Melissa to autograph. I stood back and watched the worshipful faces of these young girls and boys looking at my daughter.

That's when it really struck me that my daughter was becoming a rock 'n' roll star.

I listened to the fans' chatter.

"She's so beautiful."

"She's so poised."

"She's not stuck up at all."

They even pronounced Auf der Maur right. It felt like I was watching a movie . . .

On Saturday night in Tampa, Courtney slipped her panties off from under her little girl dress—and threw them at the audience.

She tried to get Melissa to do the same. Melissa was embarrassed and refused.

For some reason, Courtney never introduces the other two band members, drummer Patty Schemel and guitarist Eric Erlandson. Just Melissa, who in addition to playing bass sings with Courtney. And it's always along the lines:

"She's from Ca-na-da. She's pure. She's polite. She's a virgin. She doesn't do bad things."

A radically different rock'n'roll star.

—Nick Auf der Maur, column for the Montreal Gazette, *March 15, 1995*

CHAPTER 16

Down Under

JANUARY 1995

BY THE END OF 1994, AFTER ONLY FOUR MONTHS IN HOLE, I'VE POPPED MY big rock-band cherry playing in front of sixty-five thousand people, gone on tour with the darkest industrial machine monsters out there, played *Saturday Night Live*, and am now about to set sail around the globe for more.

Immediately after the holidays we're scheduled to fly Down Under for Hole's first tour of Australia, followed by a week in Japan. But first I'm heading home to Montreal for a brief Christmas visit.

At the airport I pick up a copy of that month's *Rolling Stone* with Courtney on the cover for my mother. The article features full-page solo black-and-white photos of Courtney looking glam and a small one of the band. It's the first glossy touched-up photo I've seen of myself as a member of Hole. In the photo I'm wearing my most prized vintage '70s items: platform knee-high leather boots, a tiny leather jacket, and a suede miniskirt. I look comfortable and surprisingly grown up and confident. As I stare at the photo I am seeing and meeting my new self at the same time. I'm already a veteran in front of my own camera and am now somehow able to slink right over into the public gaze, too.

The *Rolling Stone* article is titled "Courtney Love: Life Without Kurt." In a positive and glowing account, journalist David Fricke depicts Courtney as a survivor who has talent and guts. Then, about halfway in, he asks, "Did you consider breaking up Hole for good?"

When *Newsweek* found out she was my mother in the middle of the Katherine Ann Power thing, she was just mortified. Because people have met me song. Or the girl in [Bob Dylan's] "Leopard-Skin Pill-Box Hat." Or the girl in "Sad Eyed Lady of the Lowlands." All these girls riding the Jersey psychosexual aspects of r Not that I'm so desirable. the kinder-whore thing thought I was so hot. Wh

xxxx Hole as one: Bassist Melissa Auf der Maur (who replaced Kristen Pfaff), guitarist Eric Erlandson, drummer Patty Schemel and Love (from left) xxxxxx

look used to more appealin; see a 14-year-o fanzine acting it pisses me o started, it was : *Happened to* thing. My angl Then again Joe pointed this ever since he'd had little baby blocks and toy. had to do with patent-leather s being allowed dress. Never ha specific dolls. insisted on tal lessons when I v which caused a in our house. gender specific. *Do you feel loc look now?* Sometimes just wear regu onstage. Then by not being can I still pull i my costume, m cause my thin sage. But the mixed up with the idea of a ing to be appealing to get a *How much of your early mus especially that version of Mit Sides Now"* [a k a "Clouds"]

who were her clients: "If that's your product, my friend ..." The only advice she ever gave me in my life was "Don't wear tight sweaters. They make you look cheap." highway in a Bruce Springsteen song. And then I came around. "No, no, no. I don't want to be the girl. I want to be Leonard Cohen!" We had *Blue*, the Joni Mitchell album, when I was grow-

"Absolutely" is Courtney's response. "But Melissa is very talented, and if I don't nurture her, she'll go out on her own and be great. God, it was Billy, of all people, who suggested her. Billy is always right. He wasn't right about who I should marry, but he's always right."

I read and reread this statement a couple of times. What is really being said here?

The Wonder-Twin Power-Duo Shtick that Courtney has been developing for us onstage is right here on the page. It feels both complimentary and

---

Hole, photographed for *Rolling Stone*, 1993. Photo by Mark Seliger.

terrifying. On the one hand, she is saying that in some way I helped save the band. But her words also make me feel deeply unsettled, like I'm under threat of being owned or captured by someone who won't let go out of fear that I'll achieve my own independent success. The deeper I get into this band, I sense, the scarier it's going to be to find a way out.

Crediting and chiding Billy in the same sentence also strikes me as odd. It's a public jab at a person who I think may still be in love with her. Perhaps this is a way for Courtney to keep their connection going. She knows he'll be reading every word she said, especially in her first major cover story.

Crediting him for being right about me but not about whom she should marry is also a strange thing—to say the least—for a recent widow to say. I read this as Billy had wanted Courtney to marry *him* instead of Kurt. In light of how her marriage ended, I wonder if Billy wasn't right about that, too.

The *Rolling Stone* article reveals a lot about my new boss. And between the lines, I learn a lot about my role in this band.

New Year's Eve 1994–1995 will be my last New Year's in Montreal for many years. It draws a line in the sand between the old life I am almost completely leaving behind and the new adventures that lie ahead. It's surreal to meet up with my friends for drinks in the old bars. I'm a girl in a rock band now, recounting the things I have seen on the road. Already, I feel alienated from the social scene in Montreal.

At the very top of the new year I fly to LA to join the band, where we head out for our first full overseas tour. We start with Big Day Out, a traveling alternative-music festival that is like the Lollapalooza of Australia.

Big Day Out is every band's dream tour. Held in the month of January, at the height of an Australian summer, it functions like a two-week vacation for performers. Because of the amount of time it takes to travel to Australia and the big time difference once we arrive, the promoters spoil the musicians by giving us endless days off before, during, and in between shows. It's an enticing trick to get all of the desired bands around the globe to come. The nickname for the fest, I soon discover, is "The Big Day Off."

Courtney, Patty, Eric, and I are picked up at the airport in Melbourne, where we are greeted by sunshine and big smiles from the fans waiting for us outside.

"We love you, Courtney!"

"Hi Frances!"

"Can you sign an autograph?!"

Our first couple days are free for exploring the chill surfer town. We're put up in a nice hotel. I get a city map and roam around to soak in all the new experiences. I instantly love the people and the vibe. The fans and the local bands remind me of the Montreal alternative-music scene, but with funny accents. Seeing everything through the lens of a Canadian, I quickly declare Australia to be "the tropical Canada!" and Melbourne as "the Montreal of Australia."

The country seems to have a pervasive, underlying essence of "relaxed" as opposed to Canadians' underlying sense of "insecurity." "I'm sorry" and "Eh?" are the most commonly used Canadian nervous expressions, which epitomize the humble search of approval we all seem to have. It strikes me that Australia has the added advantage of being isolated from all other über-Westernized places, especially the United States, whose presence looms large over Canada and creates an underlying insecurity complex for some. But not for this girl, daughter of serious pro-Canada, anti-US parents.

Australia is a welcome counterbalance and relief after my outrageous deep dive into the US tour experience. I am terrified of the corporate landscape in America, having been warned by my parents about the capitalism that ruled the United States. The members of my band seem horrendously broken from some of the extreme forces in the United States as they transformed from neglected, poor broken kids to superstars with even worse habits. The Nine Inch Nails tour with the gross goth boys and their backstage dominatrices certainly didn't make my US immersion warm and fuzzy. But Australia, like Canada, is filled with happy people, happy crowds, and what comes across as a blissful existence. That feels immediately healing and also expands my understanding of what traveling in a rock band is: an opportunity to shadow another world.

When you go on tour in a foreign country, you weave in and out of daily experiences with local promoters, crews, and other musicians. Over a period of weeks you become familiar with a new culture through a very specific perspective. Everything from how the audience reacts, to how the local crew treats you, to how the local press, interviewers, record-company executives, and local bands receive you adds up to a rarefied way to get to know another culture. And in Australia, where the experience is dragged out over two weeks for the Big Day Off, you're able to hang around and get to know the people and the culture at a leisurely pace.

I find I have much in common with the Australians I interact with. In particular, I become instant friends with Steve Pav, the main concert-promoter rep, who becomes my first nomadic friend on the road. We both love taking photographs, and he occasionally hijacks my camera and takes pictures of himself to surprise me with later. He has a natural skater street-fashion sense that I find cute, very much like a Beastie Boy. During the tour his buzz cut flip-flops between bleached-blond white and aqua.

Pav isn't much older than I am, but he's been singlehandedly responsible for bringing all the '90s alternative-rock acts from America to music lovers in Australia, including Nirvana, the Beastie Boys, Red Hot Chili Peppers, and Mudhoney. He is the cultural attaché for all of us, a sort of ambassador for alternative rock in Australia and a hero to local music lovers. When I learn this, I feel an extreme affinity with him. Probably somewhere in there I fancied myself playing a similar role in Canada for these bands, which I'd sort of been doing when I introduced myself to Billy and apologized on behalf of the entire city of Montreal. I consider that to be another Australian-Canadian connection, that there are people like me here who are trying to foster the same exchange.

One night off in Sydney, Pav brings me to the beach, where I go into the ocean. I rarely do this because I don't know how to swim and I'm slightly afraid of the dark, but when I immerse myself it fulfills me, connecting me to the overwhelming power of Mother Nature.

The sky is dense with stars, and the full moon is huge. I lay on the beach at three in the morning, soaking up the moon rays.

When I was twelve, I stood on the sidewalk across from the huge, quiet public park across from my family's house. Staring up at the clear night sky above, I focused on the first layer of stars, trying to see past them to the next layer, and the next and the next. I could see that these layers went on and on, into infinity.

Infinity. My mind found comfort in that notion.

The concept enveloped me like the Milky Way itself: a sparkling, tripping immersion into something much bigger than anything on Earth. When I think of how prescient dreams and ethereal experiences entered and impacted my life, I believe it began there, when I found a new way of being and seeing in the stars.

We are magic. We are made of stardust. We are light in the night sky. We are all connected to each other and the infinite solar system. This is the light in which I have glowed since birth. I suppose it's the light I now crave, and the light I have followed in the dark nights of my life.

As I gaze upward from that beach in Australia—in my childhood safe place, pondering infinity—I realize that, with the time change, it will take seventeen hours for this full moon to reach North America. It takes the entire planet only twenty-four hours to turn a full circle. That's fast.

Earth feels like a small planet right now. And I am upside down on it for the first time, the farthest I've ever been from where I was born and raised. It's a moment of feeling at home on Earth. The infinite sky holds these feelings of expansiveness and connection beautifully.

✖

The Big Day Out Festival this year is a weird lineup of bands, in some ways stuck between the late '80s and the early '90s. The headliners are the Cult and Ministry, whose heydays were during my high school Thunderdome goth-club days. The festival bill also includes the new SoCal faux-punk sensation the Offspring—you may remember "You Gotta Keep

'Em Separated." They're followed by Luscious Jackson, a feel good rap/pop all-girl band signed to the Beastie Boys label, Grand Royale, and the Seattle scene's Screaming Trees, a rock band fronted by poetic tortured soul Mark Lanegan whose struggles with heroin addiction are known to everyone who follows his music. Hole and the UK band Primal Scream are sandwiched in between these acts.

When we show up at the festival grounds on the first day, the backstage village is buzzing with the usual preshow activities. Only this time, it's festival-size with gorgeous tropical vibes. Just like at the Reading Festival, the stages are erected in the middle of a large field.

It's common for the bands on the bill to watch each other's shows from the side of the stage. It's a way to get a good look at each other and also to show interest and respect. On the first day I see members of the Cult watching our set from my side of the stage. I instantly recognize the lead singer, Ian Astbury, from years of magazines and music videos. He has a rather intimidating presence, with long raven-black hair, a cowboy hat, a sleeveless leather vest over a bare chest, and a large pendant hanging around his neck. It gives him a mystical air, but when he approaches me backstage after our set he is neither standoffish nor pretentious. Instead, he greets me with a warm smile. He tells me he watched us play and was a fan and thinks I am especially good.

That night he dedicates their biggest hit, "She Sells Sanctuary," to me, and the crowd goes wild. Astbury and I become backstage friends on this tour. He says he can tell immediately I am "spiritually involved"—possibly a witch, he says, and he's had many witches in his life, starting with his grandmother and then several girlfriends. He feels comfortable telling me about his recent stint in rehab, his marriage, and his new child. We have a sweet, pure connection.

I am so lonely and isolated on this tour, literally wandering festival grounds, making friends with men who are ten years older than I am and ten years sober because I can't relate to anyone in my immediate environment. My bandmates are either detached or fireballs of chaos on a course of self-destruction, while I am trying to slow myself down and have a creative, personal experience that I can document in photographs and hold with me for the rest of my life. Despite having had heavy mystifying dreams in my twenty-two years, and big feelings about the esoteric sides of life, I haven't talked to many people about the complicated thoughts that haunt me, and I welcome these new conversations—no less with a man from a band he named the Cult.

I had very little experience with this level of drug use when joining the band just six months ago. Unfortunately, I soon find out that many of the other people on the tour are deep into heroin and how accepted and common it is among so many of the US and UK bands. Back in Montreal I knew a few heroin users, but they weren't shooting up at the bar. They were hiding their use.

The first thing to know about junkies is the hiding. The hiding and the lying.

I know heroin has been a real struggle for Courtney, but until now it has more or less been out of sight, out of mind for me. Sure, I've noticed her staying in her bedroom and hotel room a lot. I knew she wasn't only reading magazines when she was locked up in her room for twelve hours at a time. Around this time in Australia, I also start picking up on her nodding off and having pinpoint pupils and touching and rubbing at her face, which are all physical symptoms and behaviors of heroin use.

Something I hadn't thought about prior to joining this traveling circus is that when you travel on planes and buses and cross borders as a daily lifestyle, juggling an addiction becomes a complex strategy. The level of dramatic hustle to acquire drugs so that the show can go on from day to day is happening in the hotel hallways, buses, and backstages of our world tour. It requires a complex ruse to stay alive and is exhausting and dangerous for all involved.

My understanding of the game is that it involves two steps: either score the drugs or illegally score "legal" pharmaceuticals to hold you over until you acquire your next batch; and above all, don't die.

When users are on tour alone they can hide in a bathroom or hotel room. When they're on a huge festival tour—which I hadn't known, because I'd never been on one before—they don't have to hide anymore. They can do it together. I guess there's solace to be found in mutual despair and destruction and escape. Enjoy the high together? Why not.

One night I open the door to our dressing-room trailer to get a beer and find six or so people slouched on the couch and floor. I catch blurred glimpses of colored straps and belts around their biceps and delicately held syringes. Drug paraphernalia is littered across the catering table next to the cold cuts.

Their calm and focus are ominous, too. Unfazed by the world outside of their circle, they don't even notice me come in.

My whole life I have been insanely needle phobic. Vaccines as a kid were a *huge* ordeal for my pediatrician, Dr. Lupu, to perform, and getting blood drawn made for embarrassing amounts of talking it through with the nurse. "Are you sure you won't slip and puncture *through* the vein?" I still ask. This was what always gave my mother great confidence when she assured her friends I'd never succumb to heroin. Now, here I am in a band with people whose favorite pastime is injecting themselves with needles, and sometimes dirty ones, too. WHAT THE FUCK!

My visceral reaction is to register the scene, grab a beer, and leave the trailer. I know I don't want to hang out there. I also realize I'm going to have to start processing what's actually happening around me, which I haven't fully grasped before.

A few days after the dressing-room incident, while we're checking out of a hotel one morning, I overhear our tour manager talking to a crew member about one of the headliners on the bill, a long-standing junkie who's been using since the '80s.

"Oh, man," he is saying. "His tour manager has to change his clothes and bedsheets because he shits the bed when he's high."

I can't get this image out of my mind. A musician shoots up and gets into his hotel bed, and the tour manager has to go in and literally change his diapers. Where is the dignity there?

There is no dignity with junkies. Yet I'm going to end up building five years of my life around them.

Self-portrait onstage with Courtney Love, 1995. (*top*)
Patty Schemel and Courtney Love onstage, 1995. (*bottom*)

Japan is a starkly different experience from Australia. First, because we start the tour in Osaka, where a natural disaster has just occurred. Just two weeks earlier, an earthquake that registered 7.2 on the Richter scale hit the city of Kobe, twenty miles from Osaka. Six thousand people died, and one hundred thousand were evacuated.

In Australia, we were on standby to possibly cancel the Japanese tour. The powers that be have decided it's safe to move forward with our visit, but we're on guard and get familiar with all the earthquake safety gear and instructions in our high-rise hotel rooms. I've never had to deal with the threat of earthquakes and aftershocks before. Always in awe of the powers of nature, and of messages from beyond the human realm, I take this as a sign: you are not safe.

Japan is a big culture shock for me. I haven't been anywhere, other than Africa when I was two, where Caucasians are a distinct minority. My band members and I really stand out. We're taller, louder, and messier than most everyone else. The language barrier shows up in unexpected ways, too. In hotel lobbies and outside of the clubs, fans are waiting for us to autograph items, and these exchanges occur mostly in silence, with animated hand gestures that feel like miming.

But it's the audience's behavior at shows that shocks me the most. During a performance, the crowd stands in rank-and-file lines without moving or screaming or showing any emotion at all, other than some restrained and polite clapping between songs. I've never seen anything like this. Japan forever remains my only experience of a rock crowd that doesn't go wild.

I can tell that Hole is not as widely celebrated in Japan as we are in the United States or Australia. Our shows are in smaller venues, and there aren't as many interviews or photo shoots lined up for Courtney. Our daily schedule is usually printed out and slipped under our hotel room doors every morning, including the lobby call, sound-check time, and press schedule, which is typically split between us as a band and Courtney on her own. I'm used to seeing a long list of promotional requests, but only one photographer in Japan is scheduled to do a photo shoot with the band.

Getting dressed up in Courtney's hotel room is a blast. I wear brown bell-bottom corduroys, a leopard skintight top I got at a cool boutique in

Australia, and a vintage green leather jacket. Patty wears red lipstick for the first time and a big faux-fur gorilla-style coat. Courtney is beginning to explore designer-only outfits, putting on a satin miniskirt and vest set, exposing plenty of skin. Eric, as always, wears jeans and a T-shirt. We roll around on the bed and pose in front of the beige wallpapered wall while the photographer shoots with a large-format old-school camera that I admire.

Years later I'll hear that he told foreign music press he'd been the only rock photographer in Tokyo who'd wanted to photograph Courtney because others viewed her as an "evil woman." Did they take Kurt's side and blame her for his misery, or was a woman like her just deemed unacceptable in their culture? I'll never know.

On our one night off in Tokyo, we're invited to see R.E.M. play at the famed rock arena Budokan. It's fascinating to witness an audience of fifteen thousand remain obedient and largely silent. I watch as Courtney sings along strongly. She knows every word to every song. It's motivating and invigorating to see her passion for R.E.M. I know how much she wants Hole to be this big and play these rooms. *Are we on our way to this?* I wonder. And, *How can we get there with all the pain and struggles currently plaguing the band?*

Courtney's love for front man Michael Stipe is sweet as pie. He's a man of such integrity and is so seemingly together, he appears to be a good influence and friend for her. She beams when she watches him perform and also when they speak later backstage. I immediately connect with the redheaded bass player, Mike Mills, who sings backup vocals and is wearing a bright, sparkly fringed suit. I also marvel at the hospitality and cleanliness of R.E.M.'s dressing rooms. This is another marker that makes them seem like well-adjusted grown-ups compared to all the other musicians I've encountered so far.

For our own show in Tokyo the next night, I've invited some friends of friends from Montreal who are teaching English in Japan. Courtney also has some special guests at the show. Michael Stipe has a night off from the

R.E.M. tour, and with him is everyone's pseudoheartthrob of the moment, actor Stephen Dorff, who's on a press tour for his latest film. Dorff is handsome in a classic "James Dean meets Kurt Cobain" kind of way, with shaggy blond hair that's parted in the middle and bleached blond at the tips. He's wearing a Nirvana *Bleach* T-shirt. I suppose he thought it was a way to impress and bond with the famous widow.

After our underwhelming show, where both band and audience seem confused by their roles, we all head back to the hotel bar for drinks. The top floor of our hotel has a panoramic view of Tokyo, a vast expanse of lights, and Courtney's charm is turned up for her special guests.

R.E.M.'s sound and career in the 1980s, like that of the Pixies, paved the way for the alternative pop-rock bands of the moment. Courtney has said before that "making friends with Michael Stipe" is a proper step toward the kind of fame she wants, and she is lucky to call him a true friend. At the hotel bar she drapes herself over Stipe's lap, holding his hand, while she and Dorff share a cigarette. Dorff makes attempts to flirt with me, which I take as a compliment. Still, I'm wary of male actors as candidates for crushes or dates. Theirs is a different world entirely, even if it intersects with mine in a similar pop-culture ethos of the moment. Our job as musicians is to be ourselves to the umpteenth degree, and theirs is to be a chameleon, able to embody many characters. As a musician, I strive for a what-you-see-is-what-you-get existence. With actors, you never know if what you're getting is real.

At the hotel bar I bounce between getting to know the famous Americans and the anonymous Canadians I invited to the show. We chat about their typical Canadian youth plan, which involves traveling and working a couple of years abroad after or instead of university and before "settling down." When one of the Montrealers gets up to go to the bathroom, I notice Courtney following him out and pulling him in close to ask a question. When he returns, he discreetly tells me that Courtney asked him for help getting drugs.

"I told her I wish I could help, but it's next to impossible to find illegal drugs in Japan," he explains. "You could get thrown into jail just for trying."

I take another sip of the delicious sake that seems to flow continuously to our table. I'm starting to sense how tricky the drug situation will eventually become on our international tours to follow.

The Canadians and I are the last ones left when the waitress tells us that the gentleman with the shaved head has taken care of the bill. Michael Stipe will forever live in my mind as everyone's dreamy alternative uncle who keeps an eye on the kids.

A few years later, one late night in a Hollywood bar, he'll ask me why I always carry a camera. No one has asked me that question before, but the answer will come quickly.

"So, if an alien race ever comes down and specifically wants to know what it was like to be a woman in a band in the 1990s," I'll tell him, "I'll have all the evidence they need."

CHAPTER 17

Hole Goes to Therapy and Gets Unplugged

FEBRUARY 1995

"How is everyone feeling?"

I'm staring out the window of a nondescript office in a sky-rise in Midtown Manhattan. New York looks cold and gray on a February day, but still the quintessential classy cityscape. Patty is sitting cross-legged next to me on the gray couch. Courtney faces us, with her leg swung over the arm of an overstuffed armchair, smoking a cigarette and flipping through a fashion magazine. She ignores the question. Eric is hunched over on a smaller chair next to her, staring at his shoelaces.

None of us utter more than a mumbled, "Okay . . . ?"

"Is that a difficult question for you to answer?" Dr. Cooper, a middle-aged woman in a prim pantsuit with blown-out silky hair and black-rimmed glasses, prompts us to say more.

"I just don't know what the fuck we're really doing here. What are we supposed to say?" Courtney replies, relatively politely (for her).

"Your managers asked me to meet with the four of you," Dr. Cooper says. She's the picture of professional poise and confidence. "To see if I could help work out any tensions or unexpressed emotions in the band."

Courtney glances up from her magazine. "Well. As you may know from the news, my husband committed suicide last year, my bass player died of a heroin overdose, and I'm a single mother trying to get my band's record out into the world in an attempt to save my life."

I admire her honesty and her no-bullshit manner. It's something you can always count on with her, a small island of safety in a raging, unpredictable sea of moods and actions.

Plus, Courtney has a point. What *are* we doing here? How is a session with a random band therapist going to change anything right now?

Even if she's helped other rock bands, we're not just any band. We may be on a fast train around the globe with no plans to stop to reflect on our interpersonal relationships, like other bands have been. But what makes us unique, other than being three-quarters female, is what Courtney just alluded to. The majority of Hole is still in mourning, barely able to comprehend the loss of its former bass player and the lead singer's husband. My three fellow band members are in shock, and I'm treading water in the wake of their numbness.

In earnest, Patty makes an attempt. "Well, ever since Kurt and Kristen died, we haven't talked much. I feel like it would help to connect more on the sadness we have . . ."

Patty is revealing a sweet, sensitive side, and it makes my heart open up to her more. But her attempt to express confusion and sadness lands a little flat in the room. The vulnerability seems to ruffle Courtney's feathers. She shrugs the sentiment off her shoulders.

Dr. Cooper directs her next question toward Eric, who replies meekly. This immediately triggers Courtney and him to bicker. Their tension, fraught as usual, starts to dominate the session. They're definitely the parents here, which makes Patty and me their "redheaded stepchildren," a joke that never grows old between the two of us.

I feel the need to share something to avoid coming across like an embarrassing, useless void. "I'm new, and just observing it all," I say softly. It's my default excuse for being so quiet and aloof. Silence fills the room now. It seems clear that no one's really up for playing ball.

It's a quaint notion that our new managers have, to send a band living in the wake of death and with active drug addiction to a session of "talk" group therapy, thinking it will help our cause. Most of Hole's experiences during the *Live Through This* journey so far have been shrouded in drama and emotion. I wonder, haven't these managers dealt with extreme drug addiction before in their other bands? Maybe, but they've certainly had no experience with this kind of beast of a band in the heart of a pop-culture storm of this proportion.

When the awkward session finally ends, we stumble out of Dr. Cooper's office in the direction of the elevator and never look back.

"Well, *that's* over and done," Courtney says with a sigh of relief. "Now we can go back to our real job."

We are on a serious mission now. We're booked on *MTV Unplugged*, which is the reason we're in New York this week. *Live Through This* has been getting a lot of traction, and we've just found out we'll be headlining this summer's Lollapalooza with Sonic Youth. *MTV Unplugged* is going to be both a musical challenge and an opportunity for us to shine.

Yet as always, Kurt's ghost looms like a gigantic shadow over our band. Nirvana's *MTV Unplugged* session was released a couple of months earlier as an album and DVD, a major deal following Kurt's death, and is already a huge posthumous success. The Nirvana single "About a Girl" is dominating the radio and MTV airways. Hearing Kurt's voice within stripped-down acoustic production, live in front of a studio audience, has made the whole world of grieving fans intimate with his raw humanity. Putting his live-wire widow and her band into the same exposed setting, on Valentine's Day 1995, is eerie, and bound to exude primal pain.

On the way to the practice space, Patty and I giggle in the back of the van about the nickname we've come up with for the therapist we'll never see again: Agent Cooper, after my favorite *Twin Peaks* character.

The only way to face the dysfunction of this band is with humor. And music. Thank Goddess for the music.

The room at SIR studios in Hell's Kitchen, complete with a stage, is ready to plug in and play when we arrive. Frances is already there with her nanny. She runs up to greet Courtney—"Mama!"—and jumps into her arms. Courtney scoops her up and brings her center stage to play a little acoustic guitar for her. I head over to my station where I find a cool vintage Ampeg flip-top amp waiting for me, along with a very large acoustic bass sitting on a stand by a stool. I've never played an acoustic bass, and it's my first time collaborating in the studio with the band and a producer. It's an open invitation for me to expand my musical horizons and my first time preparing for a professionally filmed concert.

"Melissa?" a man's voice asks from behind me.

When I turn around I see a warm and wonderful bearded face smiling at me, like a young bohemian Santa Claus.

"I'm Hal, Hal Willner." He speaks with a terrific beatnik drawl. "I'm producing the show with you all."

Exciting! I think. *A real producer!*

Hal's assignment for the week is to refine a raw rock band into an acoustic and classy production. The acoustic part of this is within Hole's comfort zone, since most of the band's songs have been written by Courtney and Eric on acoustic guitars. Transposing the electric guitar solos, hard-hitting punk-infused drum parts, and Courtney's signature scream into an acoustic medium turns out to be the fun part. The lower volume makes it kid friendly enough for Frances to be there throughout the days, often sitting on her mother's lap while we run through the songs. She tries singing along and following Courtney's fingers on the frets of her guitar like a game of chase. Things feel hopeful and stable in these moments.

The strings, harp, and horn section join us later in the week, following our songs from sheet music on music stands, which makes the enterprise seem all the more wholesome. It's almost like being back in music class in middle school. It feels exactly like what I was trained for.

The performance itself takes place in front of a seated audience at the Brooklyn Academy of Music, an impressive concert hall. I've been able to secure a handful of tickets for some Montreal friends who've come down for the special event. Seeing them smiling from the front row makes me feel cozy and proud to share this moment.

The final set list features eight Hole originals, including "Sugar Coma," "Asking for It," and "Doll Parts," along with covers of Donovan's "Season of

the Witch," the Crystals' "He Hit Me (and It Felt Like a Kiss)," and Duran Duran's "Hungry Like the Wolf."

The songs will never be formally released beyond that spring's airing on MTV, but bootleg versions of some of them will live on in the gutters of YouTube for those who deep dive for such relics. I'm happy they were professionally filmed, and I'd like to show them to my daughter someday. I'd even like to see the recording released as an album or concert film one day.

Hal Willner was best known as the musical producer of *SNL* and the one to support and nurture many complex artists, including Marianne Faithfull, Lou Reed, William Burroughs, and Laurie Anderson, before he died of complications from COVID in 2020. With him lie so many memories of musical legacies, including a high point for Hole, a ragtag band of kids that was struggling to just exist. During our brief time together in 1995, his gentle hand and brilliant mind made us shine.

Hal Willner, Drew Barrymore, and friends in limo, NYC, 1995.

CHAPTER 18

Engaging with Hole

SPRING 1995

I hop out of a cab onto Sixth Avenue in Midtown Manhattan in front of an imposing office building.

"Q-Prime Management, please," I say to the doorman.

He points to the elevator. "Seventh floor."

Upstairs, I walk into a legit rock-management office for the first time. The walls are lined with framed platinum records, mostly of Def Leppard and Metallica. These names are globally recognized, but from a time that means very little to me, other than what I believe our generation, and the band I'm now in, is the antithesis of.

"Hi, I'm Melissa. I'm here to see Peter," I tell the receptionist at the front desk.

Almost immediately, I hear his boisterous voice. "Melissa, come on in!"

It's Peter Mensch, head honcho. "Let me give you a tour," he offers.

We pop our heads into various offices as he introduces me to the team. There's Tony who deals with tour logistics, Linda who coordinates with the labels, etc., etc., etc. I take a seat in Peter's corner office. He has an imposing presence. His shaved head highlights his very big blue eyes, hooded by bushy black eyebrows. He definitely works out regularly at the gym and has a sporty spring to his step.

Peter oozes confidence and rock-and-roll know-how. We start with some small talk.

"So, what brings you to town?" he asks.

"I'm looking for an apartment. I'm moving here this summer," I explain. "It makes more sense to base myself out of here than Montreal, and I've always wanted to live here. I'm staying with some friends in the East Village and flying out to meet the band in Europe next week."

"Great. Let me know if there's anything you need while in town." He is courteous, and it's nice to know a grown-up in town, I suppose?

"Listen, Melissa," he now cuts to the chase. "I'm glad you could come in. We've got some business to settle." He lays his hand on a stack of paper. "It's time you sign a contract with Hole. Make a commitment to joining the band, formally. Not just as a salary touring member, but as a real band member." He hands me a contract, typed up and ready to be signed.

I'm twenty-two years old. I've signed an apartment lease before, but receiving a two-inch stack of black-and-white printed words from anyone is as alien to me as being handed a gun.

"Okay," I say tentatively. "Well, I have no idea what all of this says, so I'm going to have to get a lawyer to look at it."

I surprise myself with this reply. I hadn't thought of getting a lawyer until this moment, and in fact know only one, another redhead named Richard Grabel whom I met at the bar at Maxwell's at a Girls Against Boys show a couple months back. He represents them, Sonic Youth, Brainiac, and other legit bands that I love. Maybe he'll help me?

"A lawyer? Why do you need that?" Peter laughs. The pause that comes next is accompanied by a long stare from his ice-blue eyes. "What else are you gonna do?" he asks. "Go back to Montreal and be in a band with three other Melissas?"

It takes a moment for this to register as an insult. What a fucking bully.

"I don't know," I reply. "Maybe."

Little does he know, this doesn't sound like a bad idea to me. Yes! That can be my plan should this insane band not work out for me. I could wrap up my photo degree and get moving on my master's in fine arts. I'd continue with my passion for music and get involved in a thriving art scene as both a photographer and a musician. I'd have creative control of my fate, which would be a luxury compared to this giant stack of papers threatening to lock me in and determine the next five years of my life.

I step back into the city streets with a plan to contact the trusted redhead indie-rock lawyer, but not entirely sure what I will ask of any legal counsel. At this point, it's the thought of being a grown-up that counts.

CHAPTER 19

The Abscess and the French Hospital

APRIL 1995

Growing up in Montreal, bilingual in French and English, makes me a tad more Eurocentric than my band members and our road crew. My university studies in art history, with a deep focus on the Romantic periods of art, also mean that our upcoming six-week European tour promises to be the most exciting voyage of my life.

We're scheduled for more than a week each in France, the United Kingdom, and Germany, plus dates in Italy, Spain, Belgium, and the Netherlands. The cherry on top is right in the middle of the tour: a show in Zurich, the capital of the Auf der Maur homeland of Switzerland. Imagining what I'll see on days off and during show days before sound check, the people I'll meet, the world history I'll learn, and the art and architecture I'll see cracks my heart wide open. On our flight across the ocean I devour every detail of our Xeroxed ring-bound tour-schedule booklet as if it's an irresistible novel.

After a day in London to perform on the *Top of the Pops* TV show, we board our UK double-decker tour bus for the overnight drive to Paris. We'll kick off the real tour there with a sold-out show at Le Bataclan, a historic and glorious Victorian theater on Boulevard Voltaire in the Eleventh Arrondissement. I wake on the bus at the crack of dawn, crawl out of my bunk bed, and check into our Parisian hotel. My own hotel room, with a sweet view of the iconic Parisian streets, is such a luxury.

Down in the lobby the next morning, the concierge circles some key destinations on my map that I hope to see before sound check. I start with a standard Parisian breakfast of *pain au chocolat* and a café au lait at a nearby café and then a quick visit to Le Louvre.

Back at the hotel later, I run into Craig, our tour manager. He's carrying a stack of papers and looks frazzled.

"The show is canceled tonight, Melissa," he says, as he rushes past me toward the elevators.

Canceled? What?

"Go out and enjoy Paris," he adds. "I'll keep you all informed as I know more."

I'm more or less used to not asking too many questions of "the powers that be," but I want more information. This is before cell phones, so I head up to my room and call the front desk.

"Can you connect me to Linda Manz's room, please?"

Linda Manz, a child actress discovered by seminal director Terrence Malick, who went on to play a troubled teen in Dennis Hopper's cult classic *Out of the Blue*, is Patty's pseudonym of choice. Mine is April Wine, a Canadian 1970s rock band that was huge when I was growing up. Literally no one recognizes my real name at this point, but the tour party thought it was safer for all of us to use fake names when we travel to avoid any weird fans finding us. Courtney is proper famous, and superfans of her and Kurt are everywhere. She lives between two fake names: Mary Black and Sharon Rose.

The phone rings. And rings. Finally, Patty answers, sounding groggy. I've woken her up.

"Hey, it's me," I say. "Do you know why the show is canceled tonight?"

"Hmmm . . . it is?" Apparently, she hasn't heard. "Well, I noticed Courtney seemed in pretty rough shape when we checked into the hotel late last night. Let me call the nanny and see what she knows."

I sit on the bed, staring out the window. In the gray sky and classic Parisian street life and expansive rooftop view, I feel the ghosts of Anaïs Nin and Henry Miller teasing me and my wanderlust. Like all good hungry romantics of my generation, I did a proper deep dive into Nin and Miller in my late teens. *Little Birds* and *Delta of Venus*, Nin's series of erotica short stories, spoke to me, as did *Henry and June*, the compilation of her diary entries tracing her love affair with Miller and his wife, June. As a young woman I had struggled to understand my desires, or lack thereof, of traditional intimacy. The kind of poetic and strange romances Nin wrote about in her books and journals about her experimental relationships appealed to me.

I imagine walking out of my room and into Café du Dôme, the renowned intellectual gathering spot for writers and artists at the turn of the last century, its reign of romance culminating during the Roaring '20s and '30s between world wars. I can spend this free day in a bistro with my diary and camera, exploring my deepest cravings for a life of romance. Maybe I'll find a handsome man with slicked-back hair, wearing a vintage trench coat with a notebook of his own in his pocket. He will take me for a long walk through alleyways, into basement wine bars, and finally up to his studio apartment. I take drags of his cigarette and share our late-night glass of wine. Standing in the arched doorway to his kitchenette, we begin to kiss, passionately licking and kissing every part of each other's exposed skin. I bite his neck, he pulls back, and I bite again. We run our hands firmly over the seams of our clothes that cover our most erotic private parts. We take breaks from kissing to talk about the infinite universe. We doze off, fully dressed, in each other's arms on his daybed. I want—

RING... RING...

The phone snaps me out of my fantasy.

It's Patty. "Courtney's really fucked up. She's got an abscess the size of a football on her ass. You can get them from dirty needles . . ." Patty trails off a bit, before the conversation crosses the threshold into these dark details for the first time.

I sit quietly, absorbing this detail. It's gross, graphic, and tragic. *Why are we on tour?* I think. *She needs help. She's a drug addict. She could die!*

"This shit is out of your control, Melissa," Patty says. Her tone exudes protection, and maybe some knowledge that I don't yet possess about these kinds of situations. "Go out and find some inspiration."

✕

Thanks to my rock-band lifestyle, I'm still up well past midnight. Still no updates. Restless, I turn on the TV. The few channels still broadcasting at this hour all feature French porn. I've never watched or even been curious to watch porn before. But Paris, being the City of Love, seems to offer porn for free on the airways for everyone.

I am transfixed by the actress's hairdo. It's perfectly feathered and parted in the middle, in late-'70s and early-'80s style. The lighting of the sex scene is very blue. I wonder if it's natural light and how large of a production crew was used to film these two people having sex. It's very graphic, with a lot of close-ups of penetration. Watching it repulses me. *What am I doing here?*

I pull out my camera. The woman's face on the screen contorts with fake pleasure. I snap about a dozen shots of the TV screen before turning the camera on myself.

"I HATE THIS," I seethe and project toward the lens. I want to save myself, warn myself of this, while holding myself accountable for arriving at this place tonight.

✕

In the morning I head down to the lobby, looking for answers. Our tour manager, Craig, is speaking to a gentle-looking Frenchman. "Melissa, this is Doudou, our French promoter," he tells me.

"Bonjour," Doudou says with the warmest of smiles. "Doudou" translates into English as "Soft Soft," which makes for the sweetest first impression.

"Allo . . . Je m'excuse pour le disaster . . . ," I say with a smile.

"Ah! Vous parlez français!" he perks up.

"Oui, Je viens de Montréal." I hope my French apology for the disaster will make our band seem a little more human and lovable in light of having just canceled half of our French tour so far.

"Oh, ça va, Mélissa. We just want Courtney to get better—do not worry about us!" He says this in very thick accented English for the benefit of Craig. His humanity is palpable and sends me off on a more hopeful day.

"Hey, can I come hang in your room?" I ask Patty on the hotel phone in the lobby.

"Sure. We're just watching *Barney* and eating french fries."

Inside her room are two double beds. The nanny and sweet Frances are cuddled up on one. Frances is just two years old and full of sunshine. I join them on the bed.

"Can I have a fry?" I gesture to the room-service tray.

Frances nods her head and smiles.

"Yummy! Thank you, Sweet Banana," I say, calling her by the pet name I've given her.

Patty is lounging on the other bed, lighting up a cigarette and drinking a Coca-Cola out of a glass bottle. I take a seat next to her.

"Courtney has been admitted to a hospital. Craig was there earlier. I spoke to him, and he says they're treating the infection," Patty reports. "She's tough, but she must be freaking out. We may want to go check on her."

My compassion for Courtney wells up. She must be really lonely in there and scared. Nobody's really fucking helping her. The tour managers don't know what to do.

A certain kind of mind fuck develops when you're one of the few nonusers in a small, tight group of addicts. If you're a caring person, you inevitably become the one who carries the concern for everyone's well-being. Not in a professional or a financial sense, like the managers and promoters are always focused on, but in a purely humanistic way. At times, I seem to be the only one who's genuinely concerned about the physical, emotional, and spiritual safety of every vulnerable person in this band.

Nothing makes sense. Was this what I was dreading when I initially said "No, thank you" to Billy when he presented me with the idea of joining the band? Courtney is as powerful, intelligent, fascinating, and expressive as anyone I have had the chance to share my life with yet. She's also on the verge of death. Sadness, stage diving, overdose, or infection could get her at any moment. Her addiction and lack of family care or guidance are shocking. Are we all supposed to just sit around and watch it happen? Be compliant and support this behavior?

I'm not in Paris. I'm in purgatory. Hovering in the in-between.

Should I protest and quit the band to make a statement? I wonder. *Get on a plane and go home right now?* To leave will mean to abandon it all and clear my conscience. It will release me from supporting or facilitating the bizarre infrastructure that's keeping these people sick and onstage. *If I quit, they could fill my spot quickly enough. But if they cancel the tour and ship her home, she could descend into even more drugs.* All the options and possibilities are coming up fast now.

Then a new voice steps in. The clear message I'm receiving is: *Surrender. Surrender. Surrender.*

What is happening here in the eye of this storm of our generation—the power, the tragedy, the chaos, the magic, the music—is too special to not have a mindful person present to capture it for the little girls of the future. For Frances.

I wrap this integrity around me like an armor. I want to be a voice of reason, a voice of meaning.

I will not sacrifice myself, I promise myself. *I will protect myself. Trust yourself, Melissa.*

"Okay. Let's go see her," I say.

✕

The hospital where Courtney's been admitted is old-fashioned and romantic, like something out of a World War II movie set with its high ceilings and decorative wood moldings around the windows and doors. Wrought-iron candelabra light fixtures hang from the ceilings.

Seeing Courtney in bed in a hospital gown, helpless and attached to IVs, is shocking. I've only ever seen her act fearless in the way she handles her body, like when she stage dives.

"Great, you're here. Get me the fuck out of here" is her greeting as she bolts up out of the bed. "The swelling has gone way down. I'm totally fine."

She rips her IV out of her hand in one swift move. She doesn't even look down while pulling it out, or notice the blood that spatters on her gown.

Being needle phobic, watching this makes me go weak in the knees. I feel myself starting to leave my body. All I can come up with is the simple question: "Are you sure?"

But she's already out in the hall, and Patty is way ahead of her, not looking back, headed for the staircase that leads down to the main level. She seems to know exactly what she's doing. There's nothing for me to do except follow.

Patty and Courtney are already flagging a taxi when I arrive in the entry hall. Enough people are milling about to create a distraction from the fact that a patient has just exited the building in a hospital gown. A medical-staff member catches up with me as I reach the front door and blocks my exit. She waves a clipboard and a pen in my direction. I suspect she's trying to hand me a medical-release form.

"*Vous devez signer!*" You have to sign!

The thought of being responsible for Courtney, should anything happen to her, terrifies me. Adrenaline takes over. I brush past her. "*Non, merci,*" I say, rushing through the front door. No, thanks.

Outside, Patty has hailed a taxi. Courtney is already in it, and they're waiting for me to catch up.

In the safety of the taxi, I give the driver the name of our hotel and nervously sit back. My heart is pounding. A hospital escape isn't something I ever thought I'd be part of. It's hard to rationalize, from any point of view.

Courtney immediately dives in. "So, I wanna talk business. I hear you're getting a lawyer. You better not get greedy."

She's referring to the contract that I have stalled signing, while reserving my right to get my own music lawyer. *Wow, this woman is good at deflecting*, I think. It is a terrifying prospect to talk business with her, especially right now. I mumble some niceties, and she carries on about something to do with song publishing and the last band members, blah blah blah. I do my best to tune it out. The disconnect between her fragile health situation and the legal contract binding me to her is too absurd to even entertain.

That night I call Patty before going to bed. I need to connect with her, to express my rawness and my concern for Courtney to someone.

Patty is used to this chaos. She tells me that staying in the hospital would have sent Courtney into a state of drug withdrawal, making her escape essential. I can feel her treading carefully with these details, as if she doesn't want this news to break me or make me consider leaving.

I'm grateful for her honesty. "It's so dark, Patty," I say.

"I know. But Melissa, you have so much light in you. You've brought so much to our band. We love you."

In the morning I wake to a printed "day sheet" slipped underneath my door. Despite the slight delay due to "medical issues," the European tour is kicking off tonight in Toulouse.

I order room service and begin to pack my bags. The show must go on.

CHAPTER 20

Funny Shit and the Smoking Vagina

APRIL 1995

Tempodrom, Berlin. I'm in awe.

The German rock circuit is legendary among American bands. Nowhere else in Europe can a band spend up to two weeks steadily fueled with bombastic crowds, hearty food and beverage, and good paydays. And Berlin is a city that inspires quiet questioning. The human capacity for evil and survival feels infinite here. It makes a young bass player feel small, in a wonderful way.

It's the last night of our sold-out weeklong German tour. Hole's concert is in a huge circus tent located in the center of Tiergarten (which translates to "Animal Garden" in English), Berlin's most popular inner-city park. The largest urban garden in Germany, it covers 520 acres. The venue crew are moving gear in an intense pace and beam with electric power and dedication to their mission. They make us feel welcomed and treasured. The Tempodrom hosts alternative-rock acts from around the world. It's punk power at its peak.

Our Tempodrom show is energized, raw, and wickedly great. We are relaxed and at our best. This tour has hooked me. Touring Europe is all I ever want to do.

Backstage after the show, my new local friends offer me a hit of their joint. Pot is the most common substance after alcohol in the music scene, but my band members like harder stuff and pot fucks up my brain, always has. *Not* right for my brain chemistry, which by contrast will happily receive psychedelics anytime.

Courtney is in a great mood and can feel the impact she has made on this stoic country with a big appetite for the kind of power that we deliver. Together, lubricated by the after-show social scene, we accept their sweet hospitality and take one toke of the joint, each.

Only this one time. It never happens with me and Courtney again—weed is not our kind of high.

Sweaty, filled with adrenaline, makeup running down our cheeks, we kick back and sink into a rare chill-out moment of camaraderie. I am drinking a cold and delicious German beer, while Courtney fills her mouth like a savage animal at the deli platter. She is always starving after the show.

I observe her as the alien marijuana vibes invade my perspective. Quietly, I admire her strong and broad shoulders and her bare, durable feet. They're wide, strong, and unusually broad too. Her hands, with very short nails for playing guitar. She has wide, stubby fingers compared to my tapered ones, which I gaze down at for comparison.

Oh my god, those are powerful hands.

She has muscular legs, no hips, and a compact ass, also in contrast to my extremely curved small waist, wide hips, and curvy butt and thighs. Her breasts are fake, something she does not hide and is proud of as she pushes the cleavage way up. I have very small breasts despite my high school silent-prayer chants, *"Grow Tits Grow! Grow Tits Grow!"* The goddesses never answered, but I am satisfied with the shape and perky breasts I was granted.

I'm now gazing into her handsome face, as she devours a turkey sandwich.

Was she born a man? I wonder. I'm definitely high. My brain is playing tricks on me now. How do I know anything for sure?

The idea shocks me. It's not something I've ever contemplated before, yet at the moment seems undeniable.

"You wanna see my party trick?" she blurts.

She sits on a folding chair and lifts her legs up onto the craft-service table. She pulls up her satin slip—no panties, which is common for her—and brings her lit cigarette down between her legs. Then she attempts to take a drag of the cigarette *through* her vagina.

"I can do this. I'm just out of practice," she says, as she tries to insert the glowing butt into herself.

This view into her genitals snaps me out of my strange suspicion. You cannot fake a vagina, or a baby's birth. Nor did I know you could smoke a cigarette from it.

We are a true fucking circus act.

The tour ends back in Paris, where we make up for our canceled shows and perform on a prestigious live prime-time television variety show called *Nulles Part Ailleurs* (Nowhere Else).

Backstage at Canal+, the French TV station, Patty and I have a lot of extra time and space in the huge dressing room that we share. With time to kill, we primp ourselves in the large lit mirror and introduce ourselves to new fictional characters: I am Roberta Flat Nose, and she Patricia Pig Nose.

Our index fingers manipulate our noses in the direction of our characters' namesakes. I photograph and she videotapes these improvisational slapstick-comedy skits. Our characters bond over exaggerated tales of our bonkers bandleader, the strange out-of-place boy in the band, the psychotic fan, the weird new cultures we're visiting, the unbearably cheesy industry person, and the erratic "hurry-up-and-wait" lifestyle of being on tour.

We giggle through our downtime and get lost in absurdist humor. Patty is a closeted natural stand-up comic. Our fast track to becoming close friends is making fun of ourselves and others and, most of all, our situation.

We can survive all of the ridiculous fucking things happening around us by filtering them into these skits. On this world tour, Patty and I build a foundation that keeps us close friends, band members, and soon-to-be roommates for the next few years.

CHAPTER 21

Hole Is a Band; Courtney Love Is a Soap Opera

JULY 1995

"I HATE THIS FUCKING PLACE!!!" Courtney roars into her mic.

It's July 4, kickoff day for Lollapalooza 1995 at the Gorge Amphitheater, in George, Washington. Twenty thousand sweaty summer music fans fill the festival grounds. This famed outdoor venue about 150 miles east of Seattle is considered one of the most majestic settings in the world for seeing music. A bright sun beams down over the panoramic Columbia Canyon and River vistas.

But for this band, the ghosts of Seattle loom large.

"FUCK YOU!" Courtney screams as she kicks into our set.

We are coheadlining the biggest alternative touring festival in the world with Sonic Youth, the godparents of all things alt rock, experimental, and art noise. It's been more than a decade since their impressive ascent from the deep NYC underground to glossy music videos to a contract with the highly regarded DGC/Geffen Records, which is also Hole's label.

Sonic Youth, fronted by spouses Thurston Moore and Kim Gordon, are by all standards the '90s gatekeepers of independent music. Moore and

Gordon are the king and queen of what's cool and of the "We don't give a fuck about success" ethos that all of us musicians in this movement follow and embody. The irony is that we're all currently on heavy rotation on MTV and mainstream radio airwaves and playing around the globe to massive audiences.

So what exactly do we make of not wanting success now?

Despite our collective loss of innocence, the meat market that is alternative music, and the chaos always spiraling around our band, the 1995 Lollapalooza lineup is fantastic. On the main stage is Sonic Youth, as is everyone's beloved Pavement and the recently arrived fresh-faced Beck, a.k.a. "Loser" hitmaker. My personal favorite, and still forever underground, is Jesus Lizard, the Chicago-based Touch and Go one-of-a-kind legends with all the right parts. They have a dream heavy-hitting rhythm section, spaghetti western meets alt-rock jazz guitar, and a partially naked, savage front man, David Yow, who first terrified me with an unforgettable performance years back in Montreal when he stripped down to his underwear, sweating and stumbling into the crowd, wailing, "I can't swim!!!"

Also on the main stage, and indicative of the open-minded '90s music scene, is Moby, an underground rave deejay who's blowing up in a new ambient-electronic artist kind of way. He's way over my "rock guitars only" head. It will take me years to understand his pioneering relevance. Only his sampling of the *Twin Peaks* theme catches my ear. There's also Cypress Hill, the Los Angeles weed-loving hip-hop group, with their towering inflatable Buddha and massive bong stage props, still riding high on their "Insane in the Membrane" hit. Opening the main stage every day are Boston ska heroes the Mighty Mighty Bosstones.

In addition, there is a side stage with standout acts like Blond Redhead, Helium, Mike Watt, the Dirty Three, and the Roots; there's also a circus sideshow tent, body-piercing tent, misting tent, and loads of pop-up vendors carrying '90s souvenir-style merchandise. It's a real grunge paradise.

But the most exceptional act on the lineup is Sinéad O'Connor. The festival marks her return to the American public eye after being demonized less than two years earlier for ripping a photo of Pope John Paul II live on *SNL* to protest the Catholic Church's history of abuse. It was a radical act coming from a revolutionary female artist with a shaved head, no makeup, and the voice of a Celtic warrior goddess. She was ahead of her time in an uptight society in denial about the abuse of power. Sinéad will continue to be misunderstood and her contribution not sufficiently celebrated until her tragic early death at fifty-six years old in 2023.

Courtney Love onstage, Lollapalooza, 1995.

In 1995 it's an honor to be sharing a stage with her, and even more thrilling when we hear from our agents that she agreed to join the bill because Hole was part of it.

In addition to performing, I'm embracing an exciting photography assignment. *SPIN* magazine has asked Courtney and me to capture the tour for them. She is to keep a tour diary, and I'm to photograph it. I love having a reason to take photos beyond my personal obsession of documenting the world around me. And this is a real professional photo gig, the kind I thought I'd be making my living with had I stuck with that pursuit.

The *SPIN* headline will read: "Want to know what it's really like being the world's most notorious rock star, out on the road with alternative music's biggest tour? In her own words, Courtney Love recounts the feuds, friendships, and frustrations of Lollapalooza '95. Photographs by Melissa Auf der Maur."

✗

After Courtney's combative greeting to the audience, we kick into a decomposed version of Neil Young's "Cinnamon Girl." It's an unusual opener for us, and I suspect it had some secret Northwest meaning to Courtney when she selected it. Perhaps she enjoyed singing the satirical line "I could be happy for the rest of my life . . ." Or was it a reference to Kurt's suicide note that quoted a lyric from the Neil Young song "Hey Hey, My My (Into the Black)": *It's better to burn out, than to fade away*? Either way, it sets the tone for the show, and we plow through an otherwise strong set. We play like we have something to prove and demons to exorcize.

Following our performance, the red glow of sunset makes way for Sonic Youth to hit the stage for the finale. "Let's go watch!" Courtney says giddily, grabbing my hand and leading me out of our dressing room. We walk up the stairs to the side of the stage to get a view of the landscape, giant crowd, and the band close up. Eric trails close behind. It feels almost like a moment of band camaraderie, coming together to watch "the elders" perform.

A few other people are milling about on the side stage as we approach the glow of Sonic Youth's colorful and innovative lightshow. A small group of cool-looking women come into view.

Eric hands Courtney a pack of Skittles from our bulk-candy tray backstage.

"Hey, Courtney, give Kathleen some candy," he says mischievously.

Without missing a beat, Courtney grabs the candy, approaches the group, and raises her arm. She releases a handful of candies with a catlike hiss, letting them cascade down like a sweet waterfall onto one of the women. The sound she makes and the claw shape of her hand suggest "cat fight," but in a crazy-lady, playful kind of way, as I perceive it.

I recognize the woman on the receiving end of the candy as Kathleen Hanna, front woman of Bikini Kill and a founder of the Riot Grrrl movement, an underground feminist punk movement that started in Olympia, Washington. Kathleen is a VIP friend of Sonic Youth and the star of the glossy music video for their recent single. In the video she's styled in nonglam "kinder whore" chic, with little pigtails, a baseball T-shirt, and star-patterned children's underwear. Her response to Courtney's animal act is a verbal attack.

"I challenge you to a feminist *debate* in any college in *America*!" she screeches, pointing her index finger violently toward Courtney. "And *I. Will. Win.*"

My first thought? *She's taking this playful act seriously? Hilarious.* Sure, there's a slight underground rivalry between Courtney and the Riot Grrrl scene, possibly spawned by the fact that Bikini Kill's drummer dated Kurt shortly before he met Courtney. The tension was most certainly ignited by the closing song on *Live Through This*, "Rock Star," in which Courtney takes the piss out of the pretentious, exclusionary feminist academics at Evergreen State College in Olympia, Washington. It was brilliant and hilarious sarcasm leveled toward a scene that takes themselves very seriously politically. At the same time, part of the politics of the movement is to actively *not* take their instruments or craft seriously because, in turn, that would uphold the patriarchy, or so I've heard.

Hanna threatening Courtney with an academic feminist debate strikes me as silly, like a case of the smart, popular kid at school bullying the dirty, smelly kid, who in this case is a drug-addicted single mother and widow.

It's important to note that in the wake of this, Hanna presses charges against Courtney for battery. Courtney appears in court various times that year with Frances at her side. An act that seemed like no more than comic rivalry, as always, paints Courtney as the demonic bitch witch. *Where's the humanity here?* I wonder.

It's an unfortunate start to the tour, as news spreads quickly around the festival and then worldwide that Courtney "punched" Sonic Youth's cool friend. Instantly ostracized, the already isolated star becomes even more of a pariah.

✗

The only friend Courtney makes, or needs to make, on the tour is the queen of deep song and pain herself, Sinéad O'Connor. They connect quickly, which isn't surprising. Both of their lives overflow with love, grief, power, and music.

Just a few days into the tour, Sinéad boards our bus for a sleepover and joins Courtney in the back lounge for the overnight drive. From my bunk at the back of the bus I can hear the sounds of old Hollywood movies blasting and the rumble of two women's voices in conversation throughout the night. I imagine they're talking about death, mental illness, and painful childhoods, things both women shared in spades. I am happy they can find sisterhood in these wounds.

We arrive at our next destination at the crack of dawn. Each of us checks into a hotel room for some privacy and bathing before heading to the festival grounds in the afternoon. When I later head down to the lobby to catch our ride to the festival grounds, our tour manager tells me that Sinéad has disappeared. Apparently, she walked off the bus that morning and hasn't been seen since.

Have I seen her? No, I tell him, not since the night before on the bus.

I wonder if Courtney will be blamed for this, too. At the same time, I don't know if she was the catalyst for the disappearance. Anything feels possible.

At the festival, when Sinéad doesn't show up for her set, we learn that she left the bus barefoot, got herself to the airport, and flew home to England. And just like that, she's off the tour.

In the tour diary she publishes in *SPIN*, Courtney helps clear up what happened that night. "Sinéad and I would stay up all night in the bus watching really depressing movies," she writes. "When we were in Chicago she bought me a beautiful book that I really needed, and then she went down to her room, and when she was all alone she ran away to the airport. She was pregnant, it was quite hot, and she was depressed. In her note that she left she said, *They can sue me. I don't care. I'll find another line of work*, which I thought had a lot of integrity to it, to be honest."

Courtney starts spending all her time off the stage either in the back of the bus, in her hotel room, or in the production office where she has access to a computer and something called "The Internet." She is writing a daily

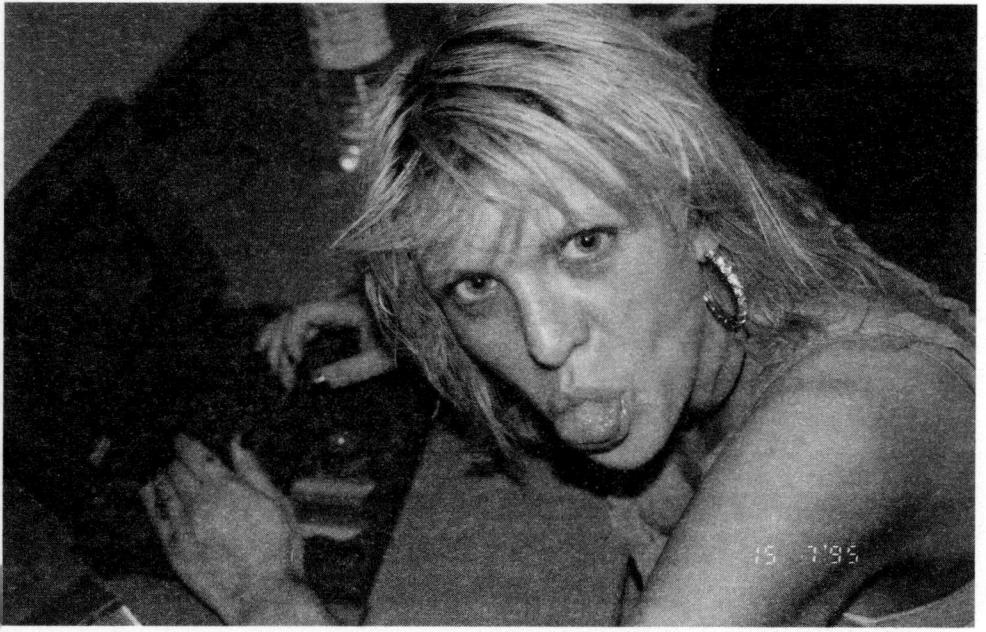

journal in something called a "chatroom." Apparently, Thurston Moore of Sonic Youth is also in there, and a duel between the coheadlining front people is brewing. It's happening below the radar, but I'm hearing whispers about it, along the lines of, "He said online yesterday that his band is the Washing Machine after the dirty Hole!"

More drama and more conflict. Just what we need.

Courtney Love at laptop, backstage, Lollapalooza, 1995.

A "Sonic Youth versus Hole" rivalry was something I did not expect, considering Kim Gordon, Sonic Youth's bass player and only female member, coproduced Hole's first album, *Pretty on the Inside*, in 1991. Sonic Youth had also been touring and label mates with Nirvana. They were friends of Kurt. Why would they be dicks to his widow?

No one seems to see what I see in Courtney, a raw and wrecked woman doing her best to stay alive with purpose. A woman who has been left by the

fucked-up love of her life. The unconditional admiration and worship people have for the man who left her also begin to seem insane. On tour with us, day to day, are their hearts not opened by the little girl, Frances, backstage? The one who's been left behind by her father to be raised by her mother's band and the rest of the traveling circus? Why is there not more compassion and care for this broken family? On this tour, I hear another calling: *Be a human above being a rock star.*

Beck backstage, Lollapalooza, 1995.

Our band's situation makes me look at people through a new lens. Who is a kind, nonjudgmental human? And who is a too-cool-for-school, hip, obsessed asshole?

This becomes the filter through which I make tour friends. Beck and I chat in the catering tents about art and oddball findings at thrift shops. Lee Ranaldo, the guitar player for Sonic Youth, is also a photographer, and we share tips about the various cameras we are traveling with. The Pavement

boys are smart nerds with a great sense of humor, and they're really good at *New York Times* crossword puzzles, which Courtney challenges them on. The most unlikely friend I make on this tour is B-Real, Cypress Hill's front man. He and his entourage watch us play most days from my side of the stage, which gets us talking about bass tones and rhythms.

Halfway through the tour, the UK band Elastica is brought on to take Sinéad's slot. They are a dynamic addition, adding spunk and pop from

---

Lee Ranaldo and Melissa Auf der Maur, Lollapalooza, 1995. Photo by David Markey.

across the pond. Like Hole, their lineup is three women and one man. Courtney engages immediately upon their arrival. The bar is raised, as she perceives singer Justine Frischmann as an equal. Courtney thrives on competition and embraces her competitors. It's a welcome addition for her.

Brits love to party, so the drinking is upped a bit backstage after Elastica arrives. They are a sweet gang to intermingle with. To pass time I make out with their cute drum tech a couple of times behind the buses.

Shortly after their arrival, drug drama ensues in their camp (good to know we aren't the only ones!). The bass player is suffering from heroin withdrawal and is sent home. I'm asked to take her place for the duration of the tour. The opportunity thrills me! More music, along with a fun challenge to learn their tunes and play postpunk, New Wave–infused catchy songs.

Except I'm informed by Hole's management that to play with Elastica will infringe on the contract I've recently signed. That spring I consulted with Richard Grabel, the redheaded lawyer with great music taste. He informed me about all the terrible parts of the contract, one of them being a five-year exclusivity clause. Meaning I would not be allowed to play music with anyone else for that long. It was a totally outrageous demand by all standards, but by that time I decided to take the easy route and just sign it, even though Richard advised me not to. He wanted to advocate for me and negotiate more creative freedom and more transparency in finances, but it seemed to me that this would only wage a larger conflict in an already full-blown war zone.

It's just money. I'm in it for the mission to get more women in rock, I tell myself. Maybe not so business smart, but possibly street smart? Are my hippie, airy-fairy tendencies an act of self-preservation or of self-destruction? It's still not clear to me.

Embarrassed, I tell the girls in Elastica that I'm sorry, but I'm not available to play bass for them. I make up an excuse that the "optics" would be confusing because I just joined Hole, and we want the public to know we are a real band and not Courtney Love's band for hire. My story checks out, because our anticipated full-band cover issue of *Rolling Stone* is on the stands right now, with the headline "HOLE Is a Band; Courtney Love Is a Soap Opera."

Journalist Jason Cohen writes in the cover story:

With Lollapalooza, Hole have plenty to prove, the latest trial by fire in a year that's been full of them. When they play and the music is allowed its own space, everything else falls by the wayside. Some of the moshing, screaming fans might respond most strongly to Love's antics, but many others are rapt, coiled and reverent, feeding off the music's introversion and aggression simultaneously. The audience really can look at them and go, "Oh, yeah, Hole is a band."

"We've stayed together because we're good," Love says, "and when we play together, we know we're good."

It all works out nicely because Moby has a great female session bass player on the tour, and she saves the day for Elastica.

Our show in Boston, my mother's hometown, is attended by my mother . . . who brings along my grandfather. Knowing this, Courtney can't resist the temptation to swear onstage in his honor.

"Hey, Boston!" she snarls into the mic, casting a glance in my direction. "So, Melissa's grandfather is here. I'm told to FUCKING behave . . . and not say fuck. *Fuck*," she continues, as the crowd chuckles and cheers. "Come on, Melissa, say it!!! FUCKKKKK!"

I shake my head with a big smile. I'm not going to participate in this. I'm just grateful my family is made up of easygoing people with a good sense of humor.

After our set my mother comes backstage to fetch me, as my grandfather waits in the catering tent. When she pops her head into the dressing room, Courtney goes straight for conflict.

"Hey, Linda, did Melissa tell you about the time she got super-fucked-up on drugs and told me she's been trying to get away from you her whole life? She was wasted, too."

This is why Courtney is known in the underground world as a hateable person—because she pushes buttons. Anyone who isn't intelligent enough to understand this is how she exists, survives and that she thrives on challenging the outside world is stupid. The endless cycle of *she loves me / she hurts me / she loves me* is something I can understand and transcend. I can accept her as she is because I believe she was sent to me, and also to our generation as part of the zeitgeist, for a reason.

"No, Courtney, she did not," my mother replies, with her most New England–y proper poise.

"To say nothing about her terrible taste in men . . ." Courtney continues to pile it on. She's trying to one-up my mother with her knowledge of me.

Unfazed, my mother and I roll our eyes at each other. My mother is a realist and was part of a wild bohemian and often intoxicated scene herself. Nothing much shocks her, even though it's clear Courtney is trying to. My mother and I both understand the depth and complexity of human behavior and how the recognition of my family's stability, compared to Courtney's estranged parents, can result in an uncontrollable urge to put a wedge between me and my source of unconditional love.

Or maybe she's just being an asshole? Hard to tell, but my mother and I tend to give people the benefit of the doubt.

We head to the catering tent to kiss my beloved grandfather, who is already chatting it up with other visitors. I rush into his arms.

"Kid! I am so proud of you!" His bright-blue eyes sparkle with an abundance of love. My mother will later tell me that on the way home from the show he glowed with pride, stating that I add "a little bit of class to that act."

The second half of the Lollapalooza tour winds down through the South toward the West. On one especially hot night in Texas, the show takes a dark turn. Courtney is notoriously confrontational with an audience. Some kind of verbal altercation is inevitable at every show, and with stage diving and crowd-surfing, things can get more aggressive and heated at some times than at others.

Tonight a chilling violence hits the stage when several small objects are thrown at her feet. She bends down to pick one up and holds it delicately between her fingers

"Are these shotgun shells?" she asks the front row.

A male voice comes sailing out of the tight crowd: "YOU FUCKING KILLED KURT, BITCH!"

For a fan to threaten violence like this at an alternative-rock concert is unheard of. It's happening now only because of a sexist culture that demonizes women. When I tell this story to people who were part of this scene in the '90s, they can't believe it. That's the level of hate this woman absorbed.

In an uncharacteristic act of stoicism, Courtney lets the brutal accusation roll off her back and kicks into our next song. As we play, our tour manager heads down to the pit between the stage and the audience barricades and confers with security.

In a rare moment of true professionalism, we play our set, but I feel an eerie silence descending on our band. The hate is so real and burning. I find it hard to turn toward the world of fairies and fantasy at this moment. Instead, I soberly glare head-on into the eyes of the crowd that's gathered to watch us tonight. *Who hates us, and who likes us?* I wonder. I can feel the omnipresent and long-standing societal hate for women, especially women like Courtney, rising from the crowd like steam.

Are we safe on these stages? I don't know. It's something too terrifying to contemplate.

As our set comes to an end, I notice B-Real and his full Cypress Hill band and crew standing on my side of the stage in a line of defense. They are large and intimidating men, staring down the front row of dinky white indie-rock boys with intent.

As I walk offstage, my friend B-Real follows me.

"We'd kick those kids' asses, but we'd get kicked off the tour . . . ," he says with a sweet smile as he hands me a piece of paper with a phone number. "If you ever need protection, anywhere, anytime, you can call me here."

Maybe these are the guardian angels my grandma Auf der Maur talks about. This thought gives me strength.

The irony is that this offer comes from someone who was a stranger to us just a few weeks ago, instead of from Kurt's friends on the tour. The stony silence from the latter seems to suggest they might not disagree with the abusive members of the crowd.

The last day of the tour is August 18, 1995, which is also Frances's third birthday. We're in San Francisco to perform at the Shoreline Amphitheatre. With the help of Frances's nanny and Hole's management, Courtney organizes a big celebration for her that turns into an unofficial end-of-the-tour party. It's a bright, sunny day with a huge cake for all, in a big white tent filled with colorful decorations and a happy clown. Everyone shows up for the sweet girl who we all know has been dealt a challenging hand in life.

I shoot a great couple rolls of film that capture images of these messy characters in the wholesome context of a child's birthday: Thurston Moore arm in arm with the big red-nosed clown; Kim with their one-year-old baby, Coco, on her hip; the girls from Elastica captured in a fish-eye reflection of a silver balloon; Courtney licking the frosting off the cake with a smiling Frances on her lap.

We were all once children. On this day, for a moment, we are a big gaggle of cultural misfits and innocent weirdos who struggled to fit in as kids shining united in that knowledge. This Lollapalooza will be the last time we're authentically together before we're destroyed by the industry and our own selves. We're lucky to have found a scene to help us belong in a world where we didn't want to work for the Man. Today is a grounding reminder that we all started with the simple desires to be loved and have fun with other weird friends. And on this day, we do.

CHAPTER 22

The Arctic Circle, Madonna, and MTV

SEPTEMBER 1995

"Hello Tuk-to-yuk-to-fuk-fuk-fuk!" Courtney shouts into the mic.

We're inside an enormous tent erected in the small village of Tuktoyaktuk, the northernmost occupied place in Canada's Northwest Territories. Punch-drunk from a yearlong world tour, we're now north of the Arctic Circle on a lineup with the biggest metal band in the world.

Molson Beer Presents: Polar Beach Party Headlined by Metallica and Hole!

We're playing to five hundred beer-enthusiast contest winners flown in from all over North America to promote Molson's new ice-brewed beer. This concert almost doubles the population of Tuktoyaktuk.

It's both the smallest audience and the biggest payday of the year for our band. The *Live Through This* tour didn't make any money. And now that I'm an official member of Hole, despite the deeply flawed contract I signed, I'm no longer making a weekly wage. Instead, I earn a quarter of whatever profits the band makes. Sounds kinda cool, but as my lawyer pointed out, what's shitty about the deal is if you're not part of the band's financial planning or oversight, which I'm not, and if you don't work directly with the managers and record label, which I don't, you make one-quarter of an amount that's totally out of your control.

This beer gig, however, was presented to us as our end-of-year bonuses. It's a refreshingly clear-cut offer, the first and last of its kind during my time in the band. Molson pays all of our expenses, including our flights to and from the Northwest Territories, and we, the band, get a paycheck of $250,000 to split equally four ways. This blows my antimoney and low-spending brain. Sounds like a good deal.

These silly Molson beer competitions in the late '90s are a quintessential and absurd example of how big biz is co-opting our cool to sell product.

Beyond the Arctic Circle . . . Beyond the tree line . . . Beyond experience . . . the Molson Ice Polar Beach Party, Labor Day Weekend 1995, with Metallica and Hole . . . Also appearing, Veruca Salt and Moist. Tuktoyaktuk, Arctic, Canada. Get up there!

The bands and crews were flown on a chartered plane from Vancouver to Inuvik and then boarded passenger buses for an hourlong drive along what could barely be called a road, which dead-ended at a tiny, remote village

---

Courtney Love signing autographs with Metallica, Tuktoyaktuk, Canada, 1995.

perched on the edge of the Arctic Ocean. When we arrived, we were shown into the gymnasium that doubled as the town's city hall, community center, and site for any other public gathering needed in town. We were instructed to sit at folding tables and chairs alongside the members of Metallica to meet and greet the five hundred contest winners who had lined up to meet us. Over the next couple of hours, we autographed each guest's poster in a veritable assembly line of delirious *Hello, Hi, Good day, eh? Welcome to the Great White North! Hi, I hope you like beer!* Greetings, jokes, and endless Sharpie-marker fumes.

The gym was the only building of any substantial size in town and a noticeable contrast to the trailer homes sprinkled around in what seemed like a random, nonlinear effort at town planning. After our gym duties, we were shown to a pink trailer home. It was the actual residence of a local family who had no doubt been given a location rental fee to make their modest home our dressing rooms for the day.

Courtney Love exiting our dressing trailer, Tuktoyaktuk, Canada, 1995.

I sat on the pink bedspread in the wood-paneled bedroom assigned to me, staring at a plastic rose in a vase. As I flipped through limited cable TV channels, I snacked on an instant-noodle bowl. The Styrofoam cup filled with boiling water somehow amplified our maligned presence in this place. Synthetic forces damaging something natural. Sitting in this room was the closest I'd come to interacting with the Native community receiving this rock-and-roll alien invasion.

I became restless waiting for the crew to set up our gear and for us to take the stage, so I stepped outside the trailer into the blustery wind. Outside, Patty was smoking with some of our entourage. I was surprised to see Montreal cultural journalist Albert Nerenberg, a protégé of my father's, here. He was always very generous when describing his admiration for Nick, his "hero."

"Melissa!" He walked over with a handheld video camera. "Can I interview you?"

Nerenberg was doing an investigative journalism piece for Canadian TV about how Molson could justify holding a massive beer promotion in Inuit territory. It was controversial, at best, for a brewing company to invade a small community composed of an Indigenous population that is widely known to struggle with alcoholism. And Tuktoyaktuk was a dry town, on top of it. Residents could drink alcohol (and did), but they couldn't buy it there.

Initially, I'd been intrigued and proud to visit this remote territory of my homeland. But once I was here, in this barren land with no trees, I understood just how controversial this engagement was. My payday tarnished when I realized it was coming on the backs of an Indigenous community that was paid off by a beer company.

The whole thing feels gross. As with most other things I've experienced this year, this is more sick, soul-sucking capitalism and consumerism at work, yet another layer of carelessness and evil greed. And our band, which plays that night for five hundred screaming fans in a huge white tent called the Big Igloo, is a cog in the machine.

✗

By the time I leave the Northwest Territories, I've spent the past ten days flying from San Francisco to New York to London to Brussels to New York to Montreal to Seattle to Tuktoyaktuk. There's still one more stop before we can rest: Radio City Music Hall in New York City for the 1995 MTV Music Awards.

The venue is a glorious Art Deco theater, and I learn it was the initial home of the Rockettes, the over-the-top dancing showgirls who hark back to the time of "old showbiz." I'm tickled to think of those pros as sisters in arms to our particular 1990s flavor of showgirl.

The show is airing live, so I'm crossing my fingers that Hole's performance will be strong and that Courtney won't let too much of her inner chaos rip and blow it for everyone. Most of all for herself. There is not—not yet—the daughter-of-an-alcoholic codependent fear that I will be embarrassed by her actions. My concern is mostly for her: *Please don't blow it for yourself*, I say to her silently. *You have the world watching you. You have this music machine behind you. You have a great record. And you have a relatively stable, devoted band trying to prop you up with these great songs that you have written.*

I don't want her, and in turn us, to sink on live TV.

We arrive for the show that evening in a limousine with Drew Barrymore, who is decked out in classic Marilyn Monroe old Hollywood chic. Courtney has added hair extensions, making for a more flowy mane rather than her usual blunt bob cut with rough scissors. I'm wearing a vintage satin slip and a tiny rust-colored velvet blazer. We—or rather Courtney and Drew, with me over on the side—have a little girly splash on the red carpet and then head in. We settle backstage, opting to watch the live show on the TV monitors in our dressing room while readying ourselves for our performance.

We've been slotted toward the end of the star-studded event. Michael Jackson has already opened the show with an extravagant medley of his greatest hits, followed by TLC, Bon Jovi, the Red Hot Chili Peppers,

R.E.M., and Alanis Morrisette. Alanis is making her debut performance of her breakout hit "You Oughta Know," which is about to add an interesting spin on the "Women in Rock" trajectory for the second part of the '90s. Something about her breakout success lands at odds with Courtney, Patty, and me. A song about being a mess after giving a blowjob to a guy in a movie theater is not the kind of revolution we're gunning for. But it's making major traction, and she's able to play the industry game. We aren't fans, but we want to be happy for the greater cause.

When we take the stage, Courtney delivers an ode to those who've left us. "This is for Kurt, and Kristen, and River," she says, speaking softly and looking wide-eyed into the camera on live TV. This is her subdued introduction to our raucous song "Violet," and her plea to bless their souls adds to the power, drama, and tragedy of our band.

> *And the sky was all fucking violet*
> *I want to give the violent more violence*
> *Yeah, I'm the one with no soul*
> *One above and two below*

Our set stands out, as always, as the messiest, but at best the rawest and "real," as we who are obsessed with authenticity call it.

The song ends like a violent purge of Courtney's insides as she screams the words. But then, instead of walking off, she stands in a trance, banging out one note on her guitar, over and over, like a monotonous religious chant:

> *God.*
> *Bless.*
> *Your.*
> *Souls.*
> *God.*
> *Bless.*
> *Your.*
> *Souls.*

The wicked widow in mourning is pushing the envelope of live TV, which works on a tight clip. With the end of the song left hanging, she pulls away, in four sloppy motions hurls her guitar onto the floor, knocks down her mic, shoves Eric into a guitar amplifier, and begins to attack the wall of guitar amps. The stage lights come up, and peppy jazz music pumps into the room in an attempt to drown out Hole's noise.

Our yearlong world tour is ending with a messy bang. Courtney is still trashing the stage, knocking over amplifiers and smacking Eric with a towel as the production prepares to cut for a commercial break. The in-house announcer cuts in with a cheerful, "Still to come, Bryan Adams, Green Day, and your pick for this year's Viewers Choice Award!"

After our performance Courtney, Eric, and I follow the red carpet along the exterior of Radio City to the media room. Music fans stand four rows deep along Sixth Avenue, where MTV has set up interview staging areas to broadcast live from the street in between acts. Iconic interviewer Kurt Loder is stationed on the main podium above street level. Courtney's eye is always attuned to power spots and immediately registers who he's interviewing: Madonna.

Never afraid to remind the world that she's unpredictable, Courtney has no fear interrupting Madonna, who still reigns as the '80s queen of pop. She bombs the live interview by tossing makeup items from her purse onto Madonna's head. Awkward laughs for all, as I move ahead, barely taking notice of it from over my shoulder. "Courtney Love is in dire need of attention right now," Madonna says on live TV as Love makes her way up the stairs . . .

Our promotional team course-corrects and gets us into the media blitz room. This is a common format for any entertainment awards show. The "talent" line up on a short stage, against an MTV backdrop, to pose for hundreds of journalists and photographers. At first, you're blinded by the flashes. Once you calibrate, you can latch on to the random questions thrown your way. All of them are for Courtney, in our case. She's the punk celebrity. We're just the band, there for show. Well, Eric and I are, anyway. Patty is missing again tonight. She's disappearing more lately. I suspect she's having an affair with the nanny.

Courtney indulges the cameras with wild and erratic behavior, including flashing her undies under her tiny black-satin miniskirt.

"Courtney! What's next for you?" one journalist asks.

"I'm gonna do a movie and write a record," she mumbles coyly. "I don't wanna jinx it. Very major, though. And I gotta write a record. *We* gotta write a record," she corrects herself. "In New Orleans. Kinda like, we're gonna write *Led Zeppelin 4* meets Moby, with really good lyrics. Hopefully."

A few minutes later, she playfully falls on her butt to take questions. When it's time to exit, Eric and I squat down on the ground on either side of her, to lift her up. She encourages us to carry her off the red carpet in our arms while she smiles and waves goodbye to the mob.

Is it just a show? Is she under the influence? I never really stop to think anymore. I just do.

By this point, I've been pummeled into a state of seminumbness, shut off from drama mode. Given the amount of daily rigor and the general nature of rock touring life, including daily travel on planes and buses, gear to set up, and frantic crowds, plus the mourning of those lost, the under-the-radar drug use, and over-the-top stage antics, all of this topped off by curveballs like shotgun shells and a Parisian hospital escape . . . I've learned to shut most things out in order to get through a day.

Occasionally, I glance over my shoulder to register a strange happening, then turn back and keep walking. *Just look away*, I tell myself. *Look away from the car crash. Don't do what the whole world is doing. Don't look.*

It's my coping strategy to stay balanced when witnessing controversial behavior on repeat, with a dash of magical thinking: *If I don't see it*, I tell myself, *then it will cease to exist.*

Shutting out reality is not something I am proud of. I don't want to turn away. But it's what I have to do now to keep up a sense of duty, optimism, and positivity.

Denial. Denial. Denial.

CHAPTER 23

The Witch of New Orleans

NOVEMBER–DECEMBER 1995

Once we've finished the *Live Through This* tour, done the crazy-ass Arctic Circle show, and completed the MTV awards, we have to get to writing the new record. The whole process feels mysterious and foreign to me. I don't know how songs will actually come into being in this wild band.

About a year ago, the film *Interview with a Vampire* was released to great success. It was based on the book trilogy by Anne Rice, an American goth author who lives in New Orleans and brought goth and vampire culture to the mainstream. This made people like me and Courtney happy, as we share a love of the '80s goth experience and believe that dark romance is good for kids (like us!). The movie was ordained by major movie stars of the moment like Brad Pitt, Tom Cruise, Antonio Banderas, and Christian Slater and introduced a young Kirsten Dunst as a girl vampire.

Our tour with Nine Inch Nails exposed us to the industrial-goth part of the music industry. Honestly, it seems more interesting than what the waves of commercialization and overnight successes are creating in our "grunge"-rock scene, post-Seattle explosion. For this and other reasons, Courtney decides to revisit her goth youth roots of the '80s. She decides to dye her hair black and move us to New Orleans for a few months to begin writing.

Every band needs its lead singer, songwriter, and lyricist to be inspired by something, and at this moment it's New Orleans.

Our team sets us up to land in dramatic goth fashion in a city that embodies its own sense of mystery. Courtney wants to focus on writing, so Frances stays out west with her ever-present nanny.

We make ourselves at home in the Garden District, in a spooky Victorian mansion that's been given a pink facelift to hide its darker past. On our first day, we visit the studio where we'll be writing and recording. It's an extravagant 1920s former Masonic-temple high-rise that's now a commercial rental property. The grand hall has been well repurposed as a recording studio. Original, elaborate Art Deco–infused wall paintings of Egyptian iconography and pyramids complete the vibe.

The creepy Victorian mansion makes me feel uneasy, but our writing space instantly connects me to the dream about 3D sound that told me to

---

Courtney Love, Eric Erlandson, and Patty Schemel in haunted house, New Orleans, 1996.

make music my life. *Here I am, in some version of the pyramid dream. May the music goddess channel through me!* is the message I hear. It opens my heart, my mind, and my ears to new possibilities here.

✘

On our first night in the pink-doily house, I am struck by how awkward it is for us to live together like a family. Sharing a public stage with someone is the opposite of sharing a domestic routine with them. Living together in the same space feels too close, even bordering on perverse. It reminds me of the time we did band therapy. This kind of earnest intimacy doesn't suit us.

The fridge in our communal kitchen is stocked by a barely seen assistant living in the servants' quarters of the house. As usual it's cold cuts, mayo, mustard, iceberg lettuce, veggie sticks, and dip, for what feels like lunch on the go all the time for a band like ours. The bare cupboards hold sliced white bread, English muffins for easy breakfasts, and chips.

Patty and I develop a morning ritual, with a cup of black tea with milk and honey for me and drip coffee with cream and sugar for her. Beyond the house's classic southern wraparound porch is a stone walkway flanked with plaster eagle statues and views of colorful mansions across the street. Patty and I take morning walks around the mansion district, which is littered with sweet antique shops and boutiques displaying silk floral robes and shawls that Courtney will soon toss around our house for added decor.

Eric pretty much keeps to himself. His room is in the far back of the house. Courtney and I both have dramatic mirrored parlor rooms with giant floor-to-high-ceiling windows in the front of the house, overlooking the front yard. Patty's room is in the middle of the house, between the boy in the back and the girls in the front. She easily rides the line between boy and girl personality, which is something I love most about her.

We're living relatively quietly, without the noise of a touring crew or a giant audience. Even though we've been set up with all we need—the house, the studio, the instruments, the engineer, the assistant, the stocked fridge—things always feel slightly hopeless. Patty, Eric, and I do our best to be a band. More

and more, the three of us silently accept the level of dysfunction we're part of. Courtney can disappear at any moment, or be angry, or—even worse—useless. These are the best-case scenarios. Her mental stability is still very much in question. She doesn't seem to sleep at night, and her daytime hours are erratic.

This isn't really working, is it? reverberates like a shared heartbeat. *We're not going to actually be able to write songs, or pull off anything that's expected from us, are we?*

At the same time, we're viscerally aware that we're at the precipice of becoming as big as any band could ever become. We're here to give birth to the next chapter. The tension of what we are "supposed" to become and where we are at the moment is ever present while we wait for Courtney to show up.

The three of us try to stay on a reasonable daytime schedule. We go into the studio together in the late morning most days and fiddle with our instruments in the imposing former hall of a historic secret society. Simply by just showing up, Eric, Patty, and I help motivate each other to be a band.

Self-portrait in bedroom of haunted house, New Orleans, 1996.

But the writing does not come smoothly or easily. We can't write songs without Courtney, and it's not our job to. Hole's songs are conceptually and lyrically driven. We need our lead singer and bandleader to, in a word, *lead* us.

✕

I quickly discover there's something very *Twilight Zone*–ish about New Orleans. I feel a spooky energy everywhere we go. I've interfaced with metaphysical presences in the "hauntings" in my bedroom back home in Montreal, but I don't yet feel stable, confident, and strong enough to look at these things head-on.

In New Orleans, surrounded by vampire stories and the grief in the band, Courtney's obsession with gothic imagery makes me uncomfortable. It goes beyond black hair or a music genre. It feels close to death itself and like our band might be summoning such forces. That's the best way I can explain it.

From the moment we move into the house, Courtney starts lighting candles, the tall glass kind that are lit in Catholic churches or sold at delis, usually with images of the Virgin Mary or saints on the front. She uses red lipstick to create her own iconography on the cylinders, like hearts crossed out with *x*'s hand drawn like a child. She places these candles all around the house, in the hallways, on the stairwell, in the bathrooms, and on the mantels. They burn at all hours of the day and night.

The whole house becomes a vigil. To a certain extent, we know that we must let her grieve, although it's never spoken about directly.

On a rare night, Patty, who doesn't drink, and I, who grew up in bars, go out for a Coca-Cola and a beer in the French Quarter. Behind the bar is a huge mirror. Through the reflection I gaze at the dimly lit room and the bar action behind me. My eyes land on a man leaning against the wall behind us. He is looking straight at me through the mirror. He is alone, but his mouth is moving in some crazy-fast movements. His tongue is slithering out like a snake.

Is this what speaking in tongues looks like? I feel a deep fright.

We make eye contact in the mirror, and I instantly feel fucking terrified. I nudge Patty. "There is a strange man behind us . . . ," I mumble. When I get the balls to turn around, he is gone.

This is the beginning of me not feeling safe.

The next day, the three of us are buying time at the studio, waiting for Courtney to arrive, or not. We're listening back to some rough jams from the night before, and I mention the strange man at the bar to the local recording engineer working with us.

"Oh, the whole town is haunted. They say the aboveground graves are part of it," he responds, casually. "New Orleans is built on a swamp. The bodies would float away and pop up in our backyards if they were buried too deep."

"This building is totally haunted," he continues. "Ghosts all over the place. I've seen them in the studio late at night."

I don't want to ask too many questions, but I believe him. My inner armor begins to grow, keeping me on guard for entities in the corners of rooms or at the end of my bed.

✕

Courtney eventually shows up to jam that night. Books and magazines in hand, chain-smoking, she strolls over to her center position.

"*Pardonnez-moi, monsieur. Je ne l'ai pas fait exprès,*" she says in strained and horribly mangled French. She looks at me as if I should know what she's talking about.

"Sorry, what did you say?" I ask.

"I'm reading up on Marie Antoinette. Those were her last words: *Pardon me, sir, I did not do it on purpose.*"

Courtney is a fast learner and a walking historian of things she has a passion for, much like my father. Flipping through a book, she can go off on a monologue, like a cool teacher at a punk school for girls.

These last words from Marie Antoinette came after she accidentally stepped on her executioner's shoe, Courtney informs us. The disgraced queen was then decapitated by guillotine and her body thrown into an unmarked grave in the Madeleine Cemetery.

"Let them eat cake!" Courtney announces in a funny French accent, tossing her hand dramatically in the air. She reaches for her guitar, indicating that we are to summon a song from the ether at this moment.

The band's style of songwriting is beginning to reveal itself. It does not come easily, or prolifically, but viscerally and unpredictably. After Patty, Eric, and I have waited around a whole day or two for Courtney to show up, one of us pulls out a riff or Patty kicks into a beat. We all fall into it and repeat the same chords over and over, while Courtney searches for a melody and a sentence or two. These become the kernels from which songs grow.

We can ride one of these strains for hours, alternating between loud and soft. Courtney goes from screaming to singing to screaming again. Her stamina for repetition is remarkable. She never grows bored. We do this over and over, massaging the single lane we find ourselves steadfastly driving in.

We each fish around for our parts, in a murky river of sound, waiting for flashes of light and improvising along the way. I find little bass-lick melodies that take me off the root notes. Eventually, I head to my own mic to harmonize, offering call-response lines or *oohs* and *aahs*. These create a foundation to support Courtney while she looks for her melodies, lyrics, and emotional intent. The engineer is instructed to record *all* of it, to be listened back to another time.

On this particular night we wind up in one deranged, hypnotic loop, playing the same riff over and over.

"Off with her head! Off with her head! Off with her head!" Courtney roars into the mic.

The Marie Antoinette theme starts making sense to me now. Courtney is doing her thing with a repetitive review of an infamous woman, putting herself in the shoes of a scandalous character. Today, she's channeling the perspective of a dethroned queen. Whether she's alone with us in the studio or in front of thousands, she is the same: on the edge and full of rage. It feels like we're having our first breakthrough.

Then, abruptly, she stops. Throws her guitar down and runs out of the studio. The rest of us stop playing and look at each other. What prompted this? We don't know. It's unsettling, and also very late. A good time to stop for the night. We wait around for a while, and then Patty and I decide we are concerned. No one has called a cab for her. No assistant followed her out. She is on her own out there.

Does she even know where we live? Will she get lost? Patty and I ride the elevator down to the lobby, but Courtney isn't there.

We step outside, look up and down the quiet street. No sign of her anywhere.

As we head back up to the studio, the elevator stops on the wrong floor. The doors open to a man and woman standing there in 1930s attire. They stare at us wordlessly. We stare back at them. They don't board the elevator. They don't move at all. Then the doors close.

It takes less than a second for Patty and me to fucking lose our shit. "Those are the ghosts!" We go screaming back into the studio to tell the engineer what we saw.

"Oh, yeah, those are the ghosts everyone sees in the building," he explains matter-of-factly. "They ride the elevators up and down. Late at night there's a ton of activity in those elevators."

Patty and I have had enough for the night. Eric, as usual, is lost in a book. Courtney's nowhere to be found. We decide to leave Eric and the engineer to solve the mystery of Courtney and the ghost elevator riders.

In the morning, we're relieved to see Courtney back in her usual habitat: lying in her bed full of books and pillows, smoking an eternally lit cigarette. Later in the day we hear mumblings from the assistant that she was found on the roof of the Masonic building contemplating suicide. Under different circumstances, I'd pause to register this as a dramatic, extreme moment. But the roller coaster I'm on just keeps going. There's no time to stop and think about it.

Keep moving. Keep moving. Keep moving.

✗

Some good news arrives: we're asked to record a cover of Fleetwood Mac's "Gold Dust Woman," a song Courtney loves. It's for *The Crow: City of Angels* film soundtrack. The first Crow film was a gothic movie infamous for the death of its lead actor, Brandon Lee, who was killed by a prop gun on set. It was released posthumously, and a sequel is now in production for release next year. We've been offered the prestigious closing-credits slot.

Ric Ocasek, front man of the Cars, will be producing. We're well aware of his recent success as the producer of Weezer's debut, *The Blue Album*, which includes my personal favorite single, "Buddy Holly."

This commission puts some wind in our sails. For a couple of days in the studio we experiment with the song. I come up with my first signature bass line for a Hole track. It's a driving, downstroked distorted bass line that takes inspiration from the moody acoustic original and makes way for a postpunk- and goth-infused heavy-rock version intro. I feel like I'm now contributing to the band's exploration of its new direction. Patty locks right in under me with a signature disco beat on her hi-hat, riding hard on the cymbals with her left foot.

Courtney, of course, fully embodies Stevie Nicks, the witchy front woman of Fleetwood Mac. She snarls the line *"Oooh yeah . . . Black widow! Black widow!"* her voice overlapping with mine as I approach the mic and add my angelic counterpart to Courtney's she-devil voice.

"Ooh ooh, shadow of a woman . . ." My first signature vocal line in a Hole track is born out of this session. Shivers of what we can become course through me.

Recording this song with Ric Ocasek a month later in Los Angeles feels like real music progress and a big opportunity and momentum for our struggling band. It also becomes a vehicle for presenting Courtney and me as a duo. The video of "Gold Dust Woman" is released in conjunction with the film in 1996, the four of us dressed in crow black, playing against a dark background interrupted by flashes of light and images from the film. Courtney appears with her black goth hair, wearing a strapless dress with bare shoulders. Several shots show just the two of us facing and circling each other closely and even holding hands, summoning sister-witch vibes. We slowly spin around each other, lip syncing, with our arms and voices intertwined, in movements that can only be described as gestures of affection.

✕

In New Orleans we're moving in slow motion, through long, slow weeks of on-and-off writing, when another huge opportunity comes our way. We've been invited to star in an episode of *The Simpsons*, the wildly popular animated series now in its seventh season.

A big envelope arrives at our house one morning containing four copies of a script for an episode called "Homerpalooza," a Lolla takeoff where Hole is the headlining band. Animation artists are already working on our characters, and the producers want us to review the lines we're being asked to perform.

They've perfectly captured our personalities. Patty is the lesbian with a pink triangle on her shirt. Eric plays noise on the guitar from behind his hair, and I'm depicted as a hippie girl talking about astrology. Courtney, of course, is completely outrageous—fierce, disheveled, cursing, chaotic, controversial, and funny. In just a few lines, she's portrayed as all that she really is. Patty and I are beside ourselves with laughter and giddiness as we read the script. Finally, the light of humor is shining on us not just from inside our own intimate, perverse little universe, but from the outside, from some of the most popular comic writers in the world.

This is as big as a follow-up record. Being featured on an episode of *The Simpsons* declares us to be as significant as any band of our generation. Our managers at Q-Prime are very hands-on and are planning for us to be the biggest female-led band in the world.

As it happens, cleaning up Courtney's persona is a big part of their project.

A couple of days later we hear that management has turned down *The Simpsons* because "it is making a caricature of Courtney." Our response is a jaw-dropping *WHAT???* Seriously, a caricature? That's precisely what *The Simpsons* is. It's a *cartoon*.

And just like that, my persona is *not* preserved in the history of animation celluloid.

To add even more kindling to this fire, we're replaced with the Smashing Pumpkins. When the episode airs in May 1996, it includes special-guest voices from all three members of the Smashing Pumpkins, as well as Cypress Hill and Sonic Youth.

In my humble opinion, management has made a big fear-based mistake by pulling us out, but I dare express this only to my confidante, Patty. They're missing the point that Courtney is *known* as a ball of chaos. That's who she is. She's a punk. And it's okay for her character to be a wild woman on *The Simpsons*. I guess their higher hopes for her to become a Hollywood movie star—which she'll end up becoming for a hot second—override our band's unpredictable cool factor. That's what I love most about us, because it's honest.

I feel deflated and suddenly confused about the direction the band will go in. So much is riding on this moment. I can't help wondering who, if not the musicians in the band, are best equipped to steer this gigantic ship?

We're a month into this New Orleans stay oozing with ghosts, suicidal thoughts, bad business decisions, and no creative flow when we find out that Green Day is playing at the Kiefer UNO Lakefront Arena, a ten-thousand-seat venue in town. Green Day is huge at this point, with back-to-back hit records. First was *Dookie* in 1994 and then *Insomniac* in 1995.

Why not go? We aren't too busy in the studio anyway. A band night out, arena rock, and socializing with punk peers will be fun, maybe even good for us.

Courtney holds a special spot for Billie Joe Armstrong, the front man of Green Day. He's a true punk from the Bay Area and Courtney often says that Kurt would be proud of Green Day... for keeping punk alive. The last time we crossed paths with Green Day was a year earlier at a San Francisco alternative-radio station showcase concert. I'd overheard Courtney and Billie Joe talking about Kurt's suicide.

"You know, I know why he did it, man," Billie Joe said. "He killed punk rock, and he couldn't live with himself."

When I asked Courtney about it later, she said, "Billie Joe's the only one who gets it. He's right. That absolutely devastated Kurt."

As usual we're late to the show; going through the artist-entry gates and in the backstage door, we run to the left side of the stage to watch from close-up. Viewing from the side stage is common for guests of the band to do at a show like this. It avoids the big crowd, and especially for a celebrity like Courtney, it's expected.

As we take our spots, looking for good sight lines, we disperse a bit. All of a sudden, I see an army of security people in Day-Glo yellow T-shirts heading straight for us. They pass right by me and tackle my three band members, one by one. Before I even know what's happening, Eric and Patty are in headlocks and Courtney is flailing her arms, trying to scratch the face of one of the bigger men who's manhandling her.

What. The. Fuck?

One of the security guys tosses Courtney over his shoulder like a rag doll. Her legs are kicking furiously. I am left standing alone, watching my three band members disappear down the big arena corridor backstage.

My heart is pounding. I have no fucking idea what just happened. I look around at the crowd, but their eyes are all focused on the band. *Did anyone other than me see what just happened?*

I head backstage to find Green Day's production team sitting around a couple of fold-up worktables stacked with phones, printers, and computers.

"I'm Melissa from Hole," I introduce myself, "and I just watched my three band members get carried off somewhere by security. Do you know what's happening?"

The tour manager bolts straight up and heads out into the hall, barking into his walkie-talkie. I follow him to a room, where the band is inside, being detained.

Courtney is fuming and freaking out, standing tall in front of the deadpan giants. "I'm friends with Billie Joe!" she screams. "Billie Joe loves me! I love Billie Joe! What the *FUCK* is going on?!"

Green Day's tour manager enters the room and apologizes. There has been a misunderstanding, he explains. We leave the arena without seeing or talking to the band. The next day, there's speculation that Billie Joe's team was afraid Courtney would bum-rush the stage. They'd asked the local team to be on guard for it, and security overreacted.

It's a fucking horrendous, nonwelcoming final tone to our stay in New Orleans. A whole new dimension is added to the danger and conflict that already surround the band. It raises the question of where Hole is safe. Who has our backs?

After five weeks in New Orleans, the pink mansion is growing old on me. I've read a variety of mystical books while bored in my bedroom, including *Many Lives, Many Masters*, a nonfiction book about how to discover your past lives through staring deep into the face of a loved one. I've made and sent multiple custom photo-collage cards to everyone back home, leading up to the end-of-year holiday season, my second one in this band. I'm feeling uninspired and a little lost, at best.

I fall asleep, always a bit concerned about what might come to me in a dream. But tonight I wake to the sound of glass shattering.

I jerk awake. It's the middle of the night, and I can smell smoke.

Through the glass transom above my tall bedroom door, I see an ominous red glow on the hallway ceiling, enhanced by a fog of swirling smoke. It registers with me that we are in danger, maybe serious danger, but the house is strangely quiet.

Holy shit.

I leap out of bed in my cotton underwear and little-girl tank top, briefly consider grabbing my diary and camera by my bed, and quickly realize there is no time for such frivolous acts. My instinct is to rush out into the hall and find the rest of the band.

We all need to get out of here.

Outside my room, reflections of red flames run across the ceiling. The hallway is filling with smoke. Through Courtney's open door I see her slowly coming to, groggy, on a bed surrounded by fire. The floor-to-ceiling lace curtains along the bay windows are already burning. Cigarettes? Candle? One of her vices, physical or spiritual, may have sparked this.

The flames dance violently and beautifully. The poetic drama of *Gone with the Wind* is not lost on me in what feels like a waking dream.

"Wake up!" I shout at her. "Courtney, *get up!*"

The fire is moving *up* the room, not across the room, before the flames run across the ceiling toward the hallway. The ceiling is high, and I calculate that we have enough time to get out unscathed.

I push open the door to Patty's room. *"Patty! Fire! Fire!"* I shout.

Patty wakes up immediately and acts fast. She runs down to the kitchen to get the fire extinguisher, while I follow to call 911 from the kitchen phone. We sprint out the front door, calling for the rest of them to come. Courtney emerges from the staircase followed by Eric.

We're all accounted for, including the mostly invisible assistant. I can breathe again.

From the front yard we watch flames engulfing Courtney's room. The firefighters show up with sirens screaming and red lights twirling, casting an eerie on-off glow onto our faces and the neighboring houses. They ram through the front door and aim their ladders toward her windows, dragging hoses behind them.

After a while, the fire is contained, but we're warned that they're keeping an eye on the attic to be sure the fire isn't spreading within the walls. It's five in the morning when we check into a nearby hotel.

This band is fucking cursed. This trip needs to end.

The next day, we grab our things from the house. I snap some photos of the black, charred doorway of Courtney's bedroom. On my way down the elegant staircase for the last time, I notice one of Courtney's omnipresent church candles. It's been blown out permanently, in defeat.

We each fly home our separate ways for the winter holidays, not sure what will come next in 1996. I leave New Orleans with a burning sensation in the back of my throat from smoke inhalation; the Witch of New Orleans sessions are over.

CHAPTER 24

For Love and Honor

NOVEMBER 14, 1996

"We've got to get control of the media," my father says. "The best way to do that is to grab the microphone. We have to have a plan."

He's talking to his friend Juan Rodriguez, a fellow writer in Montreal. "What plan is that?" Juan asks.

"The plan is that we drink, and then it will come to us," Nick says, with the tongue-in-cheek bravado of an army lieutenant. He raises his glass of local beer.

So they drink. Soon enough, Nick asks their buddy down the bar if he can post bail for them. He says yes.

Without flinching, Nick leaps from his barstool. "We're off to get arrested," he announces. And he and Juan head off to the Rialto Theater.

Nick is driven by outrage toward two writers. Their book—*Who Killed Kurt Cobain?*—implies that Courtney killed her husband. Supporting their theories is Courtney's estranged father, Hank Harrison, who is on this press tour. In Nick's mind, these two guys are impugning his daughter's reputation by association, and he won't stand for that. And what kind of father would ever support such accusations against his daughter?!

The multimedia show exploring the circumstances of Kurt's death has been canceled under threat from Courtney's lawyers and replaced by a press conference, which is underway when Nick arrives. About eighty people are in the audience, mostly teenagers. The two journalists are up onstage, along with Courtney's father, Hank.

Nick heads directly for the stairs to the stage. He's not afraid to say things that will get him dragged off. He's just like Courtney that way and even uses her tactics to defend her.

He grabs the microphone and blurts out, "I'm Melissa's mother! There are no *fathers* on this stage!"

He keeps shouting as security steps up and drags him and Juan away. As they're escorted outside, a rush of teenagers follows, asking for his autograph.

Grinning with pride, Nick turns to Juan.

"This is fun, isn't it?" he asks, with his mischievous walrus grin. "I feel eighteen again!"

News spreads fast across the networks, including MTV News. When Courtney learns that Nick confronted her asshole father, she sends him three dozen white roses with a personal note.

```
Dear Nick, the father I never had,
Thank you for defending my honor xo

                              Love, Courtney
```

CHAPTER 25

Rhythm-Section Sisters

SPRING 1996

"I've got to move to LA to be with the band."

I'm on the phone with my mother in my little New York City East Village studio apartment, my first home of my own. The space is adorned with thrift-store finds imported from my Montreal life: replicas of Renaissance paintings framed in plastic gold, faux Victorian pillows and tapestries, and my grandfather's gold American-eagle fish-eye mirror, my only family heirloom of sorts that goes wherever I go. I love to see the world through that mirror.

I'm sure my mother, who represents integrity and independence, is mortified by this news. Its far from home, and we both view Los Angeles as a snake pit for our shared values—a city full of cars and movie stars.

"You're going to need to learn how to drive, Melissa," she says. "Finally."

A woman always needs to know how to drive away from a bad situation. That's always been one of her core mantras. She's been on my case about driving since I was sixteen, when she sent me to driving school in Montreal, but I wasn't motivated enough to learn then.

I stare at the cherubs on my 1970s kitschy red-and-gold-velvet bedspread. I don't really want to leave New York. I've lived here barely a year, much of which I spent on tour, but this apartment still feels like home. It's been a wondrous bridge between my cozy big-fish-in-a-small-town life in Montreal and this new little-fish-in-a-big-ocean life of international

rock mayhem. I like it here. New York City has everything that Montreal has and then some, including cuter boys and cooler bands. I can easily meet up with other musicians on the road who are passing through town or with the creative local friends I am gathering: writers, photographers, painters, and bartenders. There is almost always a rock show to catch at one of dozens of venues. My most visited are Brownies, Knitting Factory, Mercury Lounge, Irving Plaza, and Maxwell's. At the very least, there are drinks and local rock musicians to hang with at Max Fish until four in the morning. I go out every night.

"At least I get to live with Patty. That will be fun," I say.

Moving to California was never part of my plan, but surrendering to most things being out of my control is what it means to be in Hole. Courtney has relocated to the City of Angels since ejecting herself from Seattle and all the bad memories there. And Eric, a native Angeleno, moved back there after the Seattle deaths and after falling in love with Drew Barrymore.

Self-portrait in fish-eye mirror, 1995.

It makes professional sense for us all to live in the same city to write this new record, especially since the New Orleans sessions failed so dismally. I take most of my comfort from knowing that Patty is in this same boat with me.

Since getting off tour, Patty has broken up from her incestuous (and possibly drug-fueled) "romance" with the nanny and created a well-balanced life for herself in Seattle, dating a sober woman in a local punk-rock band. My New York life is suiting me, too. I've been dating a sweet guy who works as a bartender at a classy French bistro in Soho. It's my first healthy and regular romance since joining the band. He is my age, in his last year as a photography student in university, and not fucked up at all.

Neither Patty nor I is looking to change our living situations, but we band together, literally, to oblige and obey the rules of the game. When we were in Los Angeles this spring to film the "Gold Dust Woman" video, we struck it lucky and found a perfect place to live. It's a single-family dream home for 1990s indie-rock girls like us in the hills of Silverlake, an up-and-coming neighborhood just east of Hollywood. Beck and a Beastie Boy live in the neighborhood, which adds some excitement.

The house is perfectly laid out for two soon-to-be-single women in a band. It has two good-size bedrooms connected by a big walk-in closet. I choose the one with extra closet space and french doors leading out to a large outdoor patio. Patty takes the one with an adjoining sunroom, where she can blast a My Bloody Valentine wall of sound on her stereo and smoke cigarettes in a comfortable armchair.

The living room is incredibly inviting, with big bay windows. I find a perfect faux 1970s Victorian couch and armchair set to place neatly on Patty's non-Persian rug, her only "real" home decor other than her decorative wrought-iron bed frame. Her treasured vintage bass drum makes for a perfect coffee table, while my stereo fits neatly in the built-in bookshelves framing the big windows.

The dining room features wallpaper that sends a rush of inspiration through me every time I step into the room. It's navy blue with silhouettes of big white roses connected by a thorny system of vines. We never consider using this as an actual dining room and instead make it our musical "room of one's own." It becomes a perfect homespun counterbalance to professional studios that are filled with big, impersonal speakers, amplifiers, and all manners of gear.

The first piece of gear I invest in is a Tascam 4-Track cassette recorder and guitar amp. Patty follows with Yamaha keyboard and Roland V-Drum Kit. It's an electronic kit built up of rubber pads laid out similarly to a real drum kit, with kick drum and hi-hat pedals that trigger samples into any amplification device. Patty's video cam is always charged and on the ready, too.

Our kitchen is a clean white dream of built-in cupboards that will never be filled, classic shiny white tile, a double sink, and a sunny breakfast nook where we can continue our morning rituals from New Orleans. Off the back of the kitchen we even have a laundry room that connects to a maid's room, a.k.a. traveling friends' guest room.

When we settle in, we find ourselves living mirror lives in lovely grown-up bedrooms, with perfect views of the hills of Los Angeles. Pretty houses are sprinkled along curvy streets that climb from the base of and are reflected on the shiny water surface of the Silverlake Reservoir to the top of the hills and back down again.

On a sunny morning in Silverlake, Patty and I take our typical morning walk down the hill and along the reservoir to the Back Door Bakery. She orders her usual gigantic blended iced-mocha espresso, and I grab a croissant.

I still don't drink coffee or know how to drive a car. Patty is our primary driver here in LA. She promises to take me for a spin in a parking lot later today in an effort to teach me how to drive. I've never been behind the wheel of a car, ever. But since moving to LA, I can't help but notice all the eye candy in the form of vintage cars. Most musicians and artists I know here drive something old and stylish that fits their individual personalities.

Sitting out on the deck of the café, we flip through an auto trade magazine that Patty picked up at the 7-Eleven across the street. She's coveting a

1970s vintage brown Mercedes, which screams "Grandpa!" to me, but she sees something cool in it.

Models from the late 1960s and early 1970s are the ones that speak to me, muscle cars and vintage green for certain. My only real motivation to get my driver's license is to get a car that will enhance my outfits. A mint-condition mint-green 1969 Mercury Cougar with hydrologic headlights that open and close like eyelids and super-rare sequential turn signals calls out to me.

She's the one. It's time to learn how to drive.

A woman must always know how to drive away from a bad situation. I will make my mother proud.

Within weeks I buy the vintage Cougar from an elderly woman in Long Beach. It was a prized possession that never left her garage, so it's in beautiful shape. I pay $3,000 cash. The American dollars are the same color as the car. Before I hand over the money, I take a photo of the bills lined up on the front seat. I cheat on my driving test and don't really know how to drive, but I'm not terribly bothered by this. Coasting along Los Angeles surface streets—I barely ever drive on the scary freeways—with my portable CD player, blasting my beloved Brainaic's new explosive "machines meet bleeding-hearts" album *Hissing Prigs in Static Couture*, I feel like I'm making the most of my surreal life in this weird-ass city of cars and movie stars.

We fill our idle time in Los Angeles with jokes and laughter. The video skits we used to make on the road morph into *The Chuckles Show*, a ragtag, silly home TV show. Patty pulls out her video camera as I step out of our closet in a floor-length 1960s vintage polyester dress with a pop art–style green and blue elephant design. It's a novelty piece I bought because it fits like a glove, but it's too silly to ever consider wearing in public. I pin up my fuzzy hair and stick a couple of peacock feathers into the mound above my head.

"Good day, sir. I am Elephant Castle. How do you do?" I speak in a strained international accent.

Patty pulls on a suit jacket and grabs the mic in our studio room. She places the video camera on the fireplace mantelpiece in the living room and steps into character. She is Pat, the Johnny Carson–style host of the show. She starts with an opening monologue.

Then she introduces me, her absurd, airy-fairy, flaky 1970s hippie-lady sidekick. I base my character on the *Price Is Right* woman who assists Bob Barker and start showcasing the couch as I take a seat on it, the drum coffee table, and the art on the wall.

The Chuckles Show is perfectly suited for a local cable-access station, or YouTube if it were to exist in 1996. We never entertain the thought of sharing it with the outside world, though. The videos are purely a continuation of the private universe we've taken shelter in.

While we're making homemade videos, Courtney is on a real Hollywood set. "Miloš put his name on the line for me; he's vouching for me. He believes in me!" she lets us know by phone. "This is it, my moment. *I'm taking it!*"

She's talking about legendary Czech filmmaker Miloš Forman, who's cast her alongside Woody Harrelson in *The People vs. Larry Flynt*, a film about *Hustler*'s founder. It's a bold move on Forman's part to cast her in the biggest role of her career. He's taking a chance on someone the world has not been kind to, someone who's known for the drama she embodies on a rock stage more than for her dramatic ability in front of a camera.

This means that upon moving to Los Angeles, Patty and I are formally off duty from Hole for the summer. We're still musicians bound to a legacy act, but we're basically out of work while we wait for our band leader to decide if she wants to play music, audition for Hollywood, or do whatever other mysterious things she does for weeks on end while we wait for our call.

We soon find that too much time and not enough music makes for idle hands. I'm taking photographs and keeping a diary, but I have an ever-present urge to be making music, too. So does Patty.

One morning in Silverlake, lingering in the breakfast nook, we conceive of a musical side project. We call it Constant Comment, inspired by my favorite Bigelow black-tea flavor I drink every morning. It's drums, bass, keyboards, and samples only, a simple antisong formula that comes easily, the opposite of writing songs with Hole that are expected to be radio hits.

Constant Comment becomes a way to keep our creative flames burning. I take the lead as the multi-instrumentalist producer. Inspired as an independent musician for the first time, I grab samples with my handheld cassette recorder, mostly from obscure vinyls I collect at thrift stores. One particularly inspiring record is a compilation of old radio bloopers. *One of the most spectacular kinds of automobile accidents is the kind where the car bursts into flames*, an old-school announcer says as he breaks into demonic laughter.

This one inspires a track I call "Fire Crasher." Patty kicks into an industrial beat, and I add a chopped-up staccato distorted bass line. Like most of our tracks, it is a strange, lo-fi antiradio sound. We build up to a heavy crescendo, and I find a sample to end on.

Nurses are urgently needed. Volunteer to be one of America's white-clad ladies of mercy!

The Longbeach, California–based indie label Sympathy for the Record Industry invites Constant Comment to do a double seven-inch single with the Red Aunts, an all female punk-rock band. We deliver "Fire Crasher" on a simple cassette along with a photo of us as "the band." Patty and I are in our *Chuckles Show* character costumes. I'm wearing a crooked black wig, she a bad blonde bob—reflected in my grandfather's fish-eye mirror.

Within a few weeks, we've built an improvisational forty-minute set around the experiments we've recorded at home. We take our wacky side project band on the road for a tiny three-day tour of the Northwest.

Look at us! we are saying. *We are happy and surviving, no problem, and no thanks to our bandmates.*

We spend the summer making fun out of the nonsensical things happening around to work out our fear and confusion through imagination and comedy. As time rolls on, *The Chuckles Show* becomes a long, rambling conversation between us in character.

We push the improv into fantasy one afternoon and throw ourselves far into the future. It's the twenty-first century, and I'm living in a spaceship-like glass house under a waterfall where I can commune with the stars. I am happily married, and the love of my life has built this remarkable house for me. In her fictional future, Patty is living back in the Northwest of America, reconnecting with her true grunge lumberjack roots and living on a horse ranch.

In earnest, we discuss the old days of being in Hole and laugh at the chaos that is now behind us. Our characters have made it to the other side, where we're thriving in our own remarkable ways and happy to see each other again after all this time.

"I was just visiting Courtney. As you know she's now in the White House, as *the* first lady of our fine nation," I say. "So much has changed."

"Yes, those little white gloves really worked out for her . . . ," Patty replies without missing a beat. "Cleaning up and becoming a Hollywood movie star and marrying President Eddie Vedder made it all possible. She's now the most powerful woman in the country!"

In the real future, all of these videos will be preserved in Patty's family's attic and eventually used in a documentary about her life and survival. I'm forever grateful that she saved these excerpts of our time together. It's a miracle she didn't lose them in the midst of all that happened next.

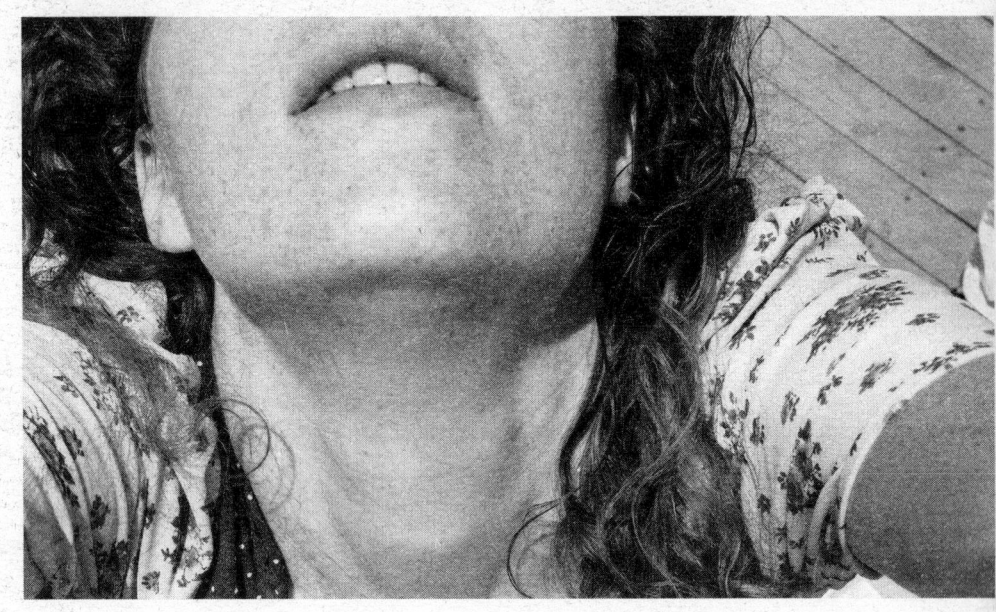

ACT III
DEATH

CHAPTER 26

Sick Nick and Music on the Rise

DECEMBER 1996

ALICE, MY YOUNG TEENAGED COCONSPIRATOR IN ALL THINGS MUSIC AND fashion, is visiting Montreal from London for the winter holidays. At her side is the love of her life, a gentle giant from Brixton named Frank. I've had the pleasure to see them a few times in the past couple years, meeting up on days off in a London pub while on tour in the United Kingdom, but it's been *years* since Alice and I have been in Montreal at the same time. This year all three of us are here at Christmastime. It's Frank's first visit to Alice's hometown, and he's eager to discover what Alice's young life in Montreal was like.

Alice was by far my most frequent weekend sleepover guest at Nick's house growing up. The most vivid memories I have of Nick involve Alice, like the homemade "TV"-show parties Nick hosted for my special kid occasions. Inspired by Nick's access to video devices, we made faux thrillers and game shows: "Psycho Juan" and "The Price Is Wrong."

So it makes sense for Alice and Frank to come with me to meet Nick for a drink downtown this holiday season. Walking through the snow and cold Montreal wind in our inadequate vintage leather boots and jackets, we meet up with him on Crescent Street, the bar strip that Nick has made legendary.

"Alice! How great to have you back!" Nick greets her. "How is ye olde London Town? Had any run-ins with Monty Python lately?"

"No, Nick, I have not," Alice laughs and mumbles, shy as always.

We chuckle down memory lane, mostly for Frank's sake. A couple of beers and snacks in, Nick changes the topic. "So, I have some news . . . ," he begins. "I went to the doctor for a checkup this week. You know how he has always been impressed with my good health, despite my *nontraditional* health regime of having a good time in bars . . ."

I sense a change of direction. His tone is less jovial, which is not like him.

" . . . but this time, he was concerned about a lump he found on my neck."

Nick raises his hand, holding a burning cigarette, up to the right side of his neck, and taps what I now see to be a bit of a bulge. It was hidden under some bloating that I'd suspected to be standard midlife puffiness.

"Turns out this is cancer."

He pauses and takes a drag of his cigarette.

Alice and I look at each other. Silently, we acknowledge that in some way we have always feared this moment. She was with me a decade ago when I dropped Nick's cigarettes down the sewer around the corner from this same bar. "Smoking will kill you," I had told him then.

I feel a numbness come over me, and I begin to float out of my body, into other parts of the room. *My father loves life so much. A bump on his neck can't really take him down, can it?* I wonder.

"Oh, no, Nick," I say. "Are they sure?"

"Yep. A biopsy has been done. It's definitely a tumor. Throat cancer . . ." He sounds upbeat, which is confusing.

My father, who relies on late-night stamina and very bad habits, is now entering a territory that may require a new lifestyle. One of health, healing, and relaxing. Can he do it? I'm not sure.

"Good news is it's treatable," he continues, "and I can start treatment immediately. Radiation for a couple months at the top of the new year. That should take care of it."

Alice and Frank remain silent, looking down into their beers. I'm glad they're here. I don't think Nick and I could have handled this level of vulnerability alone. Our whole life together has been in public. And Alice is like my sister, so it's possible he wants her here so I don't have to hear this news alone.

"Bottoms up! I'm not dead yet!" Nick lets out a huge laugh and wraps his hand around to pinch my bum with a wink. "I'm going to enjoy myself for the holidays and quit smoking as my New Year's resolution. This time for good!"

The evening grows late, with lively conversations with other bar patrons, just like old times. But a part of me stays tucked away, in a dark, silent place within.

When I share the news with my mother the next day, she responds like she's seen it coming since she fell for this wild man twenty-four years ago.

"Well, *shit*, he's *got* to quit smoking now!" she says stoically. A part of her seems to not want to take this information in. We do not dwell on it. A few days later I am boarding a flight back to Los Angeles, already a different young woman than the one who arrived home for the holidays.

Back in LA, it's sunny as usual. I take a cab home from LAX, an easy drive to Silverlake. I'm looking forward to unwinding in the lazy creative haze I left before the holidays.

"I'm home!" I call into the entryway when I open the front door. Silence. I poke my head into the rooms. All is tidy and quiet. I climb the stairs with my small suitcase and am surprised to see the door to Patty's room closed, which is unusual. We've never closed our bedroom doors before.

"Pat?" I knock on the door. "Patso? You asleep?"

No reply. I drag my bag into my room and press play on my answering machine.

"Hey! There's a fun holiday party at the Grand Royal offices! You should come! Call me," one friend says. *Beep.*

"Hey, Missy! Happy New Year; it's Brian. An exciting opportunity came in for you. Call the office!" *Beep.*

I flop on the bed. LA feels full of creative possibilities. For the first time I am relieved to be home in the city of fantasy, away from the reality of my hometown.

In the coming days I barely see Patty. When I do, she matter-of-factly explains she's been seeing someone new and has been staying with her. She doesn't share much detail or excitement around this new girl, which is out of character for her. She's been girl crazy and on the hunt since breaking up with the Seattle punk. Our connection feels strained, which also isn't typical. When I tell her about Nick's cancer, she tells me she's sorry. She and Nick share a similar sense of humor, and she loves him. We share a brief, tender hug on the stairs before she heads out yet again.

Patty is a full-time smoker herself, and I wonder if this news enlightens her. I hope so. I'm feeling concerned about all my hard-living friends right now and hating smoking more than ever.

Over the next couple of days I meet up with new LA friends, get sushi, catch a movie at Cinerama Dome, drink beers at dive bars, and go to Spaceland to see some bands. I mention to an older, more together musician friend of mine, who was born and raised here, that I'd like to find a therapist to work with in light of my father's cancer diagnosis. I've never been to therapy. This just instinctively feels like the right thing to do. I suspect his illness will be a lot for me to deal with, and I want to be prepared for the unknown. My friend recommends his Jungian therapist (bonus, she's a specialist on symbols and dreams!) who also works as an astrologer (double bonus, I'll get my chart done to offer her more context on my inner world!).

Nick's cancer will be hard enough in itself, but something else motivates me to find help. The fact that I am the daughter of an alcoholic is finally catching up with me and starting to mean something. Until now, it's been more of a vague concept. Now it feels more relevant. *Might there be a connection between this and my bandmates who also struggle with addiction?* I'm ready to find out.

The phone in my room rings dreadfully early one morning. I'm in bed, and I fumble to answer it. Through the french doors I can see another cloudless blue sky.

It's Brian Celler, the junior team member from Q-Prime management on the phone. Brian is a teddy-bear sweetheart who handles our day-to-day needs, making sure the travel team books what we want when we need it and keeping us up to speed on management, agencies, and label activities. Basically, he's our caretaker, and I am grateful for him and realize I had not called him back.

"Missy! How are you? How were the holidays?" He calls me and Courtney by the nicknames Missy and Clove, which makes me feel familial and loved and endears him to me even more.

"Back home was a little tough . . . My father has cancer . . ." I groggily fill him in.

We share some positive words about how good the treatments have gotten and what a fighter my father is. Yes, it will be okay.

"Well, I have some news that might cheer you up a bit," he says. "Ric Ocasek, from the Cars, has invited you to be the bass player on his upcoming solo album. The studio session starts next month at Electric Lady Land in New York.

"The rest of the band will be composed of other young musicians he's worked with as producer," Brian continues. "He's putting all the pieces together now, but his managers wanna know if you're in?"

I'm starting to wake up now. I loved working with Ric on "Gold Dust Woman." We forged a special musical connection on that project.

"Wow, that sounds fun! I've never made a record before. Are we sure *our* band will be okay with it?"

"Well, there are no songwriting sessions scheduled till Clove is finished with her Hollywood press junkets . . . so no conflicts," he reassures me. "I got your back on this, Missy; don't you worry. If you want to make this happen, I'll see to it."

This invitation couldn't come at a better time. I want to be playing music, and I miss New York. I long for late-night city streets to lead me to a clandestine romance. Los Angeles just doesn't have the same romance in the air.

✕

It's award season in Hollywood, and I'm catching glimpses of our lady on the red carpet. From management and from others who keep up with celebrity news, I hear that she is making a splash wherever she goes. Reviews of her portrayal of Althea Flynt, Larry's girlfriend turned wife, are across-the-board raves.

Variety writes, "Love is the revelation here, as she delivers an impulsive, nakedly emotional, quicksilver turn that brings the central romance alive whenever she's onscreen. She's a natural, the camera loves her, and she manages to express Althea's key components of brashness, insecurity, emotional fidelity and lust for life."

Courtney is doing well professionally and that makes her happy, so I know that me heading into the studio with some nonthreatening men will not stir up anything at all. When I tell Patty the news, she heads to the stereo to blast the Cars' "Just What I Needed." The pop-music fan in her spins us into a fun moment of lip-synching.

This moment almost feels normal. Almost. Something in her and between us has changed in the past couple of months, something I can't quite pin down. In the days before I leave I try to reconnect with her, but she is often out, in bed early, or sleeping late. I suspect there's something she's not telling me. I ask if there's anything wrong, but she shrugs it off with a complaint about the girl she's dating.

"I'm not sure if I really like her, but she's really into me and has been hard to shake," she explains.

It's definitely not a fiery romance, but maybe there's something about a stable normal girl, not one in a band, or the unattainable supermodel, but one who can take care of Patty that might be good?

In New York I'm booked into a two-room suite at the Gramercy Park Hotel. It's my favorite place in the city to stay and conveniently located a block away from the home Ric shares with his gorgeous wife, supermodel Paulina Porizkova, and their children. We kick off the session with a family dinner in the cozy kitchen of their classic stone town house. I meet my bandmates for the session here.

Ira Elliot is the drummer of Nada Surf whose hit song "Popular," which Ric produced, is still ringing through the radio waves a year later. Brian Baker is the guitar player for the SoCal pop-punk band Bad Religion and, more notably to me, originally from the band Minor Threat, the founders of the legendary Dischord DIY music scene in Washington, DC.

But the secret weapon for the session is Greg Hawkes, original keyboard player of the Cars. The Cars' legacy as New Wave pioneers was built on perfect pop songwriting and innovative synth sounds and hooks, so having these two members leading us "young'uns" sounds great to me.

The session spans about two weeks in the colorful big room at Electric Lady Studios in Greenwich Village that once held the genius of Jimi Hendrix. Every song is easy to learn, is fun to play, and allows me to experiment with melodic bass hooks. I'm involved with every part of the recording process, sitting in the control room excited by what I hear when Ric and Brian do their guitars and—most unique and new to me—hearing a synth wizard shower the otherwise pop-rock tracks with liquid textures and shiny frequencies.

I'm so inspired by the music that I feel melodies and rhythms coursing through me even in my sleep. In my hotel room in the mornings while I wait for room service to bring my breakfast, I pick up my bass. The rush I get as creative expression courses from my mind to my fingertips is almost overwhelming.

Bass guitars have four strings, E, A, D, G, as opposed to a guitar's six strings, and a bass is tuned one octave lower than the lowest-pitched four strings of a guitar. Guitar strings are thin and close to each other to make it easy to play them together as chords. The strings on a bass are heavy and set far apart from one another and are traditionally played one at a time. Singer/songwriters write on guitars because chords make overtones and produce a full rainbow of notes, whereas a single note doesn't offer a full range of melody options to pull from. So, as I sit in my hotel room, I resort to downstroke strumming the D and G strings together, like a guitar. I make melodies on the high octaves of the G string, while letting the D string ring out.

D is my favorite note and always has been. I'm attracted to her most when composing a new melody. A melancholic arrangement emerges as I play around with these two strings, and my first full song, written top to bottom, comes out of me one morning.

> *Last word, last card I said*
> *Every last card from your desire deck*
> *And I need you to know that I had you,*
> *But I've got good news for you*
> *I need me too.*

I've only been playing the bass for five years, first with free-flowing creativity in Tinker and then in Hole, primarily playing their songs from 1994 until now. My own skills and expression have been muzzled, and it's been deeply frustrating. I haven't been touching my bass in much of a creatively free way in the past three years—mostly repeating the same parts over and over. I imagine it's not unlike being in a loveless relationship, or like working as a stripper, performing sexualized acts for the public without any love attached to the act. I realize now this has not been healthy for me, as I start expanding during these tender two weeks at Electric Lady.

To have this channel open up between me and the endless musical equations and formulas that can be strung together to create something new and so personal feels as sacred as being connected to the universe or to a god. My body is fully engaged and throbbing with pleasure and purpose.

I wonder if this is how some people feel about sex? I'm not one for the raw act of sex. Intercourse isn't something that turns me on. I don't want anyone inside me for a few reasons: unwanted pregnancy and STDs. I had vowed to myself in recent years to have sex only with someone worthy to make a baby or a life with. I wasn't raised religious. This was my own sense of individual purpose. And possibly a direct reaction to being pursued by many men.

But I feel something similar to sexual pleasure when I'm connecting with someone romantically through words, ideas, hands, and lips. It's an attempt to create a bridge between two lone specks in the universe. Only I'm doing it now with my bass and the melodic compositions she delivers when I give her the proper attention. When I take time to listen, to feel, and to find my own way around the fretboard, I find meaning and love. For the first time as a musician, I feel held, and heard—by me and my bass.

When all the tracks are laid for the album, Ric invites me to sing backups on a few songs. "You've got a great voice, Melissa. Just play around and have fun," he says. The result makes for the first single on *Troubalizing* that will launch the album. "Hang on Tight" features me singing an angelic hook— *Hang on tight. You're running around with your face in the ground*—that wraps around Ric's signature talking style.

Like a neglected child being cared for, or a lonely woman being touched for the first time in years, I find myself melting from the tenderness Ric shows me as a producer and fellow musician. I can't help but wonder what it would be like to play in a band that functioned like this all the time. Caring, happy, healthy, full of ideas . . . The contrast is profound, and it begins to hurt.

"How are you feeling?" I ask Nick from the hotel phone. I'm afraid of the answer, but I need to know. "Are there any side effects from the treatment?"

"It's been okay," he says. I can tell I woke him. "My throat burns, and it hurts to drink any alcohol . . . and I'm still not smoking. I've been staying in this week, and taking lots of naps."

"Well, it's important to rest," I say. "I'll come home to visit next month. The band is supposed to record our new album this summer, but we still have a lot of songs to write." I tell him I've heard that Billy Corgan is coming to LA to try to write some new songs with us. I always fill him in a bit on the superficial business of Hole, but never the undercurrents.

"The Big Pumpkin! He's back—that's fantastic!" Nick perks up. "Well, Courtney's been making a real splash on the red carpets. Good for her. She's a fighter, and she can act! She deserves it." With that we say goodbye.

It's not fair that so many people I'm around play with a death wish. It's disrespectful to my father, who loves life as much as he does. When I think about going back into the dysfunctional Hole underworld, I dread going back to the strained writing process and, even worse, being around people for whom it seems to be a struggle just to stay alive.

"Kurt Cobain Had a Shotgun, and I Had Cigarettes"

The girl on the phone sounded sweet and sincere, expressing her sympathy.

Her mother had read two weeks ago in this column that I had cancer. The girl told me she had spoken to me once before, almost a year ago, when she called up to ask to speak to my daughter because she liked Melissa's band. The girl sounded as if she was perhaps 13 years old, and she presumed I remembered our last conversation. She sounded a bit nervous, so to be polite I pretended I remembered her. Frankly, I was really touched that she felt compelled to call me and express her sympathies.

We exchanged pleasantries for a minute or two, then she really threw me for a loop when she blurted out: "Do you think it has anything to do with Kurt Cobain's death?"

Well, I know people are into conspiracy theories again, and kids are into the X-Files, morbid things about death and stuff like that, but this was such a preposterous connection, so out of left field, that for once I felt at a loss for words.

Of course, I didn't want to insult her the way I would if an adult had asked me something similar, so I hemmed and hawed and stammered something about there being a world of difference between blue cheese and baseball.

And then, just as we were about to ring off our conversation something occurred to me.

"Yes, there is a connection, or at least something similar," I said. "You see, Kurt had a smoking gun. I had smoking cigarettes."

—Nick Auf der Maur, column for the Montreal Gazette, January 29, 1997

CHAPTER 27

Making *Celebrity Skin*

SPRING 1997

"Where did you get *these*?!"

This is the first full sentence I dare utter to Stevie Nicks. Respectfully, I pick up one of the dozen suede high-heeled platform knee-high boots lined up in a perfect row, like a rainbow of earth-tone leather and suede, in a labyrinth of shelves and racks.

"Oh! Pasquale made most of them," Stevie says. She smiles like she's making me privy to an insider secret. "He's in the foothills in East LA. You've gotta call him. He'll make all your boot dreams come true!"

Until now, Stevie Nicks was entirely Courtney's fetish. The high priestess of rock became her muse after Courtney moved to Los Angeles, got clean for Hollywood, and became determined to make a hit follow-up record. Hole's new album is meant to be Courtney's "California" album, her love letter to the golden and perverse myths of the state. And there's no female rock star who's more California than Stevie Nicks.

I'm relieved that Courtney has found her vision for the album, which allows us to move forward. This comes perfectly timed with the twenty-fifth anniversary of Fleetwood Mac's *Tusk*, which is being celebrated with a remastered release of the album and a VH1-televised performance. Hole was invited to a private run-through of the upcoming show in the hope of inspiring our upcoming recording session.

This is how Stevie, Courtney, and I have wound up together in what amounts to a giant closet in the belly of an industrial-size bunker behind a rehearsal studio in the San Fernando Valley.

Management has arranged this meeting for us and also hired powerhouse producer Michael Beinhorn to help Hole create the most polished hit album possible. He's produced albums that generated breakout radio hits for Soundgarden and Soul Asylum, and the hope is he can do the same for us.

"Listen closely to the kick drum and the bass," Beinhorn tells us as we watch Fleetwood Mac rehearse. "It's the space in *between* that makes this rhythm section pop masters."

Patty and I listen closely, squinting to see across the big rehearsal room. We focus on the subtle kick-drum moves of drummer Mick Fleetwood, who looks like a wizard, and the fingers of humble hobbit bass player John McVie. I learn more about pop music in one sitting than I ever have before. The trick is to make the music brilliantly simple, especially when it comes to the rhythm section. It's simple, I realize, but not easy.

In the past couple of months since I returned to LA, much shit has happened. The Silverlake fantasy home has gone dark. Patty pretty much checked out, physically and emotionally, in my absence. My instincts hadn't been wrong. She'd been hiding on-again, off-again heroin use for the last many months.

This part of the story is still painful for me to revisit, and I believe the details of Patty's deterioration are hers to tell. She'll later write about this time in her memoir, *Hit So Hard*:

> Melissa came back from her trips home to find that I had changed. "You started to shut the door," is how she put it, referring to the door to my bedroom, which we both used to keep open so we could shout across the hall to each other. Literally and figuratively, I shut her out. What had once been a sisterhood now felt merely polite. I was so glad to see her when she got back, but I was in the thick of a binge and I knew Melissa couldn't know about it.

But she did, of course. I couldn't hide the obvious. I wanted to be high so I avoided talking with people who might require an upbeat demeanor during our conversation, or expect sophisticated answers to complicated questions, such as, "Where were you last night?"

Oh, I gave it my all anyway, always projecting my voice in an over-the-top greeting (how I imagined a sober person might sound, like I was auditioning for the school play). I kept it simple with Melissa.

I learned what it felt like to be lied to on a regular basis, and it was terrible. I had no experience with this level of betrayal of trust. Weeks of this led me to finally draw a line and rat her out to Courtney and management. It was a relief when management stepped in. They booked Patty into a thirty-day rehab program at a treatment center in Pasadena, sent a car for her, and paid for it all. She gracefully agreed to go and get clean in time to make our next record.

I went to visit her a couple of times in the sunny garden visiting center. The Patty I'd known was not the one who showed up. This Patty held herself differently, like a dog that was ashamed of destroying the couch. She seemed to embody shame, guilt, and embarrassment all at once.

"How are you feeling?" I asked her. Patty and I didn't usually talk openly about our problems. Like my father, she preferred to stay superficial rather than deep. But I wanted to know how all this started and what had happened in the months that we had drifted apart.

She stared at her feet. She couldn't look me in the eye. "I fucked up," she said. "I couldn't help myself. And the girl was a bad influence. But I blame myself. I gotta clean up."

She told me that while I was in Montreal for the Christmas holidays she had helped her brother out by letting him go through withdrawal from heroin in our downstairs guest room. During that time, she too had begun to slip. She admitted that the mysterious girl she had been seeing the past few months convinced her that she could keep a high-functioning habit secret by smoking heroin instead of injecting. It didn't work. She got hooked deep.

Sitting with this version of Patty was like meeting a bad zombie ghost of our *Chuckles Show* host. It was tragic to see her drained of any laughs and light. And it chilled me to the bone to be faced with evidence of what could happen so quickly, under a shared roof.

Courtney, by contrast, has gotten her shit together. Her Hollywood phase is now in full effect. She chain-smokes Marlboro Lights instead of the harsher Reds, goes to the beach at seven in the morning with a personal trainer, and then goes to an audition before gracing us at the studio to crank out the hits. She's beaming and in love with Hollywood actor Edward Norton, who completes her new look.

It is as remarkable and stark of a transition as Patty's. Fucking wild are these women that I have fallen into a band with.

It's been hard enough to be in a band that's overshadowed by the celebrity punk widow of the biggest rock star in the world. But now a Hollywood movie star? Courtney is a whole new person. She's now a presenter at the Oscars, nominated for a Golden Globe, and on the cover of mainstream celebrity magazines, not just music magazines. She doesn't even look like she's in a rock band anymore. How is this going to play out? It's anyone's guess at this point.

By now it's been three years since *Live Through This* was released, and management and the record label are becoming impatient. They recognize the star power that comes with Courtney's Hollywood blitz, but they also need her to make records. That's where her career has been to this point and where the money is for managers, agents, and record labels—and for her band. Money from touring, record sales, and radio play. The pressure is on us to produce a follow-up.

Unfortunately, there is no real joy in writing songs together. Even more morose is that in our months off, we have each surrendered to this solemn knowledge and have been coping with it in our own ways. Going into the studio together now feels like being forced into an arranged marriage to get the job done.

✗

All of our gear is set up and ready for us at the spacious SIR studio in Hollywood. So is a week with Billy Corgan. He's been brought in to move this project along. Knowing Courtney as well as he does, Billy is aware of her talents and her limitations. His love for her is true, and although they have never written together before there's no doubt he'll get songs out of us.

I'm always happy to see him, but the last thing we want or need right now is for a much more successful male peer to come in and fix this band. For one thing, it perpetuates the myth that women in rock and roll need men in order to succeed. And on a more personal level, Hole is already sick enough of the whole world thinking that Kurt Cobain wrote the songs on *Live Through This*. Whenever some asshole says that to me, my answer is, *That makes no sense*. With due respect to Kurt, Hole's songs are so simple that no one would need him to write them. Some of them, like "Miss World," an amazing anthem of our time, are just ONE RIFF. A lot of people can write a pop-rock song like that. The sophisticated thing about Hole's songs is Courtney's lyrics and her delivery. She can do that effortlessly. She would have been more likely to write Kurt's lyrics than he would have been to write her music, and no one ever suggested that Courtney wrote Kurt's songs.

In light of all this, I can't believe Courtney is going to let Billy come in now, especially after all the personal drama they've been through. But she wants to make a Top 40 record, and this is how it's done. You hire the hit doctors and the producers, and you swallow your ego and bring in the guy who can help. It's the exact opposite of what I want, which is to be myself and to believe I'm good enough whether two people like me or two million people like me. But I'm in the minority here.

Eric, as the band's cofounder and the boyfriend whom Courtney left for Billy before she left Billy for Kurt, has the most right to take issue with this plan, but he appears at peace with it. These are not extended conversations we have as a band. Things just seem to happen, without any detailed discussion or explanation.

In the studio with us, Billy is a gentle alpha. His professionalism and songwriting talent are well known, and he knows how to get shit done. He plows through existing guitar riffs and song drafts, and from his brief time with us the kernels of some great songs emerge, including "Celebrity Skin" and "Malibu," which will become the two hit singles from the album.

Patty is fresh out of rehab and on her best behavior, which is quiet and distant at best. Smoking and caffeine are her most engaged pastimes when she's behind her drum kit or at the wheel of her vintage Mercedes as she drives between our house and the rehearsal space. She doesn't venture much beyond these two sites. It's hard for us to be happy together when we're in the band environment. The general malaise of the band is enough to prevent us from having fun or sharing anything meaningful, and there's an underlying vulnerability and shame around her coming clean.

Patty and I are mostly expected to wait on the sidelines while song arrangements are being worked out on the guitars, but most of the magic happens for Courtney when we're fleshing the riffs out with volume, rhythmic pulse, and grit. She's always performing like it's her last night onstage in front of thousands. That's what gets her ideas flowing. Countless hours are spent playing the same two parts back to back—verse, chorus, verse, chorus, louder, softer, louder, softer—in a hypnotic rotation. The pace is strangely meditative and healing, connecting us in the only way we can find connection right now.

The sessions with Billy go quickly and efficiently. New songs begin to appear. Patty and I, in a rare moment of inspiration, offer some drum and bass ideas of our own that we turn into songs: "Awful," which Courtney will refer to as "Melissa and Patty's riff" and "Use Once and Destroy," which Courtney will forever call "Melissa's song." The latter is one of my favorites on the album, not only because it is bass-driven and represents what I would've brought into my own band if I had full creative freedom, but also because it utilizes Courtney's inspired ode to Marie Antoinette from New Orleans:

> *All dressed in red, always the bride*
> *Off with her head, all dressed in white*
> *Off with her head*

We're in the midst of a group writing session when Billy turns to me and asks, "Melissa, do you have any songs?"

His question catches me off guard. Since my songwriting revelation at the Gramercy Park Hotel, I've continued writing at home alone, but I haven't shared these songs with anyone yet.

"I've recorded a few shitty demos . . . ," I reply quietly. I hope my voice hides my nervousness. The idea of something as personal as my own music entering the vortex of this band unnerves me. But this is Billy asking, the person who inspired my whole journey in music and brought me to this band. His opinion means more to me than anyone's.

"Great. Bring them in tomorrow," Billy casually says, before moving on to the next task.

The next day I meet Billy before rehearsal. Playing for the man who awakened a music explosion in my heart years ago makes me sweat—and I am literally a girl who doesn't sweat. He listens closely, gives simple supportive comments, and effortlessly selects "Good News," my first song.

"This one is great," he says. "It's a contender for the record."

Later that day we play "Good News" for the whole band. "Oh, I love it, Melissa—so pop, so Christie McVie!" Patty says. Billy adds it to the growing lists of Hole songs to share with our big-shot producer who'll be arriving soon.

And just like that, a piece of my heart finds a place in this band. And with help from my spiritual fucking cowboy, no less! Once in a while the world is a beautiful and poetic place, even when you are playing in the band Hole.

Michael Beinhorn is known to make hits, which makes him very expensive to hire. But the label has approved a ridiculous, practically open-ended budget to get this record made.

Soundgarden's and Soul Asylum's mainstream popularity created a successful, predictable formula that we are now expected to repeat. It's to start with a grungy first couple of records and time "in the van" (on the road), which then rightfully earns a band the street cred it needs to build up enough momentum to launch into "hit-radio" territory, a.k.a. Top 40.

None of this was part of my equation when I fell in love with music, and joining the ranks of what seems to be more and more trash out there now is not my idea of cool. So many bands are popping up out of nowhere now and going from 0 to 100 overnight. For the past couple of years, the machine has been signing anyone with long hair, a plaid shirt, and a guitar. Grunge one-hit wonders have been exploding out of the major-label machines.

My creative frustrations and deep discouragement around all this inspire me to take on a role of angel protector for some of my favorite still "unsigned" bands. Brainiac and Girls Against Boys are both on Touch and Go, the solid indie label I'd once aspired to sign with. I warn them to avoid temptation from the vapid, soul-crushing big-label system and consider sticking with the music-loving indie-label people who've proved themselves over and over again.

This sense of urgency and warning is amplified by a tragedy in the late spring. While we're smack in the thick of making this corporate-drama album, I get a call one morning before sunrise from a friend in Dayton, Ohio. In tears he tells me that Timmy Taylor, the visionary glam punk front man of Brainiac, just died in a car accident in his hometown. He was driving home late at night from a party, celebrating the band's signing away of their souls to Interscope Records after an aggressive bidding war between a handful of majors, when he lost control of his car and crashed into a lamppost. His car burst into flames. It was devastating to hear and meant the end of Brainiac. A techno pop-art treasure of our generation was stopped dead in its tracks at the height of its creativity.

Simultaneously, big local hometown news lands on my doorstep in the form of my childhood sweetheart, Rufus Wainwright, who moves into our guest quarters. Rufus has been discovered in a Montreal jazz bar and is stepping into the big leagues as one of the first signings to DreamWorks, David Geffen's new imprint label. Wunderkind producer John Brion has been lined up to make the record in a glorious studio, with a full orchestra to call on.

Rufus's once cute big ego has inflated out of control. So have his sex, drug, and debaucherous tendencies. So now Rufus is abusing crystal meth on the ground floor, while Patty is just barely over shooting heroin on the second floor. The guest room is turning into a questionable-pastimes haven.

Rufus manages to carry his self-destruction well. And honestly, he's the least of my concerns. I simply accept that he's decadent, and I'm happy that he's been signed; after all, he's hands down one of the most talented musicians I know—and being famous is all he ever wanted. Or maybe as shit keeps piling up, my patience is beginning to wane, and I just don't have the bandwidth to worry about another person playing with fire.

Less than a week later, Jeff Buckley dies in a mysterious drowning in Memphis. The "curse" surrounding some of the most extraordinary musicians of my generation feels ominous and real. Darkness presses down harder on me and on my feelings about the direction of our once inspired music scene.

On day one with Beinhorn we immediately have a sense of what working with him will be like. He is an odd duck, short and muscular and dressed all in black with very small wire-frame glasses. He's clearly a confident leader, professional but eccentric, a bit of a mad scientist with tunnel-vision focus. His goal is to create hit after hit that will land well with the current pinnacle of power in the industry, which is Radio. These radio gods are omnipresent in our world. They can make your career or leave you in the dust.

Beinhorn tells us that he has booked us into his favorite luxury studio, Conway Studios in Hollywood. A studio like this costs upwards of many thousands of dollars a day. Once the money clock is turned on, we're under big financial pressure in addition to hitmaking pressure. The stakes just shot up even higher, and it's intense.

Thanks to our sessions with Billy and preproduction with Beinhorn, our songs are written and ready to go by the time we head into the studio. In this type of recording, each band member tapes their parts individually.

Drums always go first, because they're the foundation of each song. Once the drums are laid down, the bass track is next—the glue that holds all the parts together. Guitars, which are numerous in rock music, follow. Multiple layers, textures, and solos are included. In Eric's case these tracks are graceful and subtle rather than the shrill ego type.

The icing on top is the vocals, which go last. Courtney has months before she'll need to show up and deliver. In the meantime, she's fully occupied with her newly reformed Hollywood lifestyle.

With a big layer cake to create, Patty is first up in the hot seat. She is still emotionally fragile, and I can't help but feel nervous for her. Her general mood has been humble and subdued since rehab. I sense an underlying apologetic shame with all she does. I'm concerned about how wounded Patty will cope with these drumming demands. She's under great pressure, in a very expensive studio, with what—we are beginning to realize—is a zero-tolerance producer who expects nothing but perfection.

Recording studio, Los Angeles, 1997.

Beinhorn expects Patty to hit her drums perfectly, like a machine.* She's not at the top of her game, but she *wrote* these drum parts and she knows them inside out. But under the pressure of trying to deliver what Beinhorn wants from her, she buckles.

Beinhorn, we learn, has a reputation of firing drummers for recordings and bringing in the same go-to ghost drummer he uses on some of his albums. At first, during a couple of days of endless take after take, we think he's riding Patty hard to warm her up and check the sounds of the drums more. Before long, it begins to seem like he's not satisfied with what he is hearing.

Patty believes she's gotten caught up in an intentional hit job and that Beinhorn has wanted her out to begin with.

"He's an asshole. He's an asshole! He's making me fuck up. He's not letting me get my parts done!" she says. "He wants me out, to bring an ape with a mullet in to play my parts!" She gets shakier and more upset by the day.

It seems terrible to be putting her through this endurance test right now, and nobody's really there to protect her. Courtney is rarely around. Eric and I are there more, but it's not in either of our natures to stand up to authority. There's room for only one authority figure in this band, and she is busy doing other things.

I can sense Patty is slipping, giving up, giving in, and I know very well that she uses drugs to cope with stress. Over the course of just one week I watch her become a shell of herself, giving up before she can succeed, if that's even possible, because Beinhorn does seem impossible to please. His vibe is military general without much room for personal feelings or vulnerabilities or weaknesses.

"We're gonna have to fix this," he starts saying. "Chop it up; put it through some programs. I'll fix it."

---

* Again, this part of the story is heart-wrenching, and is not really mine to tell. I'll do my best to recount it from my slightly removed perspective, and I recommend you read Patty's own detailed account of it in *Hit So Hard*.

This talk about cutting things and using computers to fix it is humiliating to Patty. It suggests that she can't do her job, can't play the parts she *wrote*. She prides herself on being a great drummer, something that girls aren't known for.

Management and the record label place all their trust in a producer, so no one on the greater team is targeting Patty outright. It's just a bad combination of a producer's standards, the corroded soul of a band willing to follow whatever it takes to be "big," and a very broken and vulnerable drummer. After a few weeks of this torture for Patty, Beinhorn breaks it to the rest of us that Patty "just doesn't cut it."

"I'm gonna fly my guy Dean in," he informs us nonchalantly. "He's played on all Ozzy's solo albums. He'll have this done in two days, max."

He doesn't even flinch when he says this. He has no understanding of the emotional landscape of this band or that the equivalent of a nuclear bomb has just been dropped on our beloved, if broken, Patty, our female drummer, punk rocker, and gay-pride hero.

Understandably, she's destroyed. It's heartbreaking to watch.

At the band meeting where he explains this to us, Courtney is sober and the most together I've known her to be up to this point. Being Ms. Hollywood and a perfectionist, she sees this as a very matter-of-fact professional decision.

"We're not going to tell anyone," she says to Patty, trying to reason with her. "They're called 'ghost drummers' for a reason. No one's going to know that he played on this. Don't worry, Pat . . ."

But it's no use. "Fuck this shit! Hate this shit!" Patty shouts, storming out of the meeting.

I can defend Patty by accusing the producer of being heartless and missing the point of the sacred makeup of a band. I can even try to plead with him that this could kill her. But I know that nothing I say is going to change this situation. The machine is too big. Courtney's been convinced by the powers that be, and there is no way I can change anybody's decisions. I am not powerful enough. I'm not even a legal founding member of the band. It's up to Eric and Courtney.

This shit is out of your control, Melissa. Ironically, Patty was the one who told me this in Paris.

Just as with the Paris abscess situation, when I first faced the reality of living with junkies and being part of the enabling machine, I can either leave and go back to Montreal in protest or finish what I started. I've actually worked hard on this record by this point, and I would like to see it through.

At the same time, I want to support Patty, but she makes it impossible for someone like me to comfort her. She's clearly using drugs again and has disappeared. I hardly see her at home. There's still the illusion that she will come back in a few months and be "all better again" when the record is finished and the promotion machine starts up with photo and video shoots, but deep down I know that's not going to happen. She's not going to survive this blow.

To cope with all this, I find an escape in a slightly deranged romance. There's a very famous Hollywood actor I've met a few times at intimate VIP dinners, and I experiment with a behind-the-cloak-of-night illicit affair. He shows up way after dark in the yellow muscle car he calls the Banana and waits for me. He's a very sexy man of mystery and deep pain, which is all too tempting. My kinda guy!

I know he's bad news. But everything feels like bad news nowadays, so communing with others who share that melancholia seems to suit me well right now. This incestuous Hollywood movie-star fling seems like yet another symptom of the drama-filled, sad, vapid life I am beginning to lead. It's such a cliché and so far from the girl I was when I moved here.

I pretty much won't see Patty again for more than a decade, with the exception of the album-cover photo shoot. She does show up for it, but by then she's already turned into a ghostly version of the Patty I knew. The saga of the ghost drummer turns the real drummer into a ghost, and a part of me disappears forever, too.

CHAPTER 28

My Bass and the Rise of the Digital Soul-Sucking Monster

SUMMER 1997

BASS TIME. IT WAS NOW MY TURN FOR THE ALBUM, THE SECOND LAYER OF the cake. The ghost drummer with a mullet had already come and gone, shadowing Patty, who was never home anymore. She was out of communication with everyone.

I arrived on the appointed day to record a full album of bass playing in a professional studio, onto two-inch tape, through the highest-quality preamps, mics, and vintage tube amplifiers. I stood tall for the occasion, in vintage strappy high heels, a suede miniskirt, and a tiny crop top. I was prepared for battle.

"I've never met a bass player who looks like you," the gentle British engineer said on my first day of tracking. I didn't take his comments as creepy or sexual, just as truth that it's not a common look for a rock bass player. He'd been around the block with Rush, Alice Cooper, Suicidal Tendencies, and Ozzy Osbourne, so he would know.

For the next week my bass became my sword, and the wall of sound that came out of her my shield. I created a force field I wanted to project across the room to include every member of our Hole army, across the City of Broken Angels and Evil Empire Dictators, across a nation that seemed to lack any systems to nurture and protect the most common needs of its citizens, a nation that doesn't provide the decency of affordable health care or schooling. The nation my mother left in protest in the 1960s and the one my father despised and told me I must always leave and return home. This sound wave built me a psychedelic dream-beam bridge all the way from Los Angeles back to my majestic city of Montreal, where the ghost of the girl I used to be waited for me after my long upside-down journey away from and back to home.

I dug deep into Beinhorn's military vigor. He whacked a drumstick against the soft padded edge of the recording console with all his might in an effort to push me along.

"PUSH! Ride the TOP of the drums!" he belted with a big smile. He played me rare recordings of Led Zeppelin soundboard mixes, just drums and bass. I began to *see* the placement between Bonham's wild swinging bass-drum beats and John Paul Jones's unrelenting melodic bass-guitar movements. I became the heart of a rhythm section in that studio. I felt it grow BIG inside me, filling me with light, with power, with music. With love of my life and myself.

I aced my bass parts with more passion and success and vigor than I'd ever displayed. I was performing for no one but myself. This one was for me.

Good news for you, I need me too.

This alchemic process of tracking music began to change me. I felt my inner strength, desires, and abilities emerging in real time. In that studio, I became one with myself for the first time. Knowing what I was born to do and what I was capable of in this big bad world. It was an arrival that was long overdue.

Celebrity Skin became my highest recording achievement as a bass player to this day.

I was loving everything about my musical experience with the band.

I was hating everything about my personal experience in the band.

Both things were equally true at this time.

✕

After finishing my bass parts, I faced months of free time while the wall of guitars was built for Courtney to spin her intricate web of guttural social commentary.

I would swing by the studio from time to time to check out the process. Eric was deep in, as meticulous as ever. The sounds he produced were gorgeous. I hoped he was having his moment, stepping into his power light, as I just had. He is, by all means, an overlooked guitar player and songwriter of our generation, with incredible work on all three Hole records. But like me, how could he shine in a shadow of someone so large, who *also* struggled to be recognized for her talent?

✗

I was sipping on a fresh juice in Conway Studio's tropical courtyard one day, chatting with studio staff, when I noticed a couple of young men making trips in and out of our studio room with big boxes under their arms.

"Who are these guys in black?" I asked Beinhorn. "What's in the boxes?"

He launched into a tech monologue about a topic even more alien to me than Hollywood. From what I could gather, a new digital world was landing upon us musicians. It was called Pro Tools, a digital recording process that was developed in the early 1990s. The more user-friendly version 2 had just arrived, and Beinhorn planned on applying it to our masterpiece. Our recorded tracks were right now being transferred onto a digital hard drive that would be driven to a compound up in the Hollywood Hills, where they would be transferred into Pro Tools to get "polished."

His monotonous lesson started to really creep me out. It was hard to believe this machine would make our album even more perfect than what an as-good-as-it-gets studio session could offer. What could possibly be better than the glorious old analog board and the abundance of two-inch tape, not to mention the rainbow-ribbon vintage microphones and the endless positions in the room that captured every angle of sound? How could moving the sound into a box smaller than a toaster make it better? I feared how much "better" this album could get.

"Can I visit this tech palace to learn more about this exciting new technology?" I asked. I was semimocking, but it was also an honest request.

I drove my 1969 Cougar up a steep, windy hill off of Runyon Canyon and pulled up to a modern white minimansion. It looked like something right out of *Miami Vice*.

"Hey, you must be Melissa," a young man greeted me. "Welcome to our sound lab."

He was kinda cute, dressed in black with slicked-back hair. I followed him into the main quarters of the big house. What would have been a living room with wall-to-wall white carpeting had been fashioned into a large space littered with workstations and more men in black working at large computer screens. The Miami vibes and ultra-focused worker bees hinted at cocaine. I kept my eyes peeled for mirrors and razor blades.

The guy introduced me to a tech who looked just like him. "Let me show you what I'm working on," the clone of the first guy offered, eager to impress.

I was confident that I'd played my bass parts perfectly. Michael had told me as much and had no complaints. So what more could be done with them? This whole setup reeked of fake shit.

The tech zoomed in on his computer screen to show me sound waves that represented the drum and bass tracks. There were short, colorful blobs for short sounds and long blobs for long, sustained sounds. He zoomed in and out to show me how the drums and bass were represented by visual sound waves mapping out the structure of the whole song. As a visual person, I had to admit that seeing the full image of the song was kind of cool.

"I'm making sure that every kick drum and every bass note line up perfectly like a machine," he explained. "Beinhorn likes things to be perfect."

My understanding of sonics and engineering was limited, but I understood on an emotional level that this threatened to take the humans out of our album. "What about the human touch?" I asked. At this point I wasn't hiding my confusion. "Won't it wipe out the magic? Like sterilizing feelings that come from human imperfection?"

He stared at me with a blank expression. I guess he was just a technician who had been put on the job without any knowledge of why sometimes imperfect might be better than perfect.

As I got back into my car, I couldn't shake the feeling that too much money, too much technology, too much fame and ambition were corroding the soul of the band.

I turned the chunky key into the stiff ignition of my vintage vehicle. Her purring hum of an engine, the sound of a rugged, tried-and-true machine of the past, drowned my disdain for the future. Still, as I drove away, I knew that the rise of a digital beast, the Evil Empire, was upon us.

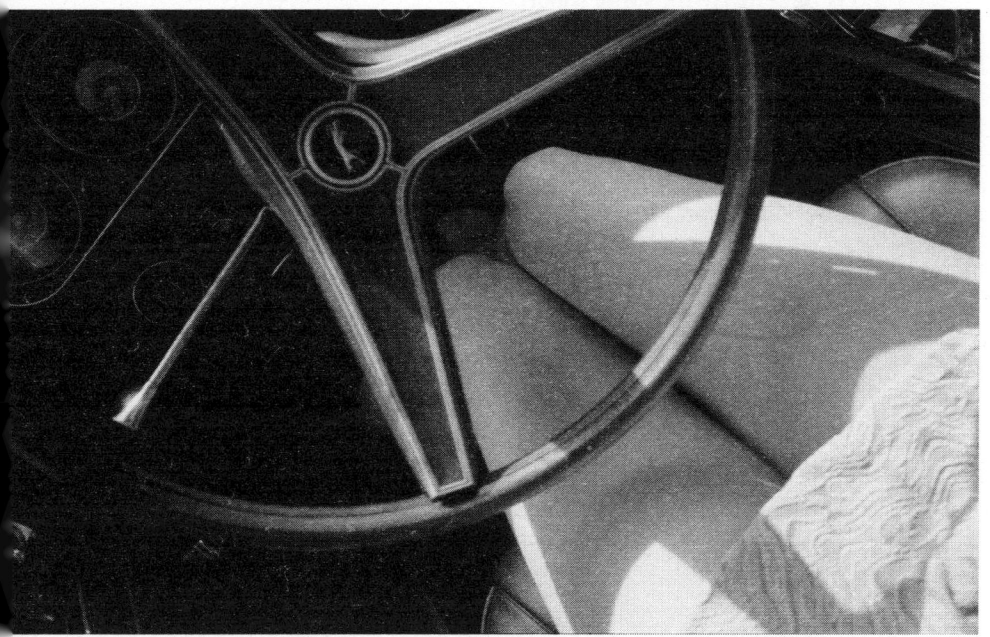

Self-portrait in Mercury Cougar, 1997.

Romantic-Comedy Interlude

A Play in Three Acts, Starring Adam Sandler,
Chris Farley, Ben Stiller, and Owen Wilson
(with a Cameo by Jim Carrey)

During my melancholic years in Hole, I was lucky enough to brush shoulders with the greatest comedians of our generation. Thank the gods of comedy for some relief!

Act One

SoHo, New York City: On the night of Hole's run-through performance for *Saturday Night Live*, the producers arrange an odd double date (someone's inside joke?) for Courtney and me with Adam Sandler and Chris Farley. We eat some Asian fusion in SoHo, then head to an empty club. The wonderfully warm and courteous Sandler grabs a couple Sam Adams beers to chat with me about Canadian comedy. Across the room, Farley and Courtney roll around wildly on an otherwise empty, illuminated discotheque dance floor. This vision of them giggling with absolute awkward joy is burned in my memory forever.

Act Two

Ben Stiller invites me on a double date, along with his friend actor Owen Wilson and Owen's pretty model girlfriend. We see *Titanic* at the Mann's Chinese. Blockbuster relevance is way over my indie-art head, and over dinner at Musso & Franks afterward, I can't keep up with the Hollywood trivia game. Romance never strikes between me and Ben, but that does not stop him from being an upstanding gentleman. In light of my father's cancer diagnosis, he sends me an advance copy of a book about SCTV, our beloved Canadian late-night sketch-comedy show, as a gift to my ailing father. This kind gesture leaves a permanent mark of love for him on my heart.

Act Three

Courtney plays the lead actress in *Man on the Moon*, the Andy Kaufman story starring Jim Carrey. She brings me as her guest to a fancy Hollywood film party at Donatella Versace's home. While she's busy making the rounds, I find a Victorian love seat to sip champagne on. I'm dressed in my most romantic vintage silk slip.

From across the room, Jim Carrey sends me a great compliment. "*You. Are. Art. Art on a chair.*"

My cool-chick persona crumbles. "I'm Canadian! I love comedy!" I blurt out like a goofball.

Only for Canadians and comics do I reveal my true sweetheart little-girl self.

CHAPTER 29

The Hollywood Hills and My Father's Halo

AUTUMN 1997

After Patty disappeared, I packed her things into boxes, hoping she would come for them at some point, and gave notice to our landlord. Finally, I was out.

I moved into a picture-perfect little house in the Hollywood Hills, a petite one bedroom with a front yard and a big pine tree. It was a New England–style cottage, with echoes of my cherished grandparents' home on Cape Cod where I spent every holiday and summer vacation of my youth. The house was on Little Laurel Canyon Road, right below the famous Country Canyon Store that all the 1970s hippie musicians like Jim Morrison and Frank Zappa frequented for their groceries and their sustenance. My new landlord was eccentric, to say the least. He was a magician (I *loved* that) who worked at the nearby Magic Castle and owned a row of three little cottages on this discreet block.

I was in love with my little dollhouse. She was just right for the new me. All of my everything fitted into her perfectly. I took the time to paint every room a custom color: My bedroom was moss green, with gold stenciled fleurs-de-lis. Womb-like pink with gold trim was for the living-room parlor. The kitchen was bright yellow, with a built-in nook to have my morning tea and write in my diary, the kind of sane home environment that had been lost in Silverlake. There was an attic space that served perfectly as a little guest room and a walk-in closet for my ever-expanding vintage clothing collection.

Living in Hollywood definitely supported a Hollywood lifestyle. Chateau Marmont was right down the block, followed by the Mondrian and the Sunset Marquis. The Viper Room, the Whiskey a Go Go, and Troubadour Club were all close by with shows to attend nearly every night.

I was living the life, as best I could. I turned my camera on myself to capture this new place and time. But in the prints I picked up from my favorite photo-processing lab down the street, I could see the Stoic Princess I was becoming. Losing my baby fat on face and body, I was slenderer without wanting or trying for it. Age combined with stress was changing me, inside and out.

Two things were keeping me grounded in hard reality: First, therapy. I'd started doing weekly sessions with Tanda, who had a dark, witchy vibe. Always dressed in black, with a head of wild, curly black hair, she met with me in a home office behind her LA bungalow filled with plants, flowers, and black cats. I'd been seeing her for about nine months, since my father's diagnosis. She had also been hearing a great deal about the ins and outs of the band's chaos and drug addictions.

And second, the sobering fact that my father's cancer battle was not going well. He was suffering from the side effects of his first round of radiation, and the cancer had spread to his brain. Being off of Hole duty for a while meant I was flying home more regularly. As much as I didn't want to admit it, or even say the word, it was beginning to seem more and more like Nick was dying.

On my next flight to Montreal, I listened to music, but mostly I felt numb. I was heading home to accompany Nick to a new treatment of highly targeted radiation to his brain. I stared at the blank page in my diary. I could not find the words to reflect on my family life, in addition to my band life. I had no access to those sentences. They sat deep inside me, hidden from myself.

In Montreal, Nick and I caught up over lunch at one of his regular spots. As we ate, he filled me in very simply about his upcoming radiation session. "They're gonna put a halo on my head," he said with a chuckle.

"Well, that will make Grandma very happy," I added, and we laughed about the Catholic fervor and eccentricity of the Auf der Maurs.

Early the next morning we took a taxi to the hospital. I waited in the hallway while the doctors informed him about the full-day procedure. It would start with an MRI for an up-to-date image of the tumor. Then a metal halo would be mounted on top of his head. This apparatus would be used to lock him into a radiation machine that would target the tumor in his brain with laser focus. The most important thing would be for Nick to not move during radiation to avoid having the rays penetrate the wrong part of his brain.

The "metal halo" (every time it was named, it inspired an infinity of goth song lyrics in my mind) looked like a crank-style medieval torture device. It was fastened to a patient's head by literally tightening four screws around the skull.

My father and the doctor emerged from the procedure room, laughing of course. It took a moment to connect this sound with the image in front of me, which was terrifying. The metal halo had been attached, and blood was dripping from the two screws in Nick's forehead. It looked like the stigmata in Jesus's palms combined with the crown of thorns and immediately evoked thoughts of Auf der Maur Catholic iconography.

"How do I look, Melissa?" Nick asked, again with his signature chuckle. He planted his fedora on top of the halo.

I laughed an awkward, nervous laugh I did not recognize as my own. "Does it hurt?" I motioned toward his head with my hand.

He sat down next to me. "I feel fine. The doctor tells us that we have a couple of hours before the radiation machine frees up. Let's go to the bar for lunch."

Pedestrians gave us confused looks as he exited the building wearing what was clearly a complex piece of medical machinery. This offered a reality check. It *was* a big deal, even if Nick was making light of it all. I could admire the denial that allowed him to do this. At the same time, I feared what would happen if he began to look squarely at the truth. Imagining that reckoning made me feel queasy, and I had to shut out the thought.

At Winnie's, his usual lunch spot, we saddled up to the bar. Everyone in the place, customers and employees, "knew" Nick. Unlike the strangers on the street, the people in the bar didn't seem surprised to see a metal device screwed into his skull. Through the looking glass of booze, his enablers could hide from the seriousness of the situation with their jokes.

The day was becoming even more surreal.

Nick took off his fedora, ordered his "irregular" vodka soda with a splash of cranberry on the rocks, and began to read the paper. I made small talk with the patrons and green-eyed bartender who had been there for most of my life. They were all up to speed on my rock-star happenings. I filled in the blanks. Yes, I am living in LA. Of course I miss Montreal. We're completing the new album, then yes, we will go back on a world tour. Yes, it will be exhausting, blah blah blah. Our small talk only added to my numbness. I felt like a windup monkey performing for the children.

Nick took a sip of his drink and winced.

"Are you okay?" I asked.

"It's fine. It still burns a bit from the throat radiation," he explained.

We finished our lunch as if everything were normal and headed back to the hospital. I was allowed into the room while he was being laid down and locked in for radiation. Then I followed the technician into a neighboring room, where we watched the procedure through a little spy-camera TV monitor. A couple of zaps and we were out. We crossed our fingers, hoping for the best.

A month after treatment, it became clear the radiation was not working as the doctors had hoped. An experimental procedure was recommended. It involved manually removing the brain and throat tumor, which meant cutting out parts of Nick's mouth, tongue, throat, and palate. He told me this in a quick phone call to my little LA home. We kept it simple and light, which felt more painful than the truth itself. The world around me was growing darker. Not being able to share the fear of it, other than in therapy, was suffocating me.

Back in Los Angeles, Courtney had aced her vocals for the album, and I was called in to add harmonies. These would be the melodic sprinkles on the top of the cake before the album went off to the mixing stage. But going back into the studio meant I couldn't be in Montreal for Nick's procedure. My mother agreed to be there in my stead, a beautiful thing for her to offer. Nick, not wanting me to miss a beat of my professional obligations, was grateful to have her by his side.

"Melissa, your mother is the only woman I have ever loved," he reminded me. I'm remembering this only now, his words momentarily unlocked from a deep recess in my memory. He'd shared this heavy secret with me only a few times, on the few occasions when we got drunk together.

In the studio this time it was just me, Beinhorn, and an engineer in a small room together. Just as I'd loved laying down my bass tracks, I equally loved recording my vocals on every song. I stepped into my power again. I learned about mic technique and placement and explored various vocal textures from airy to chest voice, depending on what a song needed.

We focused on the chorus sections to lift, a standard formula for pop songs. Each song got layered harmonies, sometimes with three-part harmonies, with each single melody doubled or quadrupled by my own voice. Beinhorn's love of gloss worked well with my talents. No one doesn't love harmonies in a pop song.

For some of the more peppy choruses, Beinhorn used my voice as a tool to sweeten up Courtney's lead track. On these songs, I became a ghostly, shadowy, sweeter version of her, a process that came naturally to me. It was my superpower, and it felt good to sparkle and shine like the ether of the stars above . . .

"That's a wrap! Incredible, Melissa. It's been such a pleasure working with you!" Beinhorn gave me a high five on my last day in the studio.

"*Merci, bienvenue et au revoir!*" I said. "Let me know when the album's mixed. I'll show up for the photo shoot!" I was relieved to finally be done with it all and also deeply satisfied. I wasn't clear if the joy I felt came from using my voice as a tool or from putting my personal imprint all over an album that had taken such a toll on my musical soul. As I walked out of the studio on that final day, it felt that both were momentarily giving me a reason and a purpose to feel and be alive.

✗

Music had always been my savior and my shelter, a true magic act in that way. When I was a tortured teen, my headphones gave me the escape. In the studio, I created the illusion in real life. But back in Montreal, reality was coming at me hard and fast. Nick's experimental surgery had gone terribly wrong, and my parents were both in deep distress.

"He's permanently disfigured, Melissa," my mother sobbed over the phone. "The pain was awful, *so awful!* The procedure, *brutal*. He woke up screaming after the operation. He was hysterical. Ripped his IVs out. He was hallucinating from all the pain and the fucking painkillers. I think Nick is glad you weren't here for it . . . I am glad you weren't here."

I felt my vision start fading to black. From the sound of it, whatever life Nick had left had been ruined. He would be unable to eat, drink, or talk properly ever again. To remove the whole tumor in his throat, the doctors had to carve out parts of his throat, palate, and the back of his tongue. Marred, mangled, and destroyed. I was fucking terrified. My father as he'd always been was not coming back, and I would have to go back to Montreal to face this.

After a year of brutal treatment, it had become apparent that his medical team was losing hope. They had tried everything and run out of options. I felt the numbness returning, creeping in slowly until it became all of me.

Nick was a man who'd always devoured life with such passion and intellectual engagement, and this stage of the illness flipped a switch inside him. I watched him begin to withdraw. Piles of fan mail from his readers and voters continued to mount around him, but it didn't bring him the pleasure it had when this battle began. Our afternoons together devolved into silence. His slurred voice only enhanced the need to hide his deformed face. He was now emotionally *and* physically stunted in his communication skills. I made him his kiwi smoothies, the only thing left that he could almost enjoy. He struggled to swallow and choked often. His house was still and deathly. We barely spoke.

Over my short life so far, I had grown accustomed to not speaking openly with Nick about feelings. I thought of all the things I had never asked him, like *Why did you drink so much? What were you escaping from? Are you lonely? How did you feel when Mum told you about my existence? Did you know I've been scared to talk freely with you my whole life?* and *Are you scared to die?* With time running out and the environment so sullen, I came to the fast conclusion that none of it mattered. I gave up on communicating feelings altogether. Just being there for him was all I could do.

In what would be Nick's last column, he described his new level of introspection: "When I lie down for a nap or for the night, waiting for sleep to claim me, 81 thoughts race through my head. I sometimes sense the damp, humid presence of death."

The doctors should have left him as he was. He could have at least drunk and smoked his way out of this world. Instead, the Nick I'd always known "left the building" long before his body gave out.

CHAPTER 30

Introducing: Death

MARCH 1998

"I want to end it," he said. His voice sounded bleak.

I pressed the phone receiver tightly against my ear. I wanted to be sure I was hearing this right.

"Yah, okay, Nick." That was Huey, my father's close friend, speaking. I recognized his voice right away.

"Huey, I want to end it *now*. I want out."

I was sitting on the floor of my bedroom upstairs in Nick's house, eavesdropping on the black rotary phone. I'd picked up the receiver to make a call and entered this conversation purely by chance.

I twisted the phone extension cord around my index finger and sat very still as I quietly listened in. I'd been stretching this long cord all the way from Nick's bedroom down the hall to mine for private phone time since I was a teen. As an adult it felt strangely embarrassing to still be trying to find privacy, or in this case to spy on my father.

Since his operation, Nick had been permanently positioned downstairs on the living-room couch. If the TV wasn't on, then the radio was blasting classical music or the news. Otherwise, he was sleeping. The living room was always bright in the daytime, thanks to a glass atrium addition that was added when he bought this house a year after my parents divorced. A large top-floor skylight brought additional light down to the living room. Years ago, Nick had inadvertently created a lovely, minimalist bachelor home for spending the last days of his life.

Exactly a decade ago, Nick's father, my Swiss grandfather Severin, had died peacefully in his sleep in a guest room in this house. Although he spoke very little English and my father spoke no Swiss German, they slipped right back into Nick's early childhood years when they lived off the grid together at the Auf der Maur mining cabin in rural Quebec. They were compatible—if silent—roommates during their last year together.

My grandfather's funeral was the first I ever attended. I was sixteen. The service was held on a gray morning downtown at Mary, Queen of the World, the seat of the Roman Catholic Archdiocese of Montreal. Big Roman columns lined the front of the building. Above the enormous doorway were statues of men draped in robes and strange hats, holding crucifixes, babies, books, and goblets. I counted thirteen of them silhouetted by the cloudy sky. Were they judging earthly people like us? I wondered what they would have thought of my grandmother Auf der Maur coming to say goodbye to her ex-husband.

"The angels are here with you, my dear Melissa," my grandmother said as she approached me in the aisle of pews. "I see them on your shoulders. They are smiling!" A giggle escaped from her wildly scratchy voice and thick accent, which felt very out of step with the mood expected for a death day.

The phone became Nick's only connection to the outside world. It rang often, but he rarely answered it. When I was in the house I answered calls and received best wishes, most of which I responded to with, "He's resting and can't talk at the moment. Thanks for calling; it means a lot to him."

During the week I was there he took only three phone calls, all from Canadian men of stature who piqued his energy enough to engage: Brian Mulroney, the former prime minister of Canada; Conrad Black, a newspaper mogul and Nick's only real right-wing friend; and Mordecai Richler, famed Jewish Montrealer and literary luminary. I overheard his side of their brief calls and watched Nick try to come to life for them.

These would be his last conversations with these peers. I knew they recognized him as fearless, full of heart, and bold in ways they might never be. They knew he was one of a kind in the Canadian journalistic and political landscape of his generation. The mutual admiration between him and these men meant a lot to him and revealed what mattered most to him—politics and writing—at the end.

Huey, at this point, was one of the few people Nick would accept as a visitor. Huey was a bar buddy and had been a loyal friend to Nick for the past few years, most recently driving him to and from the doctors. He was an uncomplicated man who asked few questions. Huey was smaller than me and looked like Joe Pesci, with strong cologne. I felt good around him, because he made my father feel good, or at least at ease at this difficult point in his life.

"Nick, are you *sure* you want to do this?" I heard Huey say on the phone.

"Yes. I don't want to live like this. Would you?!" I could feel Nick's rage, even through his slurred speech. "That's that. I've got what I need." He slammed down the phone.

I gently placed the black receiver back into its cradle. My first response was shock. I felt waves of it moving through my body.

Confusion came next.

Did I just hear what I think I heard?

Yes, I realized. I'd just heard my father tell a friend he wanted to end his life. Thoughts started coming at me hard and fast.

First, *Why?* Nick was in very compromised shape, without a doubt, but his death wasn't imminent. He could conceivably have kept living in this condition for months, or maybe more. I couldn't understand why anyone would choose to rush toward death. To me, dying was a natural process, not one under human control.

Then, *This must be even worse for Nick than I'd realized.* I knew his condition was terrible for him, but I hadn't known he was feeling desperate enough to end it. Knowing this made me feel deep empathy for him. I could understand how such a force of nature, someone who loved life as much as Nick did, wouldn't want to continue if he couldn't eat, drink, talk, or spend time out in the world, even if I would have made a different choice.

And finally, *Of course he would want to check out now.* Choosing to die with dignity and control was perfectly true to Nick's character. He wasn't going to let the universe decide his moment or manner of death. He was going to conquer the universe himself.

Just the other day, a priest had appeared at the front door. My grandmother had sent him to perform Nick's last rites, in advance, out of precaution.

"No!" Nick was furious with his religion-obsessed mother for this act. "He cannot come in. This is *my* life, and I will die how I want to die."

"I'm sorry, my father can't take any visitors right now. Maybe another day," I told him, though I wondered if by doing this I was denying my father something essential to the end of his life.

What do I do now? I asked myself as I sat on my bedroom floor.

I had the sudden thought that I might not have enough life experience yet to be considering all this. Twenty-six was considered an adult by most standards, but in some ways I felt like a girl still on her way to becoming a grown woman.

Confusing and conflicting feelings were swirling around in me at that time, and I'm unpacking them only now. I'd been a golden gift in my father's life, a sparkling, shiny star child tossed into his lap with no strings attached. As the product of a onetime encounter between two exceptional people, I came so close to not being part of his life at all. And my mother could have chosen to keep me from him forever. I was very aware of this. I had come into her life as the result of a feminist stance, politics, and intellect, but I was in my father's life purely by accident and chance.

I also knew Nick had not been lucky in romantic love. The purest form of love he'd known was with me, and I wanted to continue being that for him. I could give him the kind of unconditional love and acceptance he hadn't found anywhere else. My final gift to him could be to not make this hard for him at the end.

But when I'm being really honest, I have to acknowledge that another thought also came to mind when I overheard the phone call.

It was *What about me?*

If I hadn't picked up the phone at that exact moment, my father would be moving ahead with this without me. I would have gotten on a plane back to

Los Angeles and gotten a phone call that he'd died, without ever knowing his plan.

How dare you not include me? I thought.

Until you've been through an experience like this, you don't know how unconditional love and white-hot anger can exist so strongly at the same time. But there they both were, in equal measures. The love part of me wanted to be the loyal daughter, and the anger part was very pissed off that he would exclude me from an event that I knew would define the rest of my life.

It was a sign of Nick's emotional illiteracy that he had no concept of how doing this could affect another person. He'd always been a lone soldier, never really integrating with anyone else, and must have felt his death was for him alone. This was a sad reality to face. It was also sobering to realize that by taking his death into his own hands in the way he intended, Nick would be denying me the chance to say goodbye.

Hold on! I thought. *What do I want? What's important to* ME *in life and love and death?*

I'd become so accustomed to letting giant, omnipresent people make decisions for me and so trained to accept the actions of difficult people that I rarely stopped to consider what *I* needed.

Later that day I left Nick's house to run an errand. From a public pay phone, I called Huey at the bar where he hung out.

"I overheard your conversation with Nick," I said. "I want to be there at the end."

"Are you sure?" he asked.

"I'm sure," I said.

Huey seemed relieved. He was a good man who was likely terrified to have to keep this secret—and at this point, I really was Nick's only family. He'd kept his distance from his mother and siblings throughout his death, and I was solely responsible for him and his estate. And for Nick to end his own life behind *my* back would be to deprive me of my birthright to know my father's true wishes. Huey couldn't have felt good about hiding the plan from me. He quickly agreed to let me know when the end was near so I could be there with Nick.

Back at home, I nervously shared the news with Nick. "I know what you want to do," I confessed. "I won't let you do it without me being there for you."

Nick was quiet for a moment, then silently nodded his head.

Choosing to be with Nick at the end was my first tiny step of personal agency and individuation. It said, *I am separate from you. I am making a choice about my own future, because I know this moment will define me in your absence.* By insisting on showing up for my father, I was also showing up for myself.

"I have to fly back to LA for work. I'll let Huey know when I'll be back," I said. "I want to be here with you."

I wanted to ask if he was scared, but I was the one who was frightened at that moment—frightened to ask any hard questions of a man I did not recognize anymore. Frightened to share my own fear with someone I'd never *really* had a deep emotional conversation with before. But I knew I might not have the chance again.

"I'm scared, Nick," I managed to murmur, trying to hold back tears. "I will miss you."

"Don't worry, Melissa," he said, gently. "I'll be around."

"How will I know?"

He took his time to reply.

"I will knock," he said, with a faint but twisted smile. "Listen for me."

I leaned in for a hug and to pet the back of his mangled, balding head. It was the last, rare, tender moment I ever shared with my father, the man whose omnipresent love of life defined so much of my own life force.

My heart was cracking into pieces, but the possibility of connecting with him beyond this life opened a tiny pinprick-size hole of hope. It was a hole that would slowly but eventually expand to let in the bright light of timeless, unconditional love beyond our inadequate flawed human forms. The light came from another universe, a time and space of pure love.

CHAPTER 31

Montreal's Daughter in Mourning

APRIL 1998

THIS MAY BE WHAT HAPPENED.

"Melissa! Just hurry the fuck up!"

Despite his impatience, Nick's voice was feeble. I arrived at his home. Propped up on the couch in his usual position of the last few weeks, he didn't have much life force left.

I'd already lost Patty, my rhythm sister, to a heroin addiction that came with giving up on life. Now my father was choosing death over life. The two of them had been the crowned comedians of any room I occupied. Their big hearts grew even bigger when they were loved and appreciated. But right now, I was having a hard time accepting either of them. Parts of me were breaking alongside them.

I had started to retreat into a deep and quiet mourning in a dim world of my own, weighted down with metaphysical sludge. Everything felt creepy and haunted and unsafe, and I feared that the dark parts of my earlier dreams might return. My sense of safety had always come from a solid relationship with my inner self, but now even that felt threatened. I no longer felt a close connection to Patty or my father, and even more troubling, I was losing my connection with myself.

I wasn't sharing these thoughts with anyone at the time. Instead, I was focused on my deep drive to honor my father's last wish.

Where we going, Nick?
Crazy! Wanna come?

I could hear glasses clinking in the kitchen, where Huey was doing vodka shots with Dewey, an eccentric journalist and drinking buddy with a good heart. They followed up the vodka with what I suspected to be rails of cocaine they snorted outside of my view.

My father trusted them and probably thought they'd offer me moral support. In a way they did, because they represented the most authentic side of Nick. They were letting it all hang out that day, not holding anything back. And so was my father, broken as he was. This father of mine had summoned his Auf der Maur temper to leave this life kicking and cursing. He was pissed that he had to call it quits. Pissed that this was it and that he had done it to himself.

Hurry the fuck up. His last words.

How much morphine kiwi smoothie was enough to overdose a man who's five feet, eleven inches and 150 pounds? I had no idea. By the time I got there, Nick had already begun to feel drowsy.

Time slowed down. I sat by his side, watching and waiting. A few days ago, I'd asked Courtney and Eric, both Buddhists, to chant for Nick to pass over to the other side soon. They'd promised they would and also wrote personal letters to him. Courtney's included a particularly poignant passage where she said, "Thank you for being the father I never had. And I promise to look after Melissa in your stead, for as long as I live."

Remembering this now, I'm struck by the kindness and reassurance she offered him at the end of his life. It was a handoff of sorts, reassuring him that she would take over where he had left off. I hope it brought him some comfort in those final days. As for me, what a crazy bunch of parents I'd been offered by the universe. How perverse!

When Nick's eyes finally closed, I joined the guys in the kitchen. They were both pacing and shaking, probably from a combination of nerves and intoxication.

"I think it's done," I said. "But how do I know?"

I recognized fear in their eyes. How must I, a delicate woman of twenty-six witnessing her father dying by the force of his own hand in the next room, have looked to them? It had to have been hard for them to see Nick go, the lively leader of them all. Did they even get to say goodbye?

We seemed to be treating this evening like we had come here to just check on Nick's overall miserable condition, not to witness the *end* of it. It felt absurd. Only now do I realize the degree of compartmentalizing that had begun. I buried the details of that night deep inside myself, suppressing it as the darkest of all my secrets, probably due to both shock and fear of the dark disconnect. *Hurry the fuck up*, he said to me, no *I love you, Melissa*, or *Have a nice life* . . . My husband and I were together for almost a decade before I told him exactly what happened that day. My therapist cried, even though I'd referred to my father's death hundreds of times in our eight years of sessions, when the details came out only as I was writing this book, twenty-five years after the fact.

A gurgling noise started up in the living room, and we all fell silent. It had begun, the death rattle: the body's instinct to stay alive.

Nick lay on the couch with his mouth wide open, still breathing but with difficulty. Long pauses extended between each agonized breath. We sat on the armchairs around him and waited. My grandmother had always believed my father to be a reincarnation of Saint Niklaus, the patron saint of Switzerland. That Niklaus died of starvation by a riverbank in 1487 at the age of seventy. This Nick, the one who'd been burdened with this auspicious connection, was the father who'd always been more like a friend to me. And he was dying by his own wishes at age fifty-five, in front of me.

I could understand my father's inner struggle, because I lived with a similar duality. On one side of me has always been a timeless spirit that longs to transcend and travel the cosmos and does not easily live in earthly form. That spirit hovers over my ever-blossoming and hungry body.

On the other side, my earthly grounded body, is the soft skin, curly auburn hair, and strong hands that want to devour life fully. To kiss it all, bite it all, and suck it all in, to churn it out into visceral sounds and romantic tales that reflect the deeply conflicting energies within.

The saint and the wall. My father managed the tension between the two by drinking and smoking, and it had cost him his life. I was witnessing the final moments of his struggle now.

This moment would define the rest of my life. Even more than music would. I knew that even then.

"It's okay, Nick. You can let go now," I told him. They were the only words that made any sense at the time. "Let go."

✗

Around midnight, I called my mother. "It's done," I told her matter-of-factly. She was good with logistics, and I needed help knowing what to do next.

"I'll come right over," she said.

Soon she was by my side, with a copy of *The Tibetan Book of the Dead*. "Norma insisted you read this over his body," she explained. We had no rituals of our own to follow, no plans to move into and through this day of death. So we relied on one of my fairy godmothers to guide us. Norma, the one who had lived with us in the circus caravan in Wales and the British Postal Van in Morocco and who had gone on to find Buddhism in India, was our spirit guide that night.

We—me and my mother—knelt alongside Nick's still body, while Huey and Dewey paced and drank in the kitchen to give us space.

"Death is not the opposite of life," I read. "Life has no opposite. The opposite of death is birth. Life is eternal."

When we finished, I stepped back into reality. Or whatever this was called.

"What do I do now—call 911?" I asked.

At this point, we did a change of the guards. My mother was a more suitable person to be by my side right now than these two tipsy men in leather jackets.

"Love you, Melissa," they said as they left, their eyes glassy.

"Thank you so much." I hugged them goodbye as they cleaned up their party in the kitchen.

"Call the Auf der Maurs first. They'll want to be here before they take his body away," my mother instructed. She was thinking clearly, and I was grateful for the advice. But the next hour unfolded into what I can only describe as chaos incarnate.

"We must call the priest for his last rites!" my aunt Thais wailed on the other end of the phone when I informed the Auf der Maurs of Nick's passing. So I considered dialing the number jotted down on a matchbook for the person whom Nick wanted to lead his funeral service, a drinking buddy of Nick's and openly gay, which my father thought was a bold and brave move for a man devoted to a faith that mostly judged such a thing. "I'll call the archbishop of Canada—he's a friend from the bar!" Huey announced proudly. Within minutes, a dramatic silhouette in floor-length robes walked into my father's living room from the dead of night.

Aunt Thais arrived after him, in time to see this priest standing over her brother's body.

"Who called you?!" she blew up at him. Apparently, he was the wrong kind of man of service, Anglican instead of Catholic, despite his undeniable hierarchy in the world of religion. Why can't we *all* just get along? I was mystified as they called their *own* "better" priest, who arrived soon after.

Throughout this scene I had lifted out of my body and was perched above the room, on the beam by the upstairs overhang, looking down at the scene. In my state of dissociation, I marveled at the beauty of the two holy men standing over Nick's body in their robes with little books and beads in their hands as they collaborated on a dual version of last rites. One was there on behalf of the dead man, the other for the two grieving female family members. My aunt and grandmother cried and prayed next to Nick's body with rosaries dangling from their wrinkled hands. They seemed possessed. I don't recall exchanging a single word with them that night.

The morgue attendants arrived with a body bag and a stainless-steel stretcher. They zipped Nick's body up in plastic and rolled him out. I signed the paperwork and took note of the address where I'd go in the morning to pick out a coffin and make the necessary arrangements. As Nick's only child and sole heir, these "widow" tasks were up to me.

Before he died, I'd tried to get my father to address what to do with his library, his archives of writing, his political career, his house. "Is there anything you want me to do?" I asked him. "What should I do with all your stuff?"

He didn't care about any of that. He had only two requests for me. The first was not to give anything to his brother, or he would come back to haunt me. You see, when Nick was dying, his brother had attempted to sue him for the money that my grandmother Auf der Maur had loaned her favorite son to put a down payment down on the house he died in. My uncle was asking for his share of what he claimed was his rightful inheritance, plus 20 percent interest. My father refused to speak to him again.

His second request was, "Be sure to find the red box in my sock drawer."

So the day after he died, I opened the top drawer of his dresser. A beautiful red leather cigar box was nestled among his socks. Its interior was lined with satin. Taped inside the lid was a photo of me and my mother.

The box itself was filled with papers. It took me a minute to realize it contained every letter Nick and my mother had ever exchanged. He had saved all of her original letters to him and carbon copies of his to her.

I sat down inside his closet and started reading. As I made my way through the pile, I became witness to the most tragic love story I could have imagined. I had no idea how destroyed my father had been by failing to hold on to my mother. In his letters he was begging her, *begging* her, to stay. He said he would clean up, fix up, change whatever he needed to change.

In her letters back she had obviously already given up. She was harsh about him not being the man she wanted him to be. In the most brutal line, she accused him of wasting his brilliant mind: "You stoop so low to spend time with men of half your intelligence because it's easier, and suggests that you will never rise to the person that you could be."

I realized how ashamed my father must have felt. The letters were deeply revealing, showing me that in the end, all that mattered to him was the love he had for me and my mother.

What was I to do with this knowledge? And with the awareness that he'd wanted me to have it only after he was gone? There was no opportunity to talk with him about it now. This knowledge was mine to carry alone.

At the time, this felt like too much to take in, too soon. But looking back, I can appreciate the sweet and deep love my parents had for each other, even if it surfaced only briefly. The chances of any one of us being here, as ourselves, is infinitesimal. The chances of me being here, the product of a weekend romance, feels even more impossibly remote. That moment they shared in the summer of 1971 was something bigger than both of my parents, and I believe I came down to earth through both of them as a reflection of that love. If everyone exists for a reason, and I believe they do, I was seeking the reason for my existence now. Ten years later, my Buddhist fairy godmother, Norma, would give me the guidance I needed. We met for lunch one day when I was on tour in Europe, and I told her about the box and my destroyed father and all of the heartbreak between my parents.

She looked at me and said, in all of her hippie Buddhist wisdom, "Melissa, this is not your story. Let it go. This is your mother's box. Don't take it on."

I put the red box in my attic, where it remains to this day.

Nick died on April 7, which happened to land on Good Friday that year, three days before his fifty-sixth birthday. We cremated him forty-eight hours later on Easter Sunday, in a private family gathering in a sunny chapel at the cemetery on Mount Royal where his ashes would be buried next to his father.

As Nick's coffin was being lowered into the furnace, my black beaded necklace unexpectedly broke. The individual beads bounced around on the tiled floor, casting playful shadows.

"It's Nick!" my ninety-six-year-old grandmother blurted out. "He's laughing while heading up to his star. Stars are cars for our souls." She reached for my hand with great delight.

Nick Auf der Maur's mother, Theresa, and daughter, Melissa, comforted one another after yesterday's funeral

The public funeral was held the next day, on Easter Monday. We, of course, hadn't planned for this. The holiday hadn't even occurred to us until the deed was done. But to my grandmother, there was no more holy weekend for her son to depart. It only confirmed her convictions about his divine connection to Catholicism and the patron saint of the beloved country where she was born.

In the days after Nick's death there was a mountain of widow responsibilities and paperwork for me to tend to. A Nick Auf der Maur Cancer Fund at the Montreal General Hospital and a Nick Auf der Maur Journalism Fund at Concordia University were both created in the immediate wake of his death. There were also countless interviews and statements to give. As a good windup daughter, I spoke to the cameras and into the radio mics and expressed my deepest admiration for my father and my sadness around his passing. Still, I didn't cry.

Montreal Gazette newspaper clipping, 1998.

The early death of a man who'd been such a dynamic and loving father and such an engaged citizen of his beloved city was a tragedy, but I had a job to do. I felt I had to be Nick's daughter and step up as a public speaker, to share my heart with the friends and strangers who felt they'd also lost someone close to them. It was comforting to know how many others mourned the loss of this man who had seemed larger-than-life to everyone.

My father's life was celebrated with one of the largest funerals in Montreal history, which he and I had the opportunity to plan together. It was held at St. Patrick's Basilica, a Gothic Revival–style beauty dating back to 1847 and Nick's favorite downtown church. His favorite green-eyed bartender sang a Celtic hymn, and his chosen gay priest led the service.

The turnout for the funeral was beautiful and overwhelming. It was standing-room only, with more than three thousand people stuffing the church to its rafters and overflowing into the streets, with the doors thrown open to the sunny spring day.

Assembled that day were my music peers, my childhood friends, my father's three older siblings, his devoted mother, and my mother, who was there with her brood of Frenchmen: my lovely stepfather, Hervé; my younger half brother, Yves; and my two older stepbrothers. Courtney took the day off from her Hollywood film shoot to attend. She chartered a private plane in honor of the man she'd referred to as "the father I never had" and sat in the front row of the church in her best ladies' suit, accompanied by Joe Mama. It meant a lot to me that she came, but I was too busy to even exchange a word with her that day.

Even though all the essential people in my life were gathered in one room—possibly the only time this would ever happen—the people who defined my experience that day were not those I knew, but rather the readers and admirers of my father whom I'd never met. In the overwhelming amount of local press about his death that week, it was written, "Every friend and enemy of Nick's was there that day," which said a lot about him. His political and journalism colleagues, as well as the many engaged citizens of Montreal who considered Nick a friend, even if they had never met him, were people with whom I could share the universal truth of loss. Their presence comforted me in a way that no family or friend could.

I'd written Nick's eulogy on the flight from Los Angeles to Montreal the week before. This time, my diary pages had filled up quickly with stream-of-consciousness reflections. Delivering these words at the funeral was the only time my chiseled facade came down.

> Bonjour. Thank you for being here today.
> Merci d'être avec nous aujourd'hui. Nous sommes ici pour Nick.
> Nick was the son of a special woman, my grandmother, who's here with us today. She was always proud when she felt that Nick was helping other people, and Nick did that here in Montreal.

For the last couple of years, I had been relying on my self-protective detached, unemotional facade, especially when the going was tough. It was the precursor to the carefully constructed Bass Player–Superhero–Stoic Princess persona I would adopt to launch Hole's new album. That's who stepped up to the podium, ready to perform.

It wasn't hard for me to do. I'd relied on this persona to get me through every show with Hole, every business meeting, and every interview. It had become my armor.

Creating a public persona is what people in rock bands *do*. They spin mythology out of reality like the gods and goddesses of ancient Greece, creating larger-than-life nonhuman personae so fans can live vicariously through them. I understood early on that this was my job as a rock goddess. It was an offering I felt compelled and honored to make to the people. But it was always a role. It never felt like all of me—only a part of me.

People like Courtney and Billy and Marilyn Manson often *become* their Rock Star personae. They merge with it and become altered beings, fantasy creators, myth builders, and escapist freaks. If being a rock star is your "job," either you are likely to have to retire one day or you die "being" it. Those are the choices. It's very hard to balance the real you with this other side of you.

Until now, I'd been able to more or less manage the tension between these inner dualities. But now here I was, standing before thousands of people as a public person and also as a real person. In my pain and confusion, I had

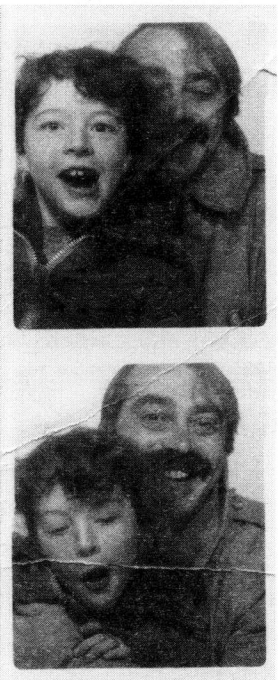

been hiding more than ever behind my public persona, but now I felt that public persona starting to merge with my real self, which at that moment was a totally fucked-up and heartbroken daughter. I could tell I wasn't going to be able to sustain the duality for long.

Reading my eulogy, I fought through tears to enunciate before giving in to my true self, a merging of the public and private me, and I let the emotions flow.

> He was a passionate Montrealer, a Swiss, a Canadian, a great friend to so many—an entertainer, a writer, a bum pincher, a politician, a brother, a celebrator, a peace disturber, a ranter, an explorer, a private man, a downtowner, an initiator. He loved to argue and enlighten people, he was a believer, a fighter, a proud person, a teacher, a historian, a little boy, a young man, a dying man, and such an enthusiastic and loving father. He loved me and I

Nick and Melissa Auf der Maur, photo booth, 1980.

love him. He was so brave and I am so lucky to be his daughter and to have been with him until the end.

Merci a tout le monde, Adieu Nick and I love you.

The service was broadcast live on the local TV and radio channels, for all his fans to see. Following the big church to-do, the City of Montreal Police led a Dixieland-band procession through the streets from St. Patrick's to the infamous Crescent Street bar block where Nick's two favorite bars, Sir Winston Churchill's and Ziggy's, would anchor a block-party celebration for him. "Gangster Politics," a young local ska band Nick had seen once and loved for their horn section, performed. He'd curated his own post-funeral party, too. It was a smashing success, with an open bar and open arms to all.

The day after the funeral, the front-page headline of the *Montreal Gazette* read, "Montreal's Daughter in Mourning," with an above-the-fold, full-page photo of me in profile, my head down in a church pew, holding my mother's hand. It was taken just after I'd read my eulogy.

I still remember how it felt to be up there before all those people, reading my words. I'd barely noticed the standing ovation in the church when I finished. I'd been overcome with a feeling of transcendence, channeling an energy from deep within, that was rising through me, and *out* of me. This otherworldly part of myself, the part that could travel through time and space and float in the ether with the stars and the lost souls, could speak to my father directly. As I read the words I'd written for him, everything else evaporated. It was just me and him and the love that remained between us.

This was my time to step into that higher power, not to crumble. I'd faced something difficult. I'd done something brave. I'd taken the high road for Nick. I'd found a way to make something come exclusively from me and not let intimidating people make the decisions for me. The way I stood up for my father on his death, and the way I stood up for myself at the same time, is how I knew that ultimately I would do what was right for me, even if it wasn't easy or clear.

I wasn't that person yet, but I was trying to become her.

If not for this moment, I would not have been able to leave Hole the following year. But I'm getting ahead of myself. In the church that day, I stepped into a new kind of place and power that was within me, yet also beyond me. And it felt like home.

CHAPTER 32

Dance with Death

LOS ANGELES, SUMMER 1998

THE INTENSITY OF MAKING *CELEBRITY SKIN*, WATCHING PATTY SLIP OFF THE deep end of drugs, and losing my father had put me into a dark dream state that I was only now beginning to emerge from. And what I woke up to was the pretty disappointing state of rock music that we were about to release our new album into. The magic of the alternative '90s wave, full of the quirky intelligence and authenticity that had epitomized Hole's 1995 Lollapalooza run, was over. Seminal bands such as Pavement, the Pixies, and Sonic Youth all seemed to have retreated from the corporate takeover of our scene.

Music styles were also shifting tremendously. The rise of mainstream industrial-goth culture, epitomized by Marilyn Manson, made for a strange brew in alternative music. The scene was flooded with wannabe goths in Halloween costumes fraternizing with bros in bum-revealing pants slapping low-slung basses. Then there were the offshoots of Green Day's punk success, kinda cute SoCal boys making joke songs. Not that I took issue with the individuals in these bands—I had met most of them along the way, and they all seemed nice enough—but the lack of sincerity and absence of poeticism disheartened me. This new landscape simply no longer felt inspiring.

Courtney thrived on peer-to-peer competition, and none of these guys were doing it for her, either. Still, I was becoming frustrated—pretty pissed, actually—as she began to focus more on her film career and less on our band. The Hollywood scene was toxic and boring to me, but ambition and fame were always major drivers for Courtney. I realize now that the underwhelming music scene we had found ourselves in must have had a lot to do with her losing interest in Hole. But at the time, it was maddening for a devoted musician to be part of.

More than anything, the end of this era felt hollow. I longed to move back to the Northeast where I could be part of an old-fashioned city lifestyle of working creatives, walking the urban streets, and musing in cafés and bars. Living in cars with the stars of "Celebrity Island," as Cecil, my art-school friend from Montreal called it, had never appealed to me. Now it felt deadly.

Los Angeles had begun to feel like a junkie training camp. In my final year there I struck up a brief and unlikely friendship with Dave Navarro, the guitarist of Jane's Addiction. He's now best known as a reality-television star, but back then he'd just come out of a long, solitary chapter of sober living and hiding from the drama of his former band, which had recently announced their first reunion tour.

Dave and his bandmates were Los Angeles locals who had become popular in the late '80s and early '90s. I'd seen them while tripping on mushrooms as a teenager, at the Rialto Theater in Montreal, and witnessed them paving the way for the new music movement of our time.

In particular, the talents of Jane's Addiction's bass player, Eric Avery, had infused major inspiration into my bass style. I hate to admit it, but to that point I had been far more influenced by guitar players and drummers than bass players. But Avery's bass lines were central to all of Jane's songs. They were fluid, melodic, and cinematic, like ocean waves for the wailing and witchy front man, Perry Farrell, to surf. His playing was total magic.

Jane's Addiction called it quits in the early '90s, probably due to the addiction issues of one or more members of the band. Some of them had been notorious junkies who'd glamorized the drugged-up lifestyle, but they nonetheless possessed explosive talent and were also responsible for the creation of Lollapalooza, which birthed the alternative-music festival culture in North America.

Navarro had been clean for years, which was a big accomplishment for a longtime heroin user. We met briefly at a corporate party in Los Angeles, and he soon started orbiting around me.

We popped up at the same parties and were friendly with some of the same industry and MTV people, which says a lot about my LA social life at the time. Dave was often shirtless with flowing, styled jet-black hair, makeup, perfectly tweezed eyebrows, elaborate tattoos, and tight leather pants—a distinctive goth-meets-rock style.

His flamboyance was both unsettling and fascinating. When he took an interest in me, I didn't entirely shut him down. Flirtation seemed to be his way of communicating, like a Peter Pan sprinkling fairy dust on everyone he encountered. I stayed fairly aloof—some would say I played "hard to get"—but it was by no means an intentional power game. It was just my true desire for independence and my wariness when it came to romantic intimacy. Dave was quite persuasive, though, and I gave him my home phone number.

This started a brief, strange, and slightly strained friendship over the next few months. He would ring me late at night, and we'd talk about our love of music and the dark, torturous music relationships we'd found ourselves in. He would ask what it was like to be me. I soon discovered he was having his first heroin relapse. He was honest about it. I knew how dangerous relapses were; that's how most fatal accidental overdoses happen (as was the case with Kristen, Hole's previous bass player). What kept me from running away from Dave was his willingness to communicate and tell me why he was doing it. This incredible self-awareness compelled me to listen and learn.

It was no coincidence that Dave's first major relapse happened in tandem with the climactic reunion of a band that used the word "addiction" in its name. It was a dangerous decision for him to return to the band, and I had deep compassion for him and all those who struggle with addiction. Still, I questioned myself. What did it say about me that I was hanging around someone who was reliving the darkest chapter of his life? Did it feel good to be the object of interest of a person heading toward the abyss?

Was I a magnet for that?

Was I seeking it?

Or both?

✗

"Drama is for people who are numb and don't feel. They need the emotional explosions to feel anything at all," my therapist, Tanda, said during one of our weekly sessions. I was always on the periphery of other people's drama, she pointed out. Her glassy words cut through my mess like a witch's dagger.

The ability to absorb someone else's psychic or soul pollution and not take it on was something I'd been proud of in the past, like a badge of honor. But now I thought of all the times I'd become attracted to the drama and it to me. From the Auf der Maur family sagas to the single mother posing naked, from the beer bottle and Billy the Big Pumpkin to the drug and fame mania of Hole, all of the defining characters in my life so far had reeked of drama.

I seemed to be stuck in an orbital pattern around a solar system of extremely over-the-top people. *What had happened to my feelings? How had I sustained the chaos and confusion of it all? Where were my feelings now?* As I asked myself these questions, I felt deeply confused about the possibility that I could be an enabler to all this drama or, even worse, numb to it all.

During one of my most memorable late-night talks with Dave, he tried to explain the difference between me and a junkie like him. He spoke with the singular wisdom of a person who had danced with the devil, who had come into the "light" of sobriety, done the hard work of therapy and the Narcotics Anonymous program, and returned to the darkness.

"Melissa, do you wake up every morning, feeling like you're connected to a higher purpose of being?" he asked.

"Yes," I replied. In spite of all my melancholy, I always felt connected to something beyond myself, a calling to be part of the world around me. *Did I take that for granted?*

"Well, that's the difference between you and me. I feel a dark hole of disconnect every morning, and I have to work every day to make a connection. If I fail to do that work, drugs are an easy fix. They're a bridge to connect me to something."

Dave's simple analogy had a profound effect on me. I've shared it with others struggling with addiction, or an addict in their life, to shed light on the fundamental struggle. That conversation about the difference between us began to defrost a part of my frozen heart.

My life in the '90s was draped in seductive drama, incredible music, and emotional roller coasters. At the same time, warnings arrived in my dreams and in the form of this glamorous, troubled messenger. I'm grateful for my intuition to let the right messengers and messages in, at the right time. They allowed me to plan what would become my escape and emotional self-rescue from the dark world that had claimed me and that I had, without realizing until now, claimed for my own.

Dreamscape #3

Your Emptiness Is Calling Me

From a bird's-eye view I see a little dollhouse in the hills of Los Angeles. Through the window, I spy a bedroom with a single bed. Its wrought-iron frame looks like it's from a Victorian orphanage, and it's covered with a handmade cotton quilt. The style is typical 1990s music video.

Suddenly, I'm thrown into another perspective. Now I'm hiding under the bed, trembling. Just as quickly, I'm back hovering above the house, witnessing a Marilyn Manson–like winged creature swoop down from the sky toward the bedroom window.

"YOUR EMPTINESS IS CALLING ME," the creature roars. Its deafening screech rumbles the building as it crashes through the large bay windows.

My perspective splits. Somehow, I'm simultaneously embodying the aerial view and the one from under the bed.

From above, I see the creature break through the window and land on the bed. From under the bed, I see shards of glass shatter across the wood floor. The creature's long, clawlike fingernails grip and rip the linens. Its body looks like a naked male, its face obstructed by long, greasy black hair. Giant leather-skinned wings grow out of its back. Strips of leather are wound tightly around its limbs. It hunches over and breathes heavily, snorting like a wolf on a hunt.

From my aerial view, I calmly watch the action unfold. But from under the bed, I'm terrified by what this creature will do to me.

Its weight makes the bed creak above me. The mattress sinks until the springs touch my back. I am trapped. I stay very still, fearing that its animal instinct knows I am just below.

What did I do for such a creature to come for me? Was I asking for it?

A deep fear of rape and death rises up inside me. I know myself to be desirable prey to such a beast. I am familiar with this force from my real life in music and felt it coming.

In a flash a chilling memory emerges: the long-haired entity that threatened me by waving its middle finger from the end of my bed when I was nineteen. If this is who's back, he is not at all playful this time and has something far more damning to tell me now.

"YOUR EMPTINESS IS CALLING ME."

It echoes like a chant.

My greatest fear is for the exorcism of my soul. Without access to my sacred, inner world, I'll be nothing but an empty earthly vessel waiting to die.

The terror of this wakes me up, both literally and figuratively. I am aware I have just received a vital message. The threat to my inner world is real.

"Your Emptiness Is Calling Me," 1998. Illustration by Melissa Auf der Maur.

Time to get in down... ↓

The Dreams
Are Broken
The Hopes
Are Lost

He's
Drawn
to my
emptyness

"Your Emptyness is calling me"

FIRE OF HELL

Sept 19ᵗʰ 98

CHAPTER 33

The Drummer and the Bass Player

SEPTEMBER 1998

AT A CROWDED AFTER-PARTY FOR THE MTV VIDEO MUSIC AWARDS (VMAs), Courtney and I were the closest things to the rocker belles of the ball. As far as pop-culture standards, it really did feel like we were on top of the world. Courtney was the most together that I'd ever seen her, and clean. Her film success had done a full 180-degree revamp of her public persona. At ages thirty-two and twenty-six, respectively, she and I both had full command of our femme fatale powers.

It was September 10, 1998, two days before the much-anticipated release of *Celebrity Skin*. The album had taken three years and $3 million to make. Its chart success was still waiting to be seen. It had all the ingredients to become a Top 40 mainstream hit, something I struggled with philosophically. I'd played my part as supporting bass player and backup singer in a band that was not truly mine and that operated in a system I never wanted to be part of. But I was keeping my doubts and ambivalence beneath the surface. This wasn't hard. My cultivated stoic self ruled all of me by now.

I arrived at the after-party dressed in some serious Flintstones chic made by Olivier Theyskens, who was one of the most exciting up-and-coming fashion stars at the time. He was a French Belgian goth boy who'd selected me as his model for his first *Harper's Bazaar* fashion spread. His clothes were powerful, remarkably well-tailored goth dreams involving a lot of leather, hooks and eyes, tiny waists, and wild structures. That day, I had the honor of wearing a rare one-of-a-kind animal-hide piece (PETA, forgive me please—it was not cool, but I was caught up in a moment!). It appeared to be made of the pelt of a deer, with glorious delicate beading and Victorian lace—part Old World, part primitive future. I wore the dress with fishnets and patent-leather knee-high Vivienne Westwood high-heeled Victorian boots.

So one could say I looked like trouble the first time I met Dave Grohl.

Dave had come out of one of the most esteemed independent music scenes in Washington, DC. At the core of this community was the music label Dischord, founded by members of the band Fugazi, formerly of Minor Threat. In the '80s and into the '90s, they mounted a sophisticated musical response to the Reagan era, not unlike the Sex Pistols' response to Thatcherism, only much more politically engaged and intellectual. That scene gave Dave the street credibility that Nirvana treasured. Before being in Nirvana, he'd been in the DC band Scream and had stood out even then as an exceptional drummer at seventeen. His talent paved his way to the top.

His band Foo Fighters had been nominated for an award that night, and we practically bumped into one another in the loud, bustling crowd. He had his hair blown out and was wearing a tailored suit, which seemed incongruous for such a sporty punk-metal guy. Perhaps these two outfits of ours, and the personae we chose to adopt for the evening, played a part in what happened next.

The evening had a hobnobbing vibe. Anyone who was anyone in the music business was in attendance. Madonna had stolen the show with the debut of her song "Ray of Light." Courtney and I had our photos taken with No Doubt's Gwen Stefani, who was also rocking a futuristic cave-woman look in an aqua fun-fur bikini top with matching hair.

The electric energy, the absurdity, the feeling of being in with the "in crowd"—all of this might've been why I abandoned my usual aloofness and introduced myself directly to Dave.

"Hi Dave, I'm Melissa. We have a friend in common—"

Before I could finish my sentence, he cut me off. "And I don't want anything to do with that person. *She* is no friend of mine." He delivered this with his characteristic charm and smile, before turning his back on me with a fling of his shiny hair.

I was taken aback. I hadn't expected the "nice guy from Nirvana" to be so rude, especially not to me, the "nice girl in Hole." Even more than being taken aback, I was insulted. I wasn't some social climber desperate for his attention. I admired his drumming, and I knew he'd been essential in elevating Nirvana's music to its next massively influential level. But I had no stake in knowing him as an individual, beyond the fact that all the older music men who'd mentored me through my deejay days and early bass-playing time in Montreal's dive bars and rock scene had enormous respect for Dave. They'd met him during his early punk days and always talked about how "nice" and "cool" he was.

These were the friends in common I was referring to when I approached him that night. In particular, I was thinking of my friend Barry "Tinker" Thomas, who'd lent his name to my first band. Barry was a gentle, stoic character, a guardian angel of sorts. If he thought Dave Grohl was nice, then Dave Grohl must have been nice.

Yet here that same Dave Grohl was, blowing me off and insinuating that he resented my connection to Courtney, who—if one wanted to go down the John and Yoko "blame the woman for ruining your favorite band" route (and many did)—had destroyed his former act.

What a dumb jock, I thought to myself. *Nothing special at all; no wonder I was never curious to meet him.*

Dave seemed to me like a simpleminded man who judged my band member, and me, unfairly. I didn't raise an eyebrow as I turned away from him, knowing there were plenty of other male musicians at the party who'd be thrilled to meet me. Only an hour later, I found myself holding hands with Flea, bass player from the Red Hot Chili Peppers, in the crowd. Ha! Totally innocent and totally silly.

After losing Patty and my father and shutting down my emotions to cope with the pain, I'd fallen into the temporary trap of a woman on display. My beauty was beginning to ensnare me for the first time in a warped feminine illness that measured my value by my attractiveness to the outside gaze. A role that her band leader and the larger music machine wanted her to play: the Babe. The years 1998–1999 were my darkest, in this respect.

The next day, the bad vibe from my encounter with Dave was still lingering. I called "Tinker," who was by now living illegally in LA and playing in a band called Bluebird. Barry had also been the tech interpreter in the 3D sound dream that changed my life.

I told him what his jerk friend had said to me. Was *this* the "nice guy" he was buddies with?

Barry had been looking out for me since I was a teen in Montreal. He had my back on this one, too. He was a man of few words, which was a big part of why we all loved him. With his tech knowledge, he spoke like a physicist and looked like a 1950s auto mechanic. "I'm going to call Dave to rectify this situation," he said. "I apologize, Melissa. This should not have happened."

He called Dave and told him in his polite, slightly robotic voice, "Hello, Dave, I am calling because you offended a dear friend of mine, and I think you owe her an apology."

As fate would have it, Dave and I were neighbors in LA—and I mean genuine neighbors, living one door down from each other on Little Laurel Canyon Boulevard. We both rented from the same magnificent, eccentric magician who owned two perfect little Cape Cod–style cottages on either side of his home. The houses were set back behind big pine trees, in their own enclave, but given LA's car culture and the fact that Dave and I both traveled a lot, we'd never bumped into each other during the whole year we'd been living on the same property.

The day after his phone call with Barry, Dave knocked on my door and apologized for his behavior at the VMAs. He explained he was in the midst of packing up his cottage to move back to Virginia that week. Did I want to join him and some friends at the empty house for his goodbye barbecue?

I walked over that evening. We hung out in his backyard with Barry and a few other mutual friends who played in local bands. Dave told me he was done with Hollywood and wanted to reconnect with his punk roots and get "real" back home.

Here was the nice, down-to-earth person I'd heard about for so long.

That night he walked me home, and we kissed on my doorstep. It was passionate and playful, with a bit of laughter about "the girl next door." Very Americana, and not my usual style of romance. We made a plan for the next night after the truck was packed up with his belongings for the move. He invited me to his suite at the Chateau Marmont Hotel, where he'd spend his last night in LA.

The Chateau was the best hotel in Hollywood. Courtney would live there for months at a time, and it was where all our fancy band press and promotional junkets were held. I had spent a lot of time there getting dolled up and feeling like I was living out a rock-star princess fantasy. When Dave invited me there, he mentioned that Taylor Hawkins—the new drummer for Foo Fighters, whom he'd poached from Alanis Morrisette's band, of all places—was staying in the suite as well. My close friend Sarah Sophie Flicker was an on-again, off-again lesbian (nowadays simply called bisexual!) who had recently decided that she wanted to revisit dating men, so I invited her on a double date with me, Dave, and Taylor.

The four of us met up at the hotel and ordered dinner and drinks up to the suite, which had a dining room, living room, and terrace. Dave and Taylor were entertaining, sporty drummer boys, both wearing a variation of khaki shorts, band sweatshirts, and Vans. It was quite a contrast to Sarah's and my more sophisticated outfits: retro-chic denim capri pants, slip-on cocktail heels, tiny and transparent flowy tops, and the perfect, tasteful amount of makeup.

The two guys were goofy and humorous, feeding off of each other in the way that only boys in bands do. It made me happy that they'd found one another. It was widely known that Dave had a hard time filling his own virtuoso drummer shoes when he started his own band, and in Taylor he'd found his perfect brother and companion for the job. It was refreshing and joyful to witness that kind of boy bonding.

After several drinks and dinner and more banter, it was a natural progression for each couple—Sarah and Taylor, me and Dave—to retire to our separate rooms in the suite for what seemed likely to be one-night stands.

I walked away the next day feeling proud that I'd shown my friend a good time . . . and also confused that the happy, goofy drummer guy had figured out my physical code. No one had ever put so much effort into making me orgasm in my entire life. I was twenty-six years old, and he was the first guy to bring me to climax. No penetration, no penis needed, just hands—drummer's hands.

As I've said, I was not that into sex. Playing music was my instinctive sexual outlet. Penetrating the audience with my bass was my true desire. But Dave, the best drummer on the planet, had opened something up in me, and the chemistry between us was undeniable. Sarah was the only person I told about this, given the history between Courtney and Dave. I knew that for as long as I stayed in Hole, any kind of relationship with Dave Grohl would be off-limits.

Plus, he wasn't my type.

✗

Within weeks of its release, the *Celebrity Skin* album was a success. The songs "Celebrity Skin" and "Malibu" were to get heavy radio and MTV airtime, and we'd received great reviews and shot several magazine covers. Courtney and I had accomplished what we'd set out to do when I joined Hole: to put women on the rock stage, show the world what we were made of, and give our male peers a new perspective—to put them in their place, if you will.

I could feel the awe and respect coming my way when I was recognized at a show or browsing in a music shop. As a female-led rock music group we were an anomaly, and there was no one in music, of any gender, who matched the extremes of our front woman. The longer we could stay in the top ranks of the scene and the higher we climbed, the more women we could inspire and convince to join us.

But our work was far from done. We were determined to keep getting our message into people's daily lives, to reach them in their homes and make fans and feminists of their children through visceral emotions, savage beauty, sensuality, and humor. All the good stuff!

By the spring of 1999, we headed to New York City for the *Late Night with David Letterman* show. *Celebrity Skin* had been out for six months by then. Our second single, "Malibu," was on Top 40 radio, and the glossy music video was in constant rotation on MTV.

By that point, because of my photography and visual arts background, Courtney had empowered me to be the visual, aesthetic contact for the band. I was overseeing some of the album design, music video making, and the set designs for the stage show. For the "Malibu" video I interfaced with the director and the editor around a very expensive video shoot that involved burning palm trees, giant billboards, and car explosions. After we shot it, I spent time in the editing bay to review some passes.

Courtney saw our edits and made some big changes. Her edits put in all these weird outtakes of me laughing like some kind of comedic goofball and one of me quite literally picking my nose. She was aiming to make me more likable and relatable. Over the phone she challenged my self-presentation, referring to "Cameron Diaz" as a woman so pretty she could do comedy and said I could consider the same for myself. I was now twenty-seven and a serious rock musician. I didn't want that. I wanted the beauty on the screen.

A woman in a band, who's in the public eye, gets trapped inside a visual representation of themselves, no matter how strong they are to begin with. Female exhibitionism has been such a ginormous part of arts and culture for hundreds of years. Being female to the public male gaze inevitably traps you in your physical form. That's how you can be on the top of the world and have all the trappings of it, or at least that's what it looks like from the outside, while at the same time you have lost such a big piece of yourself. I found myself falling into a hollow version of myself, a self that was nothing but beauty and style.

It was a slow, and steady, slippery slope, the beauty thing. I blame LA, but it wasn't always a sinister thing. "Have you *ever* tweezed your eyebrows?" asked Molly Stern, one inch from my face at my first visit to a Hollywood beauty parlor soon after moving to Los Angeles. She was an angelic and charismatic wannabe redhead with swing-dance chic. No one had ever looked that closely into my face or hair situation before. She was a

born-and-bred Angeleno, which was something I quickly learned to value highly—set apart from a transplant who came for fame. Exactly my age, she was an up-and-coming Hollywood hair and makeup artist to the stars. She loved dressing up, but more important, loved rock music—which was the gateway to our connection. I knew I'd have to start getting used to this primping thing, and she held my hand through my first real haircut and makeover. I trusted her, so I kept this soul sister close as my go-to beauty squad—we would even start a Black Sabbath cover band in the future, just for fun. I loved her so much. But still, even in her care, so much looking at myself in the mirror, photos of me reflected back in magazines and on TV, I lost myself in the surface of my existence, simply because of the role I had found myself in.

Polaroid from *Celebrity Skin* photo shoot, 1998. Photo by Guzman.

Meanwhile, so many integral things I valued most had been taken from me: Patty, my father, musical integrity, and a true art scene. To survive, I was focusing on the superficial. I'd lost my way.

Courtney got that about me. She got that my true value was not as a beauty queen. She was trying to tell me with her video edits and with a letter she sent to me soon after, which she titled "Beauty Manifesto DuJour." It's profound and glorious to read now, but at the time it seemed manipulative and hypocritical. Wasn't she the one turning into a blonde bombshell, a silver-screen star on the covers of magazines?

Look in the mirror, I thought. I had learned not to trust her, or anyone in our camp, for that matter.

Ultimately, we struck a compromise for the "Malibu" video. The final version removed some of those goofball shots and still depicts me as more casual and human, which is a good thing in the long run.

```
11/09/1998
Beauty Manifesto DuJour


Dear Melissa,
I want to explain something to you that I know
about Beauty.
   It's a fairly recent revelation (the past
year or so) but it's transgender and an amazing
thing to know. Harder, I think, for someone as
technically beautiful-lifelong-as yourself to
come to grips with-But if you can, it will see
you through the Rest of your life-including
AFTER your beauty fades. The Greatest stars, the
ones that truly endure, are the ones, beautiful
or not, who are generous with their spirits and
faces in the images they present to us.
   Sure, Joan Crawford was a brilliant mannequin-
```

but she is not loved and respected the way Vivien Leigh was.

Nicole Kidman is a Beautiful woman—so Frozen by her obvious—huge—vanity that although yes she is famous and—makes men look good, no one likes her or looks at her for modeling.

A woman—Annette Benning, Jessica Lange, even Gwen Stefani, is so much more appealing when she is uncannily beautiful on the outside AND is a little transgender and goofy about it.

That's why Drew is so loved, and why Kurt was, all that Beauty, all that crazy symmetry and Beautiful face & body But seemingly HARDLY AWARE of it. I once heard that Jessica Lange didn't even look at polaroids or spend more than 20 minutes in the chair—so comfortable was she with herself. I don't have the luxury of your bones or hers, and I know that a winning beautiful shot which shows truth is worth so much more to me than a modeling shot—I'm not a model and if I give some truth now when I'm 40 & upwards I will endure.

Because I depended on beauty PLUS personae.

As we enter into this cycle together I don't want to begin it by rolling my eyes at a sort of vanity that could become tragic in its stiffness and dependency on youth. I like you because you're a <u>QUEEN</u> you're <u>not</u> a <u>PRINCESS.</u> Big difference. A <u>Princess</u> will get married off.

A <u>Queen</u> will Rule and have what she needs and wants and get shit done.

I love that we're all a little/lot vain and foppish—so were the rolling stones—but as women I don't want to see you on a self-destructive course. I don't want to see you as a lifeless mannequin, you're one of the century's Great Rock Stars for god's sake, you don't have to play Daddy like Gwen who will end up History at the Due Date (35). Anyway. You are a <u>true star</u> not a fake, and a true star with your amount of Beauty. Can be as alien-cyber-fashion-cool as you'd like—I love that—but you've got to let it go in terms of the Ice Princess thing—<u>Give</u>.

Cause you are so much more than that. This is written in part to your response to the video, not so much that it bothered you but at how I see you being myopic & shortsighted a little bit about your own <u>appeal</u>.

DON'T GET TRAPPED By YOUR BEAUTY!! You are So much more than Beautiful. You will cause change and affect reality, just give of your beauty, you know you have it, be <u>Generous</u> with it. Boys will want to marry you. Girls will want to be you. And whip out your mannequin stuff whenever you'd like but don't be afraid of that goofy funny part. <u>That's</u> the part that's enormously sexy and appealing, your Nick part if you will. & the synergy between the warmth & earthiness and the intellect & Enigma is what makes you a star.

Mostly though just an advice letter. Something I've wanted to say for a while but didnt . . . know how. There is Nothing wrong with what you want in regards to the video, but I have a fantasy that you replace <u>all </u>the appeal with frosty Beauty—(In life too, the drive to replace is what I want to call your attention to)—Please Try for a 50/50 balance. For your own sake.

Because you are better than just beautiful.

When you're drunk and nasty & funny & making guttural noises & making collages out of garbage & jewels, you are unbeatably <u>mega</u>.

Love,
Your friend,
C

> Beauty. Please try — for a 50/50 balance. for your own sake. Because you are better than just beautiful. When you're drunk and nasty & funny & making wierd Gutteral noises & ~~you are~~ ~~totally~~ making collages out of Garbage & Jewels you are unbeatably <u>MEGA</u>.
>
> Love,
> your friend
> C.

✕

Our visit to New York City was a whirlwind of activity, with a one-day side trip to Nashville for the Billboard Music Awards. We sold out two nights at the Roseland Ballroom and swanned through a week of glamorous celebrity parties. Although I was based in Los Angeles at the time, I still had a lot of friends in New York, including a few up-and-coming female actresses, some old pals from Montreal, and a group of barfly intellectuals I'd connect

---

"Beauty Manifesto," excerpt from Courtney Love fax, 1998.

with for late-night musings whenever I was in town. I felt at home on the East Coast and longed to move back there. I was much more social than my bandmates. Before she left the band, Patty had tended to keep to her lesbian friends wherever she had them, and Eric's social life was always a mystery to me.

"Canadians are everywhere!" Courtney would say, marveling at all my backstage visitors in almost any city we played. She had a few trusted, loyal folks, but at that point in her life she was so famous that she was wary of new people.

Hole performed at the top of our game at the Roseland shows. We'd been on tour for the past six months, the songs were tight, and our sets ran more smoothly than ever. Courtney was in excellent shape, fresh off of shooting *Man on the Moon*, in which she costarred with Jim Carrey, and she was taking her health and public persona very seriously. We had a new drummer who had replaced Patty, Samantha Maloney, from the straight-edge hardcore scene in New York. She was as young as I was when I joined the band, so I made sure to take sweet care of her. It helped that she was drama free and doing a great job despite the difficult position she was in, replacing yet another bandmate lost to self-destructive behavior.

Whereas Los Angeles was an industry town where the bigwig executives came to the shows, New York was where the cool kids came out. We had so many late-night and hilarious celebrity gatherings that week, including a karaoke after-party in the West Village that turned into a "who's who" of '90s culture, including Kevin Spacey, Liv Tyler, Natasha Lyonne, Parker Posey, Clea DuVall, Christina Ricci, Michael Stipe, Gaby Hoffmann, and more.

Someone led a horrid group rendition of "Hotel California" that I understood to be a friendly nod to our latest album, a California-infused and Fleetwood Mac–inspired concept album that Courtney dedicated to "All the Stolen Water of Los Angeles, and Anyone Who Ever Drowned."

Also present that night was a mature and straightlaced actor who caught my eye. I'd recently seen him in an indie film starring alongside Viggo Mortensen, who was everyone's favorite heartthrob at the time. I asked

Natasha Lyonne to introduce me to this guy, and just like that we were leaving the bar together. The night turned into a delightful walk through the city streets, hand in hand until the wee hours of the morning . . . and a little more, but light and easy between two people on the move who were just seeking a make-believe romance for the evening.

We met up again later that week in the lobby bar of the Gramercy Park Hotel to watch Hole's performance on *Letterman*. I invited Gaby Hoffmann as a social foil to what I thought might be a slightly awkward date. Gaby brought along her new Bard College film-studies boyfriend, Tony Stone, who I thought looked a bit like a young Billy Corgan with lovely curls falling just above his shoulders and around his cherubic face—and who, it turned out, I would marry more than a decade later. We shared a few beers, and I played it cool watching my band on late-night TV, exuding the good old "I don't care about success" vibes of my clan. But now those clan members *did* seem to give a shit, and I was the odd woman out, it seemed.

High-Fashion Interlude

Milano Fashion Week, Fall 1998

This wonder tale of '90s decadence is absolutely my favorite dinner-party story.

In the fall of 1998, Donatella Versace invited Courtney and me to sit front row at the Versace show at Milan Fashion Week. It was an all-expenses-paid trip that included suites at the 1920s neoclassical five-star Hotel Principe Di Savoia, our own handsome drivers, and our own security guards outside of our hotel rooms. We were treated to the most luxury I've ever experienced. Our chauffeurs brought us to the Versace store in Milan, which was as big as a department store, and we were encouraged to take whatever we wanted. I left with two suitcases of clothes. Many pieces are still unworn in my closet today, and others made wonderful gifts to friends and cousins who could never, like me, otherwise buy Versace.

For the big night we were dressed by their stylist in one-of-a-kind pieces from their showroom. I wore a copper wire–fitted corset/tube-top elaborate piece, with wide-legged Versace black wool slacks. Accessories du jour for me at the time were always leather bands around my wrists and some kind of metal hairpiece. This time it was a copper headband with two little horns coming out of the top of my head.

Before the show we went backstage to meet Donatella and her entourage. We were brought to a private, curtained-off lounge within the big changing room where the dozens of naked models and stylists buzzed hectically. Perched on a white couch, we were offered champagne and silver platters of cocaine. What came next made us both blush.

As we politely sipped from glass flutes and felt obliged to take tiny sniffs of high-quality powder, Donatella gave a gentle clap of her hands.

"Bring in the boys," she commanded deadpan, with a strong Italian accent, to one of the well-dressed small Italian men who hovered around her.

One by one, "the boys" entered the lounge. Some were dressed runway ready in suits, and others were shirtless and in the midst of getting dressed. They were ushered into a lineup.

"Boys, you all know Courtney and Melissa from Hole?" Donatella demanded respect for her honorable guests, and as if this was the usual routine, each male model introduced himself to us, like they were auditioning.

"I'm Jim, from Wyoming, and I love a tractor."

"I'm Dave from California; surfing is my jam."

Courtney and I looked sideways at each other in disbelief and grasped hands, trying not to laugh, as we were told that all "the boys" would be at the after-party back at the Versace home, and we each would have our choice for companionship.

The highlight of the night was snorting a single line of coke, under a Picasso in a bathroom in the Versace home, with Jennifer Venditti, a woman in the fashion industry I had just met that night, who would more than a decade later become my only daughter's godmother—instant lifelong connection on the absurdity of it all. I spent much of the rest of the night trying to avoid one of the overly handsome male models who had his eye on me. Toward the end of the party I found myself telling him I was not interested and taking shelter in an intimate gathering in Courtney's bedroom that led to possible whispers of a threesome between Kate Moss, Courtney, and me.

I remember politely declining and retiring back to my room for the evening, relieved to be alone.

CHAPTER 34

My Drug? Crushes

I NEVER GOT SERIOUS WITH ANY MEN DURING MY YEARS IN HOLE. MY IDEA of a good time was to stay until closing at an old dive bar, then make out with my latest crush in an alleyway and talk about what romance and soul connections could be. I liked a long courting game, imagining that I was living in 1930s Paris like Henry Miller and Anaïs Nin, or like Gustav Klimt surrounded by muses in turn-of-the-century Vienna—only I was both Gustav *and* his muse. These encounters felt like heaven to me and a welcome distraction from all the drama and chaos of touring. I was seeking romance more than sex and was obsessed with the act of getting to know someone new. I'd approach the finish line of intercourse or a relationship, or both, but I rarely crossed it. I didn't want to be tied down or to seal the deal with any one person. I wanted to ride free around the globe.

Most of my sexuality had been fleshed out via loud rock music, in the act of both creating and experiencing it. I've always said that you can tell what someone is like sexually by the way they perform onstage. How they move and play reflects their connection to a deep desire and life force that lies under the skin somewhere in between the heart, mind, and spirit. A live show may be a shared experience, but you are alone in the way it moves you and makes you feel.

That was the pleasure I hunted for.

My dream about 3D sound was about music's power to unite heartbeats and flesh, allowing a group of people to become "one." It's a shared experience that takes you out of yourself. Until now, my sensual experiences in

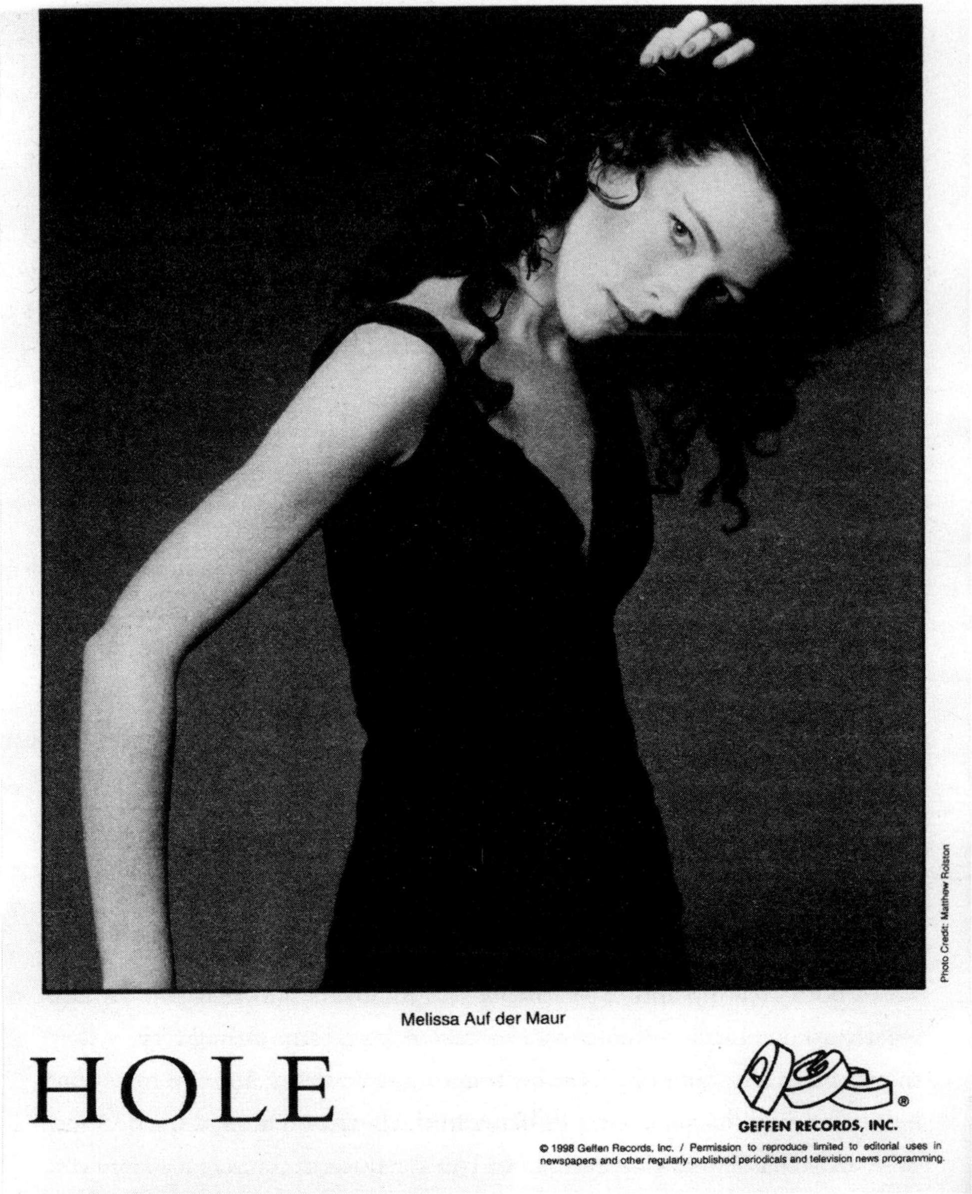

Melissa Auf der Maur

HOLE

© 1998 Geffen Records, Inc. / Permission to reproduce limited to editorial uses in newspapers and other regularly published periodicals and television news programming.

Headshot courtesy of Geffen Records, Inc./UMG, 1998. Photo by Matthew Rolston.

crowds or onstage had been more pleasurable than one-on-one intimacy with another human. This may be why, when I became so disillusioned with the music scene, my sensual, idle music hands turned to actual men. For better or worse.

Sensual decadence, compounded by my emotional detachment, likely stunted my growth when it came to love, relationships, and intimacy, but I learned a great deal about people during those years. I could play the role of therapist soul sister to my male peers in the rock scene, these wild yet sensitive, wizard-like men. They were traveling the world on a mission to find themselves through music, and I could meet them where they were because I was right there with them. My penchant for noncommittal flirtations made things easy for them at the end of a long night on the road. Being a member of Hole gave me an air of power and allure, but I wasn't Courtney, so I didn't scare them.

The men I became entangled with tended to fall into eight categories. These were the archetypes I fell for at the time:

- **The Dive-Bar Rock Poet:** An old-school Bukowski romantic party boy who came up in the Washington, DC, hardcore scene. Ethical and educated, he had endless independent music and poetic credibility. He loved French and European culture, which set him apart from the usual American man. He was also unavailable and drank too much. Incredibly sexy.
- **The Tortured Punk Poet:** He was a surfer from Hawaii who sang in a band on one of the coolest punk record labels out of the Midwest. He lived in his grandparents' house on a golf course in LA. He was celibate and unavailable, and he didn't drink, which was both attractive and suspicious. I was obsessed. A solid long-term friendship came from our time together, though. His response to an email I sent him in 2021 said, "Remember the time we sat in Canter's Deli and I asked how you were so good with people? You answered that you simply liked people a lot and there was no other secret. I knew then I could never be good with people. Ha."

- **The Short-Lived Songbird of Our Generation:** Cheekbones from heaven, hands held, diary left on my bed that I never read.
- **The Tortured Movie Star:** He was a member of a famous and tragic showbiz family and a fixture in the LA scene. His late-night appearances in my life would have freaked me out if his passionate brooding hadn't been so attractive to me, like the ghost of James Dean. His brief, unhealthy fascination with me got us into a messy place where we didn't stand a chance. Still, he was a man of outrageous depth, mystery, and beauty. He drank too much. Incredibly sexy.
- **The Dream Fanboy Babe by the Backstage Door:** Irish and Italian, he worked at his family's Detroit auto shop. His look was a '90s dream combo of Johnny Depp with a little Matt Dillon mixed in. The takeaway: midwestern after-show make-out sessions with strangers are great!
- **The Rock-Star Soul Brother:** I offered him Ampeg amplifier tubes as a gift and an opening slot at a few of our shows. Despite his hard-living tendencies, he was my dream man for real. We eventually became music collaborators and mutual supporters. He was always cool and always respectful, and his talent was above and beyond them all. I wanted to be him. Incredibly sexy.
- **The Pretty Boy Pop Rock Crooner:** Kicking drugs on the beach, holding hands, and an occasional hug.
- **The Nice, Sensitive Guy in an Indie-Rock Band.** There were so, so, so many of these—in every country, on every tour, every day of the week. They were good company and a pleasurable, safe way to explore my desires. Lovely conversations, talking shop, late-night walks on unfamiliar streets, hand holding in hotel elevators and making out everywhere. Incredibly fun, all of them.

CHAPTER 35

First Loves Save the Day

SUMMER 1999

GIVE ME AN R (CROWD CHANT: *R!*)
    - O (Crowd Chant: *O!*)
    - C (Crowd Chant: *C!*)
    - K (Crowd Chant: *K!*)
    —*What you got?!*
    (Crowd Chant: *Rock!*)
    What We Gonna Do?!
    (All together: *Rock You!!*)

Over the summer of 1999, Hole toured across Canada as part of an outdoor summer festival called the Edge Fest, Canada's wannabe Lollapalooza. As the only international act on the bill (other than the Australian band Silverchair, a teen Kurt/Nirvana look-alike band that was eerie to have so near to us), we kicked off our set each day with "Rock You" by Helix, a Canadian one-hit wonder. All the other bands were Canadian, including the coheadliners, Moist.

Yes, "Moist Hole" was at the top of this bill, a joke that was not lost on anyone who got near that tour.

Courtney, Eric, Samantha, and I were in top entertainment shape, having just spent weeks on giant festival tours around the world. For a couple of them we coheadlined with Marilyn Manson. Since the Nine Inch Nails tour five years prior, these boys in "pleather" goth garb had become kingpins of the mainstream goth-rock world, even eclipsing their NIN mentor, Trent Reznor, with alt-rock radio hits like "Beautiful People" from their 1996 album, *Antichrist Superstar*. Their current album, *Mechanical Animals*—also produced by Michael Beinhorn and released that September, just days after *Celebrity Skin*—featured feel-good hits like "The Dope Show" and "I Don't Like the Drugs (but the Drugs Like Me)."

The volatile pairing of our two bands made industry sense due to our album's commercial successes and our promotional cycles syncing up—and, as usual, potential headlines. Artistically, though, it was an unlikely marriage that brought out the worst from our outspoken, controversial front people. Manson front man Brian Warner and Courtney played up their Beauty and the Beast personae, which made for loads of drama. Plus, the level of drugs that surrounded the Manson band, in contrast to our newly "cleaner" band, was concerning. Similar to when Courtney the Widow was booked on "The Self-Destruct Tour" in 1994, we were trapped with these ogres again. It wasn't good for anyone's mental or physical health, to say the least.

We had just been Down Under for the Big Day Out festival again, with an eclectic lineup that featured us along with Marilyn Manson, Korn, Fat Boy Slim, and Sean Lennon. Following that tour we coheadlined, with Marilyn Manson, the Beautiful Monsters Tour, a US arena tour. This one was supposed to extend for two months, but it was doomed from the start. It lasted just over two weeks, cut short due to a variety of messy things, including financial disputes and a public feud between Brian and Courtney, which resulted in Hole pulling out of the tour early. Our last show of the Beautiful Monsters Tour took place at the Great Western Forum in Los Angeles, where Brian coincidentally twisted his ankle in his big platform boot onstage. The tour ended there and then.

Following that we had a killer run of European early-summer festivals and headlining shows, including a triumphant UK set at Glastonbury that we arrived at via helicopter, with a brief sightseeing twirl above Stonehenge. Michael Stipe was with us because R.E.M. was headlining the

Pyramid Stage that day. Hole was scheduled in a perfect sunset slot, and we were at top-notch ability. We had come a long way since Reading five years earlier.

After the main-stage sets were finished, I set out to explore the late-night dance-tent scene. Music had been changing so rapidly. I felt that I was witnessing the future of music at Glastonbury that night, or at least one that I could get behind. Fatboy Slim, whom I'd grown to love on tour in Australia earlier that year, seemed like the start of something shiny and bright coming out of all this new technology.

When Fatboy Slim's song "Right Here, Right Now" kicked in, the sea of thousands started dancing in ecstasy. The image of a tent full of sweaty smiling Brits was glorious and so different from what our alternative-rock scene had been built on. They were turned inward into themselves, ecstatic as a group and led by one clever and humble man, Norman Cook (originally a bass player from the '80s band the Housemartins that I had loved as a teen!). An egoless, artistic, poetic, and electronic pioneer, to me Cook represented what future could exist without "rock stars" but instead actual servants of sound who allowed us to tap into the music god within ourselves.

In that tent that day, I felt a glimmer of my dream about 3D sound that I'd had almost a decade before. *Maybe we can transcend these egos and individual dramas and morph into a collective group*, I thought. My disenchanted rock heart filled with hope.

And then we were off to Canada.

Though I've always been a proud Canadian, I'd never traveled much beyond my beloved Montreal. Montrealers are infused with a continental European-influenced lifestyle and sensibility. The rest of the country felt more like a mashup of "United States meets England" culture, with a lot of drinking. Everyone was polite and nice, of course, but on that tour, I realized I was in fact a Montrealer and not as much a Canadian.

Still, it was exciting to be one of the biggest names on the bill in Canada, and especially to be the only women playing in the sweet summer sun of my homeland. We were given special treatment at hotels, on festival grounds, and on days off. I was celebrated as a source of national pride. On Canada

Day, I went onstage in a Canadian-flag tube top, white hot pants, and knee-high red suede boots—a veritable Canadian Wonder Woman.

The intrigue and awe people had for our rare breed of female were palpable. We sang '80s Canadian hit songs to get the crowd excited, incorporating a fun cover of Bryan Adams's "Summer of '69" in which Courtney and I traded on and off for lead vocals. The crowd went wild. On that tour I got some of my best photos of Courtney performing to seas of crowds and dynamic close-ups of the fans she would bring up onstage to join us.

On July 9 in Calgary, we celebrated Courtney's thirty-fifth birthday. I threw her a decadent surprise party in the catering tent at the end of the night. All the bands and crews were invited, and a cowgirl stripper was hired as the center of entertainment. It had been a big leap for a goth-punk stripper from California to become one of the most famous women in the world, with a Top 40 hit song, a headlining festival spot, and big roles in Hollywood movies, and I knew Courtney would appreciate the gesture. I wasn't wrong. She showed genuine respect for the stripper by licking whipped cream off her fake breasts and taking a Jell-O shot from between her legs.

We were high on talent, power, and fun, with radio hits streaming out of cars and bars. This was the most professional and entertaining we'd ever been as a band, in a "rock" way, not the old "car-crash" way. But it was all pretty easy, and even a tad boring. There didn't seem to be much magic happening in the music scene or on those tours. The major-label grab bag of alternative bands seemed maxed out. I couldn't relate to the music or to any of the people in the bands anymore. It had begun to all feel very . . . empty.

Man on the Moon, her new Hollywood film, was due to be released in the fall, and the film schedule was holding up management's ability to commit to any more tours for Hole. We were being offered the highest fees and best festival billings, yet the band had become secondary to Courtney.

When I was truly honest with myself, what I wanted then was the same thing I'd wanted in 1994, when Billy let my band, Tinker, open for him. Artistic freedom was what drove me. Exploring creative ideas, in a little

Hole, *Guitar World* magazine, 1999. Photo by Ross Halfin.

apartment, with no deadlines and no platform to release them on, is what I wanted most. I longed to return to school for photography, learn a new printing technique, or—even more challenging—make my own record from scratch, with no bandleader to follow. My exploratory voice, which had begun to come alive in Tinker, had retreated into a swampy underworld. I needed to get it back.

I knew I'd been given a one-in-a-million opportunity and that I had everything an aspiring musician supposedly wants. I knew how lucky I was. Yet I was also so disillusioned and disconnected. It all felt kinda hopeless, even tragic, in a distressing "we've got it all" kind of way.

The power of being treated like a queen in my homeland made me even more aware of the trade-offs I'd made and what they were costing me. As we made our way across Canada, something small and bright started to burn larger inside me. So simple and effortless it was, for me to then realize, *Oh, cool. It's July, and it's been five years. I can go now.* My five-year exclusive contract was due to expire at the end of the month, and no one had noticed, or asked for renewal. *I've fulfilled my commitment to the band*, I thought. *I did my best and accomplished all I'd set out to do, and this is not what I want anymore.*

This revelation screamed FREEDOM! to me. I knew what I had to do.

Vancouver was our last date on the summer tour, and on the plane back home to Los Angeles, I began writing my letter of resignation to Hole. With each line, I felt the flame inside of me start coming back to life.

When I landed in Los Angeles, I turned on my newly acquired cell phone. I still had no email and had only recently graduated to a cell phone, using it for emergencies and short texts with a few people.

A text message popped up from Dave Grohl, whom I hadn't heard from in months. I read it in the town car driving back to my little cottage in Laurel Canyon.

I'm in LA, please tell me you're here and we can see each other.

Since our one-night stand almost a year before, Dave and I would occasionally text. Our exchanges were simple and didn't amount to much more than
Hi! I am making a record, how are you?
Hello! I'm fine and on tour.

Dave was, in retrospect, lightly courting me via text, but I hadn't thought much about it. It did feel like kismet, however, that his request had arrived right in the wake of my fresh secret decision to leave Hole.

I texted back, telling him I'd just returned from tour and was free that night. I suggested we meet at Three Clubs, one of my regular bars on the corner of Santa Monica Boulevard and Vine Street. A few hours later, as I was getting ready to meet him, I felt like I was harboring two secrets: first, that I was going to leave Hole, which Courtney was not prepared for; and second, that I'd just planned a clandestine meeting with one of her archenemies.

I arrived at the bar first. Rio, one of my favorite native Angelenos and bartenders, was behind the bar. As I took a sip of Rio's signature tequila cocktail with a lot of lime, I looked up at the mirror behind the bar and saw Dave walk into the room. Our eyes met through the reflection in the mirror, and we both beamed. And just like that—the same way it had happened when I'd descended the escalator at the Seattle airport to meet Hole—I felt a powerful sense of inevitability. That's when I realized, *Oh, shit. We're going to fall in love.*

I understood in that moment that love is not always what you think it is. Love at first sight is just a dream. In reality, your true love may be already right there, in your midst. Love is a mystery and something no one can fully understand or predict. I surrendered to its force.

Dave was excited to see me, and I him. He walked up with a huge smile and his giddy, nervous drummer energy.

"I haven't been able to stop thinking about you since our night together last year," he said.

I was touched by his immediate honesty and directness. It opened my heart and softened me up right away.

We had a sweet night talking about music, old mutual friends from Montreal, the new album he was in town mixing and planning to release that fall, and the big tour I was just getting off. Two people at the top of their game. Two equals. I think that felt new and refreshing for both of us. We spoke openly about our potential as a couple, and he very forwardly said he was interested in exploring a relationship with me. I was candid about my plans to leave Hole, which didn't take much for him to support.

Everything you've spent your life thinking you want, whom you want, and what actually works for you may turn out to be completely different. I had never fallen head over heels in love before or even had a real boyfriend, at least not one that lasted more than my usual three to six months. And there hadn't been many of those, either.

Perhaps I didn't know myself as well as I thought. Or perhaps I was changing and life was showing me something new, because I was ready to see and feel it. We went back to my house in Laurel Canyon and pledged to keep seeing each other as much as we could, despite our wild lives.

In hindsight, I can see that in all those years leading up to Dave, I was processing my mother's radical independence and my father's complicated emotional inheritance. I'd purposely been avoiding committed relationships, real intimacy, and sex. Instead, I was pining over unobtainable, odd, and tortured men. But the universe spins magic, sometimes.

Here was a nice, direct person who had decided he wanted me, then courted and pursued me and offered me a connection, and what felt like a cosmic musical bond helped me receive it. There was quite possibly no other person in the world who shared the same slice of madness that emerged from the nexus of Kurt, Courtney, suicide, and heroin-infused "rock music meets mainstream mayhem" we had both experienced. We never spoke about it. We didn't need to. We had both harbored something untouchable, an ache deep inside, and then—all of a sudden—we were not alone with it anymore.

Within a week after I decided to leave Hole, and as I fell deeply in love with Dave, another first love popped back into my life.

First Loves Save the Day | 355

The rotary phone rang in my Laurel Canyon dollhouse. "The stars have aligned," a familiar nasally voice said. "It's time for you to join my band."

Billy Corgan. "How did you know I'm about to leave Hole?" I asked. Truly, I was mystified by how the most guarded secret of my life could be known. But then again, he was my "spiritual fucking cowboy" after all.

"D'arcy has disappeared," Billy explained. "We're completing our new album, which will be our last album, and you are the only person who can take her place."

What timing! I wasn't even yet officially free from Hole. I still faced the daunting task of telling Courtney about my plan, and this had already fallen into my lap.

"I have to think about it, Billy," I said, quietly and slightly ashamed. "I'm about to free myself from Hole, which is no easy thing to do, and embarking immediately on another music commitment scares me a bit . . ."

There was silence on the other end. Billy was insulted and shocked, I'm sure, but then his otherworldly confidence that he always knew what was going to unfold appeared.

"Just get on a plane to Chicago and come listen to the record. We can talk about it here," he said.

I was being offered another opportunity of a lifetime, and once again, it was a hard decision to make. Especially for a girl who was seeking freedom from the overwhelming cast of characters that seemed to eternally overshadow her.

I was terrified to announce my departure to Hole, and I was also resolved. I just had to do the emotional work and find the right words to tell them. A friend offered me his family's house in Santa Barbara. I headed straight there, where I spent two days staring at the ocean. During that time I spoke to my lawyer and therapist, sketched my departure statement, and started to emotionally detach from my complex bond with the band.

I imagined Hole as a set of tentacles that had twisted around all parts of me. Then I pictured a white light from deep within the ocean dissolving them. Dave's love and Billy's music amplified that light and created an illuminated bridge I could take out of the dark underworld that had claimed me for the past five years. On the very edge of the continent, overlooking the Pacific Ocean, I felt like I was being reborn.

Meanwhile, my new, first, love was back home in Virginia. We were in constant touch by phone. Dave knew about my preparations to leave Hole. Then I told him about Billy's invitation.

"You're not going to do it, are you?" he asked.

"I don't know. I told Billy I'd think about it."

"But what about us? How are we gonna be together?" Dave asked.

This was a man looking for a devoted girlfriend, future wife, and mother of his children. I was too in love to see his quick concern about our future as a warning. Instead, I saw it as a testament to his love for me.

"Well, you're going to be on tour, and I may be on tour, too," I said. "We'll find each other in between."

I flew to Chicago that week and instantly fell in love with the Pumpkins' new album, *Machina/The Machines of God*. Their first two albums had been seminal music inspirations to my younger self, but the band had lost me a bit on the albums that followed. These new songs, themes, and textures brought together all of the best of them. My body tingled when I imagined playing those heavy riffs and melancholic melodies. The opening track, "The Everlasting Gaze," remains one of my favorite Pumpkins songs. I've always thought this album was overlooked and deserves far more attention in the context of the band's long career.

Machina was already in the final stages of production with everyone's favorite producer at the time, Flood, and was being mixed by the equally worshipped Alan Moulder. Flood and Moulder were a longtime UK production dream team known for their impressive credits, having worked with everyone from U2 to Depeche Mode, Nine Inch Nails to PJ Harvey, and later Sigur Rós to the Killers.

Once I was there in person with Billy and the music, I knew I had to accept his offer. It would be an honor to support this album. And how could I say no to joining my favorite band?

Once I'd told Dave I was making this choice for musical "rock-destiny" reasons, he climbed fully on board. The week before I joined the band in Chicago for rehearsals, Dave and I spent hours together in his basement home studio in Alexandria, Virginia. With his prodigy-like abilities, he helped me decipher the complicated bass parts of the songs I'd need to play, and he learned all the drum parts as well.

We'd spend half the day making out and the rest doing the other most pleasurable thing for both of us: playing rock music. He wasn't a Pumpkins

fan like I was, but their drummer, Jimmy Chamberlin, was one of the best drummers out there. Dave enjoyed mirroring his parts to help his love find her way through the most challenging songs I'd ever played.

I know it's hard to believe that all these magic moving parts happened over the course of just a couple of fateful weeks, but they did. The universe was speaking loud and clear to me, creating a reverse destiny that brought me back to the beginning, where it had all started. "One day you'll be

---

Polaroid from *Guitar World* magazine photo shoot, 1999. Photo by Ross Halfin.

in my band," Billy had told me at the side stage in Montreal, when I was twenty-one. Accepting this invitation was an act of fulfilling my destiny.

My bold chess move to leave one band in its prime for another would become headline news in the rock world. The rigor of playing with and touring with the Pumpkins would be a big departure from the "waiting for Courtney" rock career I'd had for the previous five years. I was about to prove myself as a musician in a man's world of epic riffs, arena concerts, and more private jets. As overwhelming as it all seemed, it was time to fax my resignation to Hole. To move forward, I had to commit to never looking back.

Courtney Says Goodbye

Sept 17, 1999

Dear Melissa,
I don't know, really what to say.
  I've been thinking about it for a while myself.
  I think you are afraid of your own Creativity when it comes to music, afraid to get past the withholding blocks. They suffocate you. Sometimes In the past 5 years certainly when it comes to harmonies & <u>singing</u> you've been amazingly forthcoming.
  But . . . Truthfully? As a bassist and . . . a writer? I've always felt you had more to give if you could stop being so "Precious" and "saving" yourself.
  Because its Evident you're not saving yourself for <u>yourself</u> which is a Great <u>Big</u> Fucking tragedy to me.
  I spent 4 years being dominated by dickhead men/Alpha Males and have moved on. I hate that you're proving the adage—We (females) are only good as salaried arm pieces for alpha male dickheads.
  I <u>wish</u>! <u>wish</u>! <u>wish</u>! you were doing this for yourself and no matter what you say or not—You are doing it because you believe—misguidedly—that Billy Corgan will "teach" you. (and that—very misguidedly he is a <u>BETTER INVESTMENT</u>)

Billy Corgan will, in a reactive/gleeful frenzy, convince you that you are valuable to him and then, I promise, he will use you up until your sell by date. And you ARE valuable to him as a commodity and you might get a song written for your "solo" effort which he will control etc. etc.

Oh Melissa, the future is <u>SO CLEAR</u> to me on this I'm <u>always always</u> right about this stuff.

Anyhow—I feel a little bit like I'm being dumped by a lover for an enemy. But I don't consider him an "enemy" and never will, he'll never ever ever possess my essence, Kurt's essence.

I'm sorry he's to possess your essence.

I wish you the <u>BEST</u> in your efforts to yield to <u>yourself</u>.

Build your <u>own</u> canon.

When I heard the little bit I heard of your own stuff I was proud of your voice and the vibe.

I wish you had put your 25% of that into this band. But you chose not to. Nonetheless—It was Great, don't let the delicate part of yourself get smashed.

NOW→ As I said on the phone

This is my <u>Stock</u>, you are about to Eve Harrington/Embarrass me & Eric publicly & make us look like the weaker band next to Billy's Band—Which is Grotesque. and a lie. And I <u>won't</u> lie down for it.

No way.

Number one reason?

Guess what I'm gonna say? . . .

WE AREN'T THE WEAKER BAND.

But you're going to make me look foolish in a very humiliating manner for a minute, and I need to spin this <u>MY</u> way.

You are going to make yourself look— Specifically? Like a Girly version of Dave Navarro, which is not a great thing, but that's your problem.

Public Perception being a very
<u>REAL CONSIDERATION</u>

In order to keep this Amicable or at least to not provoke me

You need to think about my/our "stock"

As a delicate gardenia from a Hothouse Enigmatic, frail, & rare. I'm not a thistle and neither is the name Hole, and if you want to make it look like we're some hearty common weed on the front lawn we're <u>all in for it</u> and "it" is Ugly and none of us (but Billy, who is so negative) wants it

So Let's not go there.

I will have no Public announcements on you or Billy's (poor Billy . . .) behalf until a replacement has been found for you. & a good solid replacement. Then we will ease into the shift slowly and coolly.

Do you understand this?

Before we hand this off to the lawyers and managers, let's have this dialogue.

As a matter of fact—we should <u>keep</u> the dialogue just like a good divorce. All Good divorces have dialogue. Bad nasty ugly draining painful divorces do not.

I don't agree with you

But I do love you. And I do respect you.
And I do respect the ineffable Great Melissa-ness of you and will always watch out for you psychically and on the Ground.

As long as you respect my "stock" and my reputation publicly.

Good Luck Melissa
May the spirits guide you
& Bless you & may you make those
amazing records inside of you
I love you so much
& am Really Really Sad
<3 (drawing of a crying face)
Your sister—C

CHAPTER 36

Out of a Hole, into a Pumpkin

FALL 1999–SUMMER 2000

```
BIG B . . .
I was very happy to see your sweet weirdness
this week. I felt good about what I heard, saw
and felt, so I've got a good feeling about my
brain not melting in my future with you. How
about while I vacate from reality to a tropical
no phone no Fax world, and you slave your ears +
brain with wonder Flood this week, our hands can
call lawyers to begin preliminary check ups and
such? To get us rolling towards the exciting and
new. Good listening to you!

                                    <3 Melissa XX
    -Letter from Melissa to Billy, September 1999
```

"One lump or two?" Ozzy Osbourne asked. He was pouring tea in his Beverly Hills backyard as his wife, Sharon, and I discussed having me officially join the Smashing Pumpkins. She had just begun managing the band for their new (and last) album. That's how I found myself, as a young bass player, negotiating my next contract while the front man of the legendary grand wizards of metal, Black Sabbath, served me tea.

"So, Melissa, what would you like to get paid?" Sharon asked.

It was an abstract trick question that I had neither reference for nor experience with. In Hole, I'd never advocated or negotiated for my value.

"I'm not sure," I said.

It had never crossed my mind to be represented by a manager who could negotiate on my behalf. I just took what they offered, which in this case seemed, and still does, like a killer deal.

I agreed to a generous weekly salary for a solid year, regardless of whether I was on or off tour—a retainer, which was something I'd never had from Hole. I managed to mention, sheepishly, that I had a debt to Hole's managers, Q-Prime, who had advanced me funds toward living expenses after so little money was made from the record, followed by touring. Creating *Celebrity Skin* had cost way more than it made, and Hole's standards, or shall we say Courtney's, were extravagant. Overspending on fancy hotels, business-class flights, and the occasional private plane was the norm. Beyond the concert fees that went directly to paying the tour costs and crew members, the label had to cover all these extra costs with recoupable tour support. This was a debt we'd have to pay back in time, with radio play and record sales.

In addition to the lavish expenses, the outrageously expensive album costs and top-notch photo and music video budgets meant we would not be seeing any money from album royalties, almost ever. I left that band after five years with no money in the bank, in debt, and with no Hole money coming in. It was all a wash, really, but I sure did incur some life experience, eh?

And now here I was, twenty-seven years old and ready to start anew.

"Billy will surely take care of that for you," Sharon assured me. "Consider it a signing bonus for joining the band."

And just like that I was out of debt with big paychecks on the way, poised to join my favorite band, *and* in love.

It all felt so grown-up, idealistic, professional, joyful, and smooth. Plus, it was a totally novel bonus to have met the legendary, bat-eating, rock wizard, Ozzy. I joined my favorite band with a handshake overseen by the "master of reality" himself.

"There are three rules of the band: One, you can't make a mistake. Two, you can't get sick. And three, there are no days off."

We were in the Pumpkin Headquarters in Chicago for our first rehearsal together. I looked up from checking my bass tone. Because I was never quite able to tell when Billy was being serious or slightly sarcastic, I assumed what he said was true. More or less, it turned out to be.

The song list I had to learn was long, and the days of perfecting them were longer. The catalog at this point was overwhelming compared to what I had been used to pulling from to build live sets with Hole. The Pumpkins had released five albums, one double album, an album of B-sides and outtakes, *and* a box set of even more rarities. The band was prolific, to say the least. There were nearly one hundred songs that Billy wanted to be able to pull from at any time. And the upcoming world tour was right around the corner. As the only new member, I had a lot of catching up to do.

Part of this was learning how Billy played around with special guitar tunings to accommodate and preserve his voice. Certain songs, ones with a lot of high-note screaming, were easier to sing at a lower register, so we had multiple instruments tuned in different ways: standard tuning, drop-D tuning, one tuned a half step down and another tuned a full step down—*plus* a backup instrument for everyone, in case we broke a string. That meant a total of eight basses for me. Fender Guitars had sponsored me during Hole, and I was thrilled to pick up my conversation with them and add more Fender Precisions to my collection of custom sparkle basses.

Learning all the songs with the constant changing of instruments, and planning for different song set lists every night, was intense. It expanded my mental dexterity and music range tremendously. Strong musician muscles were established that year. I loved it then and am still grateful for it now.

The Pumpkins' tour started in late February to align with the album's release date. Billy wanted to do something special for the fans, so in celebration of the release we did a week of "in-store" intimate performances in record stores. Each was followed by a meet-and-greet with fans who stood in long lines to meet us. It was a healthy promo stunt, making for great visuals of fans lined up all day around the block and followed by hours of shaking hands and taking photos with them. Ten days in a row—sometimes three cities in a day—no days off.

February 28, the album release date, found us in Chicago. I loved how patriotic and loyal the Pumpkins were to their hometown. I could relate. From there we moved on to New York, Philadelphia, Boston, Cleveland, Minneapolis, LA, San Francisco, and Seattle. We zigzagged across the country by private jet, the only way you can get to that many cities in a row, on time. This added another compelling visual of a giant rock band on tour.

Record-store empires still existed at that time but were soon to die with the rise of digital home consumption. It was the last gasp of the big chains like Tower Records, Virgin Mega Stores, and HMV. They were all huge department-style stores, laid out the way fast-fashion giants Zara and Urban Outfitters are laid out today. It was an unfortunate swap: music for fashion. I mourn the lost rituals of having real-life physical hunts for albums and striking up in-person exchanges around the music bins now that music is available at everyone's fingertips, for free at home.

After the intimate tour kicked off, the relentless Pumpkins' worldwide arena tour began. We were scheduled for more than one hundred sold-out shows in twenty countries in ten months. From the United States to Japan, Korea, and Canada, and across most of Europe and concluding in South Africa, arenas were packed with devoted fans who fed the magical exchange between audience and performers. We often opened up for ourselves with an acoustic set leading into our rock set. This often made for up to three-hour shows, unusual for any band, let alone one exerting so much energy and sound. The incredibly heavy and long sets made me sweat like an athlete, which was a new extreme for me.

Billy was happiest when playing, so we played a lot. Up to five shows a week, with very short breaks between the tour legs. It was nothing any of us were not capable of and came with the territory. I admired Billy's ambition, and was happy to rise to the occasion, but when I think of it now, it seems impossible that I would have been able to extend this kind of lifestyle into the next couple of decades, as some of my peers did. I needed to step off the circus caravan eventually and experience life in one place, where you cannot run and hide from who and where you are.

My relationships with the boys in the band were friendly but slightly detached. Once again I was the "new" member, and this time the only girl. D'arcy's departure was a touchy topic for everyone. It was yet another wound that was best avoided in the hope that time would heal the loss.

Guitar player James Iha, however, soon became my buddy and best friend—my Patty—in the band. We shared a similar love of art and film and had mutual friends in those circles. We also had compatible tastes in fashion and food. We ate together on nights off, and synchronized our outfits on show nights with custom-made color-matching outfits that positioned us intentionally as red, white, or shiny black bookends to Billy and drummer Jimmy Chamberlin, who were positioned in the middle and always wore black leather. I really connected with Billy and Jimmy only onstage, through music. This was the holiest place for me to connect, and I cherished it.

James shared my love of photography, and together we upped our photography practice on tour. On days off, we sought out art exhibits, collected old cameras in pawn shops, and walked the streets, cameras in hand. I came up with new tricks for taking photographs onstage involving timers and foot switches that expanded my skill exponentially that year. James and I both accumulated a significant body of street-photography work on that tour. It made for a beautiful companionship when Dave wasn't with me on the road.

Most of the Pumpkins fans knew I was from Hole and that Billy had discovered me in Montreal. It was like a grunge Cinderella fable, from rags to riches, fan to band. Sometimes I'd stand onstage during a show, and the surreal aspect of it nearly overwhelmed me. It had been nearly a decade ago that a young woman had apologized for an airborne beer bottle in Montreal. I never could have imagined then that I would play this level of music, for this scale of public, with this band.

The most intoxicating part of the tour was the pure relationship we cultivated with the public. Being the force that delivers a song that brings passion, direction, or meaning to another person's life and accompanies them through tough times, let alone time *itself,* is a sacred service. I knew this from being on the other side and having received music, including some of these songs, in my youth. I took this responsibility seriously, especially when I was delivering the same songs that had woken me up to this part of myself.

No longer shackled to the mic as a backup vocalist, I was free to focus exclusively on my bass. I wielded my instrument like never before. My signature move of "chopping wood with my ax" was perfected on those stages. My superhero aura was enhanced when the stadium lights reflected off the mirror pickguard on my bass and enormous beams of light emanated across the hall and onto the crowd. The Ice Princess persona that Courtney had coined was being retired, graduating into a fiery, passionate, openhearted Queen, a rider of life at its most visceral and fantastical. I wielded that light beam like a sword across the universe, a declaration of my defrosted heart.

"I Am One," the opening track of *Gish*, was the song the band had retaliated with after the beer bottle smashed against Billy's guitar and changed my life. "We've got one more for you, Montreal," he had said that night, with more conviction than I had ever witnessed a person embody onstage, in front of a sparse group of strangers, one of which had just attacked him. The rolling tom drumbeat that opens "I Am One" is joined by an iconic two-note bass lick, then joined by feedbacking guitars to create a full-band tackle of the signature Pumpkins-style song. Playing "I Am One" for thousands aligned my cells with my inner dreams and passion for music like no other magic potion could. I found my center in this expanding infinite universe for the first time. But only for a time.

The only drawback of being part of the epic Pumpkins machine was being separated from Dave. Our longing for one another was overwhelming, and mutual. The desire to stay connected every waking minute fueled a love affair for the ages, supported by global travel and "Love Faxes."

That's right, facsimiles! An unexpected mode of romantic communication came to define both our relationship and that time of our lives. We used them like lovers once used pigeon carriers, or twenty-first-century people use texting. Our cell phones made for end-of-day and top-of-the-day

Dave Grohl, Spain, 2000. (*top*)
Melissa Auf der Maur, Spain, 2000. (*bottom*)

calls, too, but the faxes became a lifeline of their own. Whenever I woke up or checked into a hotel room, my first question was always, "Do I have any faxes?" Because they were created alone in our hotel rooms, they captured the longing of solitude and the loneliness we were trying to remedy in each other. So much humor, and so much fun, ruled our love. It was genuine solace for the Ice Princess who had formed during those cold, lonely years in Hole.

The creativity our faxes tapped into was hands-on mind-blowing. Dave, with his perfect-square block capital letters, meticulous penmanship, and remarkable drawing skills, made drawings of his hotel rooms with hidden messages inserted within, or a love letter composed of twelve elaborate puzzle pieces that I needed to cut out and put together to read the text. It was yet another testament to the beauty of analog communication.

My messy, inconsistent, large, looped, and flowery writing filled up endless pages with my daily musings and meditations about life on the road without him. I supplemented them with squiggly sketches. In one, I drew masculine and feminine souls hovering above thought bubbles that listed my favorite Dave personality quirks.

In our faxes, we explored comic book–style formats, self-portraits, lists, tour schedules with notes on when we'd see each other next, and inside jokes mapping out our future together. We loved that the method seemed so silly. We were convinced we were the only ones on Planet Earth utilizing it as such. My three-hundred-page collection of Dave's and my faxes still lives intact in my personal archive. I suspect it might be the only one of its kind to archaeologically analyze what love was like for two rock stars on tour in the 1990s.

60 THINGS THAT DAVE LIKES ABOUT MELISSA
(excerpt from a fax from Dave to Melissa, 2001)

1. The way she translates anything into her own weird language
2. The fact that she's from Montreal
3. Her home-made dresses
4. Twin Peaks–Palooza

5. Her taste in music (except Danzig)
6. Morning photo sessions
7. Her choice of lamps
8. The fact that she loves me back
9. Her truthful nature
10. The fact that she hates that I smoke
11. Her influence on me
12. The way she is embarrassed for me
13. The way she is proud of me
14. The Future she has shown me
15. Everything else.

Dave tried to build his Foo Fighters schedule that year around ours, but it wasn't always possible. We had an agreement that whoever was not playing shows would fly over to be on tour with the other. Sometimes that was geographically insane, like the time Dave was at the Big Day Out festival in Australia and I had five days off between the Pumpkins' European tour, just before the US tour began. I flew around the globe, over Asia and Down Under, to be with him for just three days, then around the rest of the globe to get back to California. It reflected our "I'll cross a desert for you" style of devotion. He did it for me, too. It was always worth it.

In the summer of 2000 we ended up at the same festival across Canada, Summersault Festival. It was my second consecutive summer headlining across Canada, and my Canadian ranking of alt-rock queen was on high. The bill this year was Smashing Pumpkins, Our Lady Peace (a popular Canadian band), Foo Fighters, A Perfect Circle, Catherine Wheel, and Sum 41. It worked out beautifully. Having endless freedom, no kids, no pets, and no responsibilities to anything but your band and your true love made for a fun life. It was as if all my dreams, the ones I had never really dared to dream, had really come true. Almost too good to be true. His prolific love faxes wove themselves into my DNA's romantic fabric:

In time, I'm sure we will have claimed every city our own. This world is no longer big enough for a love so grand, it could collapse under the weight of our lofty aspirations. We must set out on an intergalactic exploration to make way for the big-bang sized love we have created.

For a guy who hid behind a common-man jock persona, his romantic poetry flowed explosively . . .

Was it love at first sight? Hmmm . . . Good question. Maybe it was love at first sight once we stopped and took a good look at the people behind the armor, that's when we fell in love. The instant I got a good look at you, the real you, that was it. It was love at first sight.

For two people who had looked into the faces of hundreds of thousands, we felt like authorities on the matter of our love . . .

I feel very fortunate to be one of the few people to have been introduced to your purity. I imagine you digging your little hands into the center of my ribcage, looking me in the eyes with the most unconditional trust, and opening yourself wide for me, like two enormous doors swinging open, and the warmest light exploding from within you, bathing and warming me. In that moment I am introduced to your truth. It's like a blessing, or baptism.

Our mutually prolific handwritten love-letter writing was a private testament for our eyes only, coming through a soon-to-be-dated technology of a facsimile pumping through international phone lines.

<u>You have baptized me with your truth</u>, submerged me in your soul, cleansed me with your purity. In your hands I will sink into this truth and purity, and in your hands I will emerge, new and, without a doubt, yours until the end of time.

—Excerpt from fax from Dave to Melissa, 2000

How could it actually last?

I could not have imagined at that high point that my grand music adventure would end bitterly or that my love with Dave would ever end. Or perhaps I did not look beyond soaring around the globe, faxing the love of my life, and head-banging my heart out to my favorite riffs to take notice of the warning signs.

CHAPTER 37

Trapped in Mythological Webs and Shadows

IN THE FALL OF 1999, DAVE RELEASED HIS THIRD ALBUM WITH FOO Fighters, *There Is Nothing Left to Lose*. The band's namesake debut in 1995, just over a year after Kurt's death, had been the surprise "OMG, the Nirvana drummer can sing!" hit. *Foo Fighters* was followed up two years later with *The Color and the Shape*, which featured radio hit after radio hit. Dave had proved himself as a frontman in his own right. His steadfast commitment and feel-good rock vibe were the antithesis to Kurt's morose anger. *There Is Nothing Left to Lose* would win him his first Grammy in 2001. On his arm as his date, I witnessed what would stabilize his career for the rest of time.

I thought I'd fallen for the nice guy who disdained Los Angeles and the limelight as much as I did. But Nice Guy Dave was not destined for a normal life "back home." As I type, Foo Fighters is one of the biggest commercial rock bands in the world. He eventually found his way back to Los Angeles and the fame game. But that came later, after our story ended.

In the summer and fall of 1999 we were basking in big love and the buzzing success of our simultaneous tours. Being with a joyful person was nice for a change, and we devoured every moment together. Y2K was on the horizon and everyone was abuzz with "end of the world" shit, but we were totally oblivious. We were even daring the world to bring it on, with an invincible "You can't knock us down; we've got all we need and nothing will take this away from us!" attitude. This new chapter promised to be one filled with more music and love for both of us than ever before.

On December 31, 1999, we rang in the new year together in a quaint bed-and-breakfast on Cape Cod, wrapped in each other's arms and staring at the cold sea at midnight, ready for change and whatever the new millennium would bring us.

Between our upcoming dual world tours, we began to make life plans together. The first step was to move me out of my little Laurel Canyon house and back east into his suburban Alexandria, Virginia, home. I was no LA girl, but I was possibly even further from being a suburban girl. With that in mind, we decided to make Virginia our home base and to also get a loft in New York City so I could reconnect with the urban life and culture that resonated with me.

As much as I was no Suburban Girl, Dave was no Big-City Boy. New York was a place he'd never loved or considered living in until he'd met me. Our geographical and cultural differences were real, but did not seem like unresolvable incompatibilities. We told ourselves that opposites attract and love rules all.

As the calendar turned over to start 2000, I couldn't help but contemplate the intricate web of '90s grunge-rock heroes that surrounded me. The rock gods of our time, and in my life, seemed to be part of a mythology that was unfolding in real time, along with huge generational and societal shifts.

Several key events seemed to have spun this web around me. There was Billy and Courtney's former love bond, which had been broken when she fell for Kurt. That was followed by Kurt and Courtney's marriage and child and, shortly thereafter, Kurt's violent death and its impact on Courtney, Dave, and the history of rock. After Kristen's death, Billy returned to find a new bass player for Courtney to get her back to the music, where she belonged. He came back around again to help write the hits on *Celebrity Skin* that put Courtney on the Top 40 charts where she wanted to be. Then he stepped back in again to claim the bass player as his own.

My new musical and romantic connections must've been difficult for Courtney to accept. I was conveniently ignoring her feelings about Billy stealing me back, as well as what she might feel about my relationship with Dave, her utmost rival. She'd been in constant battles with Kurt's Nirvana bandmates about royalties and rights since his death. I somehow justified this by simply evaporating from her life. Luckily, she was still riding high on her Hollywood movie accomplishments, and for the moment, her focus on the music was out of sight and out of mind. Surprisingly, she had very little ill will toward me in private or public. The worst thing she said about me to the press was "Melissa's gone off to be Billy Corgan's purse," which was hilarious and true to her cutting wit.

Beyond these individuals at hand, there was also the omnipresent Nirvana and the Smashing Pumpkins rivalry. They were unwillingly locked together in a generational competition over which band would win for the biggest band of the '90s in the history books. Then add Dave, the drummer of Nirvana, coming into his own power as a Rock God while in love with Billy's newly reclaimed bass player, a.k.a. protégée. Plus, to make matters even stickier, there was my Vermont mini romantic fling with Billy way back in the day that I've never disclosed until now.

It was all just so incestuous.

Astrological constellations are clusters of stars that create subjectively meaningful shapes in the night sky. All over the world, millennia ago, different peoples named these star shapes after mythological characters, animals, and objects—what we refer to today as the twelve signs of the Zodiac. In this cosmic game of connect-the-dots, certain stars are related to each other, creating zones of the sky that mysteriously coincide with the themes and events of life on earth. Each of us is born under the rulership of one of these signs—as I am under Pisces—and its themes become the themes of our lives.

I've noticed a similar phenomenon among people. There seem to be *soul constellations*—people who are connected to one another by some mysterious force, who come together for a time to fulfill a shared purpose. People within these soul constellations both teach and learn from each other—as lovers, as friends, as collaborators, and sometimes even as enemies. Something bigger than personal chemistry binds these clusters of souls together, as though the lessons *will* be learned, the themes *will* be expressed, and the destined work *will* get done . . . by any means necessary.

Remember Rufus? The boy I loved at twelve? He is a gay man who married a man but had a baby with the only woman I ever was sexually attracted to and made out with in her pickup truck. Further mind-boggling? "My mother fucked your father last night" was how Rufus informed me, when we were roommates in LA, that his mother would be the last woman to have sex with my father. Then, to further freaky things out, a few years after my father died, I made out in the rain with the grave digger who had dug my father's grave, a sexy goth punk I reconnected with from my Thunderdome teen days. Some might call these coincidences. I've always believed them to be more.

No matter how messy, or poetic, they were, these soul constellations I was part of had always felt safe. As the landscapes of both music and the world at large changed, I found shelter in Dave and Billy. We had all come into our musical higher powers and callings in the early '90s, when everything in music still felt enchanted, connected, cohesive, and independent. But by the end of the decade, the scene had become splintered, disconnected, and violated by corporations. Most of us felt disenchanted and out of place. Being with Dave and Billy made me feel like I was back where I belonged. I was seduced by their charms, talents, and familiarity.

But the world was changing rapidly. I was changing too, and my nostalgia for the not so distant past would be short-lived. The universe apparently had other plans for me. *I* had other plans for me, too.

Billy's girlfriend at the time was Yelena Yemchuk, photographer extraordinaire, exotic beauty, and glamour queen of the century. She was heavenly, and he seemed to have claimed her as his greatest possession. So would anyone lucky enough to call her theirs.

Born in Ukraine, Yelena had arrived in Brooklyn at age twelve. She grew up to become one of the best photographers I've ever known. She shot everything from documentary street photography in Ukraine to high-fashion spreads that rivaled any of the big-name male fashion photographers of the time. She and Billy had met right around the time I joined Hole, when Virgin Records hired her to photograph the Pumpkins for their third album, *Mellon Collie and the Infinite Sadness*. She became their primary photographer and directed many of their music videos. Eventually, she doubled up as the band's unofficial creative director and Billy's central muse.

I would see her around at rock parties in the '90s. She was impossible to miss. One, because she was gorgeous, and two, because she flaunted a glamour from another era. Whenever I saw her I thought of oil paintings from the turn of the century. She evoked the romance of the poets and painters in Europe that I'd always felt so connected with.

Billy and Yelena were very much in love. Their wide moon faces, of equally high cheekbones and strong jawlines, made them look almost like siblings, even down to their matching sets of front teeth, with their eyeteeth turned out like fangs, which I always admired.

"Stand Inside Your Love," from the Pumpkins' latest album, was my favorite love song that Billy had ever written. There was no hiding that it was about Yelena, because he starred her in the song's music video. I played bass in the video wearing a gigantic gothic Victorian hoop dress. The video was shot in black-and-white, in the style of a silent film, and featured turn-of-the-century illustrations by Aubrey Beardsley, who was known for depicting the grotesque, the decadent, and the erotic. Beardsley was a leading figure in that aesthetic movement and illustrated Oscar Wilde's 1893 one-act play *Salome*. A line from that play was quoted at the top of the video: *"The mystery of love is greater than the mystery of death."*

The video for "Stand Inside Your Love" depicts Yelena's character as a woman enslaved by a hideous, obese king who sits upon his toilet throne, entertained in his court by freaks and perverts. Handcuffed and cloaked in white robes, she is cast as an angelic goddess put on display to dance for him. Billy's character spies on her from behind the castle walls. He falls for her and crashes the party where she is being forced to entertain the king, dropping to his knee to kiss her bare, chained foot. They are both sentenced to death by guillotine and fly up to heaven together.

It is a romantic, artistic ode to the relationship. But the irony was never lost on me. In some ways, Yelena was a bit of a kept woman in her real life, her beautiful talent trapped in the bell jar of Billy's world. She was like a fairy nymph for people to admire, and for him to worship. I'm not claiming that he was sadistic or that she was a victim, but the relationship was not destined to last.

It was intense for me to watch such a talented and fiery woman beholden to a more powerful man, to never have to work to earn her keep or make a name for herself. It went against everything I was taught by my fiercely independent mother and against everything I wanted to be to a man. I could hear one of my mother's mantras: *No man was going to define who I am.*

Polaroid from Smashing Pumpkins photo shoot, 1999. Photo by Anton Corbijn.

Perhaps, subconsciously, Yelena became my warning sign about what I could become. I remembered what Dave had said at the beginning of our relationship, when I'd told him that Billy had invited me to join the band.

"What about us?" he had asked, so innocently.

It was a good question for a man who was coming into his passion and his role as a front man, strutting around arenas like he had never been behind a drum kit. He was way ahead of me in establishing his career, and it seemed to me that any partner he had would have to take a backseat to the level of energy he had for music. For a suburban Mama's Boy—and I say that with all the love in the world, as Dave's deep love and loyalty to his devoted mother was admirable—he'd need someone to become the "Mama."

Whenever he mentioned marriage and children, I would freeze with fright. My thoughts would go blank. *Don't move*, I would think. I knew I wasn't ready for merging with someone else in that way, and didn't know if I ever would be.

Yelena and I became very close the year I was in the Pumpkins. We spoke endlessly about photography, vintage clothes, art history, and the secret language of dreams, but discussing our love relationships was generally off-limits. However, that time spent together included witnessing each other in our relationships with dazzling men. We were both on the precipice of huge turning points, headed for serious heartache and challenges in order to step out of the shadows of these bigger, more successful men. Our dual comings of age forged a lifelong bond. She remains one of my closest girlfriends today.

The Pumpkins' shows were powerful, the schedule continuous, and it was hard not to feel like I was achieving something grand in the band led by the overachieving Billy. However, my commitment to just one year and the one world tour was clear and resolved for me. I'd agreed to come on board knowing my time in the band would have this end date. I could sense the end beginning to press on Billy, though. Even when we were on the high of sold-out shows, he was melancholic. Moody was his natural disposition, but he had not made it easy for himself by announcing this as a "farewell tour," with an imminent breakup and disbanding on the horizon. A farewell tour was a totally insane concept. No one had ever done this before. It was a strange tone for a tour to adopt and an unlikely declaration to promote, although also wise and transcendent in some ways.

After all, the twenty-first century had arrived. The computers had not crashed, despite all the Y2K hype, but something had died with the flick of that calendar page. The world as we knew it, the good olde 1900s, the glamorous century of the Industrial Revolution, two world wars, romantic art movements, and so many radical cultural shifts, was receding into history. So was the dream of our '90s music scene, which by then was pretty much dead. Safe to say we were all in the midst of identity crises.

Billy's steadfast commitment to ending the band when we started the tour seemed to be shifting as the year drew to a close. As a workaholic, he had no idea what to do next.

I don't remember how he approached me about collaborating after the end of the tour. The mention of it was so casual, something about a "new music project in the new year" after the tour ended, something that I might be part of.

I clearly remember my response, though. I reacted the same way I did whenever Dave would mention marriage and children. I would shut down and become invisible. *Don't move*, I would think. It was the opposite of how I rose to respond to demons. I wanted to disappear, which was exactly what I feared these offers would do to me.

My dreams of independence and freedom raged hard in me. The idea of merging with another person terrified me. I was also acutely aware that I had one year left of my Saturn return, the period between ages twenty-seven and thirty, when Saturn brings intense personal challenges. A Saturn return is an initiation of sorts: If you make it through alive, you rise from the ashes a deeper, wiser, more mature person. But many wild cards don't pass the test. Jimi Hendrix, Janis Joplin, Jim Morrison, Kurt Cobain, and Kristen from Hole are all in the "27 Club," dead at twenty-seven.

Saturn had no shortage of tests for me. In just the past two years, my father had died, I left Hole, I joined the Pumpkins, and I fell in love. When I turned twenty-nine in the spring of 2001, I knew I still had one year left to go, and I was on guard. I couldn't break this year. I couldn't fuck up.

Who would ever think that marrying Dave and making music with my musical hero wouldn't be good things? But the fearless, independent woman in me knew if I said yes to either, I would wind up shackled. *This is not progress or success*, I thought. *This would be continuing on, trapped in other people's shit.* That had already been my life's work, starting with my real parents and continuing with my grunge parents, Billy and Courtney. By the age of thirty, I was yearning to be a sovereign, successful, creative, authentic woman.

Despite the temptation of these wonder men, marriage to Dave (subconsciously wishing he could just be my drummer) and collaborating with Billy would have been taking the easy and passive route that had been laid out for me by these dominant males and a continuum of generations of women before me. It would have meant abandoning the process of cycle breaking that my pioneering mother had started for herself, for me, and for the women of the future. For better or worse, I understood that neither of the paths being offered to me would test me to really fucking prove myself. To do that would require me to break away to confront my vulnerabilities and inner depths and to take on a real personal challenge.

So in 2001, I tried.

Dear Billy

October 2000

Dear Billy,
When I met you I was 19 years old, I saw and heard things in you and your music that resonated deeply inside me. It was as if your music symbolized the music that lay dormant in me. In turn, I looked to you for teaching and guidance, and that's what you've given me. In many ways your development as an artist and person who has found his creative voice and vision, has been one of my greatest sources of inspiration to find and develop my own.

This year has been such a wonderful opportunity for me and I am grateful. Although the recording project in the new year would also be a great opportunity, sadly I cannot include myself. It has been almost ten years that we have known each other and since I began my artistic process, for me and I'm sure it won't come as a surprise to you that it is truly time for me to face my creative self.

From what I've heard, there are no plans to extend the tour after South Africa, so I would like to set my departure date for the end of November. However, if there are any shows you would like to book between then and Christmas I will make myself available.

Having fulfilled my commitment to promote and tour the record,

I feel it is time for me to make some big changes in my life.

This has been a difficult decision to make. I have chosen to write to you because I felt more able to express these feelings in writing.

Thank you for your understanding. I hope this decision is not too disappointing to you.

I am excited to be part of the Pumpkins Farewell tour of so many foreign countries.

                    Again, thank you for everything.
                                Love, Melissa

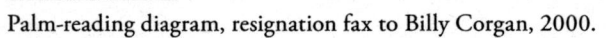
Palm-reading diagram, resignation fax to Billy Corgan, 2000.

. AUF DER MAUR HAND .

diagram #1.

#1. As you can see in my hands destiny line, it resembles a wish bone, and my wish has always been to be a fluid musical maker. The line indicates that the year 2001 ~~is~~ my year to enter the lottery of the musical gifts of the gods

So be it. I must do it!
Farewell and good luck
love always, your BAss can panaur; x Mx

CHAPTER 38

End of an Era

SUMMER 2001

THE MAKESHIFT STUDIO IN THE FAR CORNER OF OUR TRIBECA LOFT WAS NO more sophisticated than what Patty and I had set up in our Silverlake dining room five years earlier. It held my same Tascam 4-Track cassette recorder and, this time, Dave's electronic drums. We set up the studio by the manual freight elevator and the large windows that overlooked Church Street and the Tribeca Grand Hotel. The loft itself was a few blocks from the World Trade Center and located in the "Triangle Below Canal Street," a.k.a. what "TriBeCa" was named for. The once industrial and manufacturing district was at its peak as a hip neighborhood. Our favorite decadent sushi spot, Nobu, was just down the block and frequented by its cofounder Robert DeNiro, who had played a role in raising the profile of this Lower Manhattan neighborhood.

Living with yet another drummer with punk roots and a beloved brand of humor was comforting. In Dave, I'd found a nontortured male version of Patty.

Similar to me with Hole, Dave had come to fame by joining Nirvana for their second breakout album, *Nevermind*. Just as Billy had introduced me to Courtney, Kurt had introduced Patty to Courtney and said she had to be the drummer for Hole's second and breakout album, *Live Through This*. And as legend has it, Patty was almost in Nirvana . . . so the similarities and overlaps running through all of these stories and characters were undeniable.

The connection with Patty, though, cast a morbid shadow on my happy love with Dave. It was a reminder of how I'd lost her, and her tragic turn of events. By this point, she had slipped deep into the heroin streets of downtown LA. She was living under a bridge out of a shopping cart and had essentially disappeared. Not even her family, including her best friend and Irish twin brother, Larry, were in touch with her at that point. Everyone who loved her had said a prayer and hoped she'd come back one day. It was heartbreaking.

This was yet another twist in the "grunge gods and ghosts" myths that wrapped around my heart like electric barbed wire. These two drummers were important to me musically because of our natural fit as a rhythm section. But even more so, they were people I loved dearly, one that I had lost and another I could not imagine losing. They were not rock gods to me. They were humans first, which meant far more.

Meanwhile, Billy wasn't too happy with me, either. After my resignation letter, my last few months in the Pumpkins were chilly between us, though he gifted me a thousand-year-old fertility figure at our final show. It was a beautiful gesture, making my departure bittersweet.

With a new Grammy in hand, Dave had become just famous enough to be recognized at a fancy spot like Nobu Sushi. I could see him light up when the hostess knew who he was, though not in a bad way. He was always gracious, humble, and generous. But the light in his eyes was enough for me to see what this kind of recognition offered to his sense of worth and that he enjoyed the pleasant stroking of his ego. He was not a tortured star—far from it—and his natural inclination to go to this place and receive this attention kind of scared me.

When he was at home, shirtless and in cargo shorts, learning some obscure cover on an acoustic guitar for us to record just for fun, he was my dream partner. The man dreaming up a death-metal supernatural side project called Probot was far more intriguing to me than the one who could crank out pop-rock hits of minimal meaning in his sleep. We were both off tour, which was new to us, and we instinctively gravitated toward creative projects together. I had my favorite Fender Jaguar guitar drop-tuned to D to make power chords as easy as they could be, and my first Fender bass was ready to try out riffs through my favorite home amp, the Fender Blues Deluxe. It had great overdrive, so you could be totally distorted but at a low volume. The reverb and tremolo knobs could make most anything sound pretty cool.

During these empty days, I began to experiment with song ideas of my own. I hadn't done that since the Silverlake demos that I presented to Billy for the Hole album. Our Tribeca recording setup was as casual and innocent as any '90s aspiring nonpro, so it was not at all intimidating. Plus, it had out-of-this-world bonus access to the best drummer on the planet to lay down a drum track for what would become my first real rock song of my own, "Followed the Waves," which would become the first single off my first solo album, *Auf der Maur* (2004).

> *I followed the waves to you, I promised to see it through.*
> *But my heart lies to you. You'll never have me true.*

By now Dave and I were well into our second year together. I started our mornings with the ritual of taking a self-portrait of us in the big bathroom mirror. I wanted to capture this new domestic version of us. He would usually strike a humorous pose, with his toothbrush in hand and a huge toothy smile, or with a toilet plunger slung over his shoulder, acting cool. I would offer my typical esoteric gaze through the looking glass, peering into the future and my next quest. Looking at these photos now, you can see our differences back then so starkly.

Remember that the cultural context of this great love was that the '90s had just ended. For people whose identity and love of life were deeply engaged in that period, it was a huge upheaval. Those of us who came into the prime of our twenties during that time were being asked to grow into real adulthood in our thirties, while the world around us was in such a state of major transition.

American politics were experiencing a huge sea change. What had felt like the golden Clinton Democratic years—when anything was possible—took a nose-dive when Bush "stole the election" and brought back the 1980s old-guard Texan oil-baron conservatives. The socialist Canadian in me was appalled by what so clearly represented more epic corporate greed to come, and this time with big oil, the dirtiest of them all. It seemed like very bad news in the United States from my perspective. I had gone out of my way to submit my absentee ballot in the national election the prior fall, while none of my American-band bandmates or my boyfriend bothered to. The cultural divide between me and my peers began to expand. They seemed to still be taking the heyday of the '90s for granted when life as we knew it was under threat.

Threats of online banking and the internet crashing seemed ludicrous to an analog being like myself who didn't use them, but they were clear precursors of the digital hellscape to come. This rise of technology and big corporations terrified me. We'd already witnessed the objectification of alternative art freaks who'd been turned into products falling off consumer shelves as freely as Coca-Cola. We had lost the counterculture war against the mainstream.

All this was happening in real time and was hard for many to see clearly, but as someone who longed to live in an analog creative community utopia for eternity, I felt it deeply in my bones. I truly feared the world was heading in the wrong direction.

I don't think Dave felt the threat like I did. He had magically created a happy-go-lucky Foo Fighters bridge to carry him out of the '90s and into the 2000s, and his marching orders were clear: Make music, be successful, get married, have kids. Be part of the machine. The tectonic shifts of our time were profound for me, but it was business as usual for him.

"Don't you want to settle down into a cool art scene in DC or Montreal and just, like, be humans?" I would ask him. But his fire and his ambition weren't oriented in that direction.

My inner wayfinder had always been my trusted guide. I couldn't abandon her now, even for true love. Effectively, this inner conflict started making it very hard to be with me. I had become restless, doubtful, and insecure, which tells me now that I knew it wasn't working anymore. And it made Dave feel like, "What can I do to love you better? Why are you so unhappy and freaked out?"

That summer, Dave felt a strong pull back to Virginia and his real basement recording studio there. He was ready to settle in and write his next album. We both knew by this point that I could not join him to live a suburban-housewife life. It was not that I didn't love him. I did, completely. But it had become clear to both of us that I wasn't able to be my full self with him—and likely that was true for him, too. Dave was—is—a very simple person. He prides himself on simplicity. He just wanted to be in love and have a normal life, with a wife waiting for him back home, while also being a gigantic superstar. Eventually, he did find both, but it couldn't happen with me. I wanted a world of two equals going on a huge adventure into the spiritual and the cultural, with everything I needed to fly free and make rock records when I wanted to. I needed to travel the world more. Or maybe I didn't know what I needed to do. But I knew I wasn't going to move to Virginia to be his wife. Our love, as grand as it was, could not fit into our earthly existence.

By the summer of 2001, Dave's needs and my desires had become incompatible. These differences were so painfully clear that we almost didn't have to speak about them. When I heard my friend had a one-bedroom apartment opening up in the illustrious Chelsea Hotel, we made the strategic decision to downgrade from our three-thousand-square-foot loft and to set me up in my poetic artist's dream bohemian apartment while he moved back to Virginia.

The pied-à-terre I found in the Chelsea was a picturesque Victorian jewel box with stained-glass windows, a working fireplace, and french doors that opened to a wrought-iron balcony, overlooking the Chelsea Hotel's iconic neon sign. The ghosts of the great poets, artists, and punks who'd been there during the former century were alive in the hallways and stairwells. Janis Joplin apparently had lived in room 411 long before I did; many icons of the time visited her in that room, Patti Smith, Leonard Cohen, and Kris

Kristofferson among them. I would finally be landing in a place where my soul belonged after a long detour via Hole and Los Angeles.

My mother came to New York to help us pack up for the move. While I was at a doctor's appointment, she and Dave spent a few hours together in the loft. They had always gotten along beautifully. He cried with her that afternoon when he told her his side of our collapsing union. "It's never enough for Melissa," my mother remembers him saying. "She wants so much."

My mother, more than anyone, could understand this. I was her daughter, after all.

"I think it has to do with how I raised her," she told him. "I fought for my independence and wasn't going to let a man define who I was."

Our romance ended where it began, in the Chateau Marmont suite where he had first unlocked the key to me three years earlier. He was in Los Angeles working on his next album; I was the girlfriend, *visiting*. Our split was loving, and heart wrenching. Curled up on the cold tile of the bathroom floor, we cried together.

"I don't think I'm as cool as you think I am," he said. "I don't think I'll ever be able to be the man you want me to be."

I wanted him to be everything, but perhaps I was beginning to fear that he was *not* going to be as *cool* as I wanted him to be—and maybe I didn't want to stick around to find out. In the end, all he could be was who he was. That was all that either of us could be.

Dave and I had been a match made in grunge heaven, the "nice ones" in the legends of Nirvana and Hole. We'd written a sweet story, but our chapter together had come to a close. I made sure of it, despite the burning love I felt for him. I couldn't bear to drag a love this pure onto a tortured and wretched path as an unhappy wife to man who wants, and would have, it all, which I knew would eventually tear us apart. So I decided to end it on a high note, still in love. And, breaking my own heart, I chose to let go.

CHAPTER 39

It's the End of the World as We Know It

SEPTEMBER 11, 2001

"Wake up!"

My next door neighbor Steve Willis was banging on the door of my Chelsea Hotel apartment. "THERE'S AN EMERGENCY! EMERGENCY!"

I opened my eyes. I had a headache from drinking too much sake the night before at a karaoke party I'd hosted. For the past two days I'd been celebrating the opening of my first solo photography exhibit. Surrounded by local New York friends and other dear ones who'd come in from LA, Chicago, and Montreal, I sang "Paranoid" by Black Sabbath with great liberation, having taken the first step into my post-'90s music life. Photography had waited patiently for me to return to it and deserved my attention.

I had put this show together by digging through the boxes and boxes of photos I had obsessively taken over the past seven years, only I did not select a single photo of any bandmate or audience. Not a hint of a musician's mark on the body of work I decided to put forth as my first.

I named the exhibit *Channels*. It was presented at the new Secret Gallery in Red Hook, Brooklyn. I was returning to my roots of independent art spaces in up-and-coming cultural neighborhoods and communities.

The collection featured photos of hotel TV screens I had taken while on tour. They were mounted on glass and set within light boxes. I installed an old TV in the middle of one room, broadcasting a drone score I had made on my 4-Track. It glowed with a sepia-toned, pixelated photograph of a man walking on a tightrope across what looked like the abyss but was really the space between the two Twin Towers of the World Trade Center. I chose it as the leading image from the show because it represented media and precarious behavior. At the time I just liked the ominous image, but now I see it as a self-portrait.

Melissa Auf der Maur, Artist Statement

September 08–November 7, 2001

TV was not my best friend while growing up in Montreal, Canada.

My mother had issues concerning her daughter being bombarded with "Barbie" and "Three's Company." She waited as long as she could to buy our first TV. Of course once we got it, we had no cable and there were strict hours and regulations of when I could watch it at all. There were better things I could be doing with my formative years . . . like discovering a love for photography, music, art and my own inner world.

"Tightrope," from *Channels* exhibit, 2001.

So I never really developed a childhood relationship with TV and throughout college, I didn't even own one.

But then, in 1994, at the age of 22, l abandoned my photo degree to join HOLE, a hard touring American rock band and TV became a close companion overnight. Alone in generic hotel rooms around the world I developed a subtle and intimate relationship with TV.

CHANNELS is a reflection of my journey with television.*

Pairing photos into small groupings to suggest visual and conceptual narratives had always been my way of working with photography. The TV characters that made the cut for my first show were an oddball mash-up of cultural and personal references. One of the installations featured five characters caught midaction, mouths wide open: a TV psychic with fake boobs and a blonde wig; a close-up of Ben Orr from the Cars in his finest 1980s glam look from a live concert; a female scientist in a lab coat from *The Jetsons* cartoon with her arm up explaining a space theory; a naked Parisian pornstar, midecstasy, looking straight at the camera; and the first male rock star to channel goddess and Viking energy all in one, Led Zeppelin's Robert Plant, lit entirely by blue stage lights.

The back room featured the little TV set with the leading image of the tightrope walker flanked by two fridge-size light boxes, one featuring a sunset from high up in an airplane showing the curve of the earth and another of a giant wave in the ocean. This was my own secret reference to my last body of photo work, in my final year at Concordia University, titled "The Sky Is My Ocean."

After the opening that weekend, I hosted my out-of-town friends for a couple of days. On a quiet Monday night, I rented a private karaoke room on Avenue A in the East Village. Laughter is always the best remedy for a girl steeped in deep heartache and taking the first daunting step into her new life of independent art. I was aware that I was now the leader of my own life, for really the first time ever, but I had no idea what I would be doing past that night.

---

* Television is the original personal home screen (wild to think where our relationship to screens ended up now, eh?!).

The dark karaoke room glowed from the big screen that fed us the lyrics and absurd kitschy videos made for the medium. We squeezed into a black U-shaped leather banquette around a table full of beers and sake glasses. It was still legal to smoke inside, and my friends had filled the room with smoke. The haze added to the mood. Eric from Hole was there from LA, as was James from the Pumpkins, and LA-based Paz Lenchantin, a phenomenal female bass player for the band A Perfect Circle. I had bonded heavily with her as the only other woman on the cross-Canada tour the summer before. Also with us were some of my Montreal pals from the early '90s and other rock-and-roll stragglers and fixtures of the East Village scene.

The bar kicked us out at the usual four in the morning. Some of us roamed through the big-city streets till dawn. In the gorgeous autumn air, we did a loop down to the World Trade Center and gazed up at the remarkably strange grid of lights speckled over the one hundred floors. The pair of towers jutting into the infinite night sky were a symbol of the American financial dream. "Fuck money! Fuck money!" we chanted as we wandered around downtown, heading back uptown in a taxi at sunrise.

The banging on my door continued. I slowly rolled out of bed. In the living room I saw Paz on the pullout couch, also waking to the noise.

Steve was in major distress when I opened the door.

"They blew up the towers!" he said.

"What? What towers? Who?"

He brushed past me into the living room. "Turn on the TV. It's on the news."

I dug around for the remote to the all-in-one VHS TV, my first big buy with Hole money back in 1995. Clicking it on, I didn't have to scan for long to land on a disturbing static shot of the World Trade Towers from a distance. They looked just as we'd seen them only a few hours ago, except now one was smoking like a cigarette.

"What the fuck," Paz and I said in unison.

"A plane flew into it." Steve blurted. We stared at the screen. My impulse was to grab my camera *and* video camera to capture the shot on TV.

"Let's go up to the roof," Steve said. From there, twelve stories up, we'd have a direct view twenty-three blocks down the West Side. I was wearing only a tank top and undies, so I threw on a jean skirt and slipped on my royal-blue velvet Chinese slippers with the embroidered dragon on the toes. We were surprised to find the elevator jammed with people when it arrived. The next one, also full. When we finally got up to the roof, many of the hotel residents were up there gawking at the surreal view.

"It must've been an accident," someone said.

"Those poor people on the plane and in the building . . ."

The Tribeca loft I'd shared with Dave and left just two months prior had been only three blocks from the towers. I could only imagine what this day would have been like for me if I'd still been living there.

We stood in silence. I filmed, looking back and forth between my video lens finder and the real thing.

Our shock and confusion were interrupted by a large commotion. "Everybody OFF THE ROOF!!" Stanley Bard, the infamous hotel owner, came charging at us, furious. "This is NOT SAFE!" He waved his hands, shooing us all back toward the rooftop door. "Get back to your rooms!" he ordered. "This is a liability for me!"

Stanley was a frequent source of disdain in our bohemian community. He represented "the Man" to most of the weirdo artists who lived here, who were often behind in their rents and were by all measures "anti"–the Man. On the crowded elevator down we complained about him, a usual activity.

While we were riding down, the unimaginable happened. Back on my couch, we saw both towers now smoking on TV. *What the fuck just happened?* "A second plane has hit Tower 2," the announcer repeated over and over, not able to hide his distress. For any person, or newscaster, the evidence of a calculated attack now seemed clear.

Paz and I sat on the couch, looking to the TV for an explanation that would not come. I sipped my black tea with milk, and she sipped the Yerba Mate she traveled with, reflecting her Argentinian heritage.

"I wonder who's behind this . . . ," Paz said carefully.

"Those who really hate what those towers stand for, I guess," I dared to reason.

Through the french doors that overlooked the Chelsea Hotel neon sign we could see the Empire State Building. We wondered if that would be the next target. The authorities on TV told everyone to stay indoors.

I decided I should call my mother. She was at an artist residency in Banff, Canada, two hours behind me on mountain time. My cell phone was acting up, and after a couple of tries, I got a hold of her with my landline. The receptionist put me through to her hotel room.

It was early morning there. I had woken her up. I broke the news as simply as I could. "Don't worry, Mum, I'm safe," I said. I wasn't quite sure if this was true, but I didn't want her to worry.

"Don't go back up on the roof!" she instructed in a panic.

"I love you," we both said before hanging up.

Soon after, both landline and cell phones would not allow any calls to go through. Too many people were trying to get through to their loved ones and jamming the lines. Disconnected from the outside world, in the midst of an unknown future, we waited.

This just in, a third plane has now hit the western side of the Pentagon in Washington, DC.

The godlike voice of the television announced this new development. The usual buzz of the weekday-morning city streets began to diminish. Silence was taking over the Big Apple, and our hearts. Time came to a stop.

The 110-story towers have collapsed in a massive cloud of dust! came next. The image on the screen practically faded to gray. Within moments the light outside began to shift in scale. The dust was drifting uptown.

A fourth plane has crashed in a field in Pennsylvania, seemingly headed for Washington, DC.

The news was coming at us quickly, in little bits of information that painted a picture of a full-scale attack on this nation. Later we would learn that heroic passengers managed to take down those who hijacked the fourth plane, which likely saved it from crashing into the Capitol Building in Washington, DC. All other flights were grounded.

We kept shelter for the day in another dimension—a bohemian enclave inside a mythic hotel—with the TV as our window to the world. We watched the endless reruns of carnage, planes colliding, specks of people jumping from windows, towers collapsing, and dust clouds billowing. Our world had come to a halt.

What had seemed like hard-won freedom from my mythological Rock Army riddled with drug addiction, and evil corporations who had robbed us of our pure-hearted scene, shrank in importance on this historic morning. So did my heartbreak. In an instant, they'd been replaced by the bigger feeling that I was lucky to be alive.

My world had already been transformed by the power of my own freckled bass-playing hand and my commitment to independence. I had helped break my own heart and detached from those who claimed they desired me most in order to be stronger for it. But the world I'd been living in as recently as last night, a music-hungry fantasy in the land of the free, had just changed in an instant by the hand of an unknown enemy.

With that, the twenty-first century was born.

Just a few months away from turning thirty, having officially graduated from her Saturn return, the woman in me was born alongside this day. She was on a new course now, riding into the unknown.

Self-portrait at Chelsea Hotel, NYC, 2001.

AFTERWORD

Home—Planet Earth—2024

My twelve-year-old daughter, River, and I planted ourselves on the couch, with dinner on our laps, to watch the 2024 Grammy Awards together.

The show's transformation from twenty-five years ago, when Hole was nominated for Best Rock Performance, was a testament to feminine power. We saw Billie Eilish win for her tear-jerking Barbie soundtrack hit. When Taylor Swift broke the record for the most Album of the Year Awards, she brought Lana Del Rey onstage with her to share the glory of it all.

Annie Lennox and Tracy Chapman, s/heroes from the generation before mine, played "Fast Car," the timeless hit, and "Nothing Compares 2 U," a tribute to Sinéad O'Connor (RIP, misunderstood Celtic warrior goddess). Joni Mitchell received a lifetime achievement award.

The only man really featured was Jay-Z, who received the Dr. Dre Global Impact Award. He brought his twelve-year-old daughter up onstage and held her hand while acknowledging the talent and recognition his wife, Beyoncé, deserves.

Every category this year was dominated by women. It was a revelation to see women fully occupying mainstream pop culture, and to share the moment with my daughter.

"I want to release this album so I can be a better mother one day," I'd told Andy Slater, the then president of Capitol Records, when I was looking to get signed and he came to see one of my first solo shows. What I meant was I needed to become a fulfilled, whole person—especially when it came to music, my "calling"—to be worthy of being a mother. I needed to successfully step out from under the shadows of others before I could nurture another human to do the same.

"No one has ever said that to me before," Slater replied. He was more accustomed to artists who wanted to sell records, not be well-rounded people. "And who knew the bass player had something to say?"

That's how we agreed to sign me to the historic label and release *Auf der Maur*, my first solo album, in 2004. I used the Auf der Maur thousand-year-old family crest, a wild horned mountain goat jumping over a stone wall, as my logo. In the liner notes of the album I wrote: *"Dedicated to Lovers of Sound, and all the Ancestors I've never met. I feel you in my blood and soul."*

After my years in the '90s bands you know all about now, I released two solo albums, toured Europe and North America a few times over, and explored my deepest chambers of music and performance. Arriving center stage, and stepping into my own voice for a decade, made up for all my time in the shadows and supporting others. I even fronted my own Black Sabbath cover band, Hand of Doom. Ozzy made a comeback for me, as psychic singing coach.

My follow-up album, *Out of Our Minds*, was a fantasy, multimedia concept project that featured an album, a film, and a related comic book. I toured it to festivals from Sundance to Comic Con, to museums and the usual rock circuit. The fantasy metal scene is where I feel most at home. As I explored my own sounds and songs, I found that my natural frequency was way more tuned into the great metal wizards—from Black Sabbath to Danzig, Kyuss, and Type O Negative—and all the other long-haired men who dared to explore the witch inside as much as I loved exploring the wizard and warrior in me. Other than Billy's more mystical psych-rock vision, most of the '90s were a little too real, and full of pains and politics for me.

My mother's decision to become a single mother was, above all else, a political choice. My birth was a political act, not an act of love. Similarly, my decision to join Hole was a political act. It was to break the norms of women in the rock world. Making my own music was an act of love. But my journey in other people's bands was necessary to deliver me there.

In 2011, when I was about to turn thirty-nine, I very intentionally quit music to become a mother. More than a decade earlier, I'd sworn only to have sexual intercourse with someone who I was fully in love with, who I would consider moving in with, and who maybe, but not certainly, would be worthy of having a baby with. That was the intent the night my daughter was conceived. River's father, Tony Stone, and I, five years into our relationship, "opened the floodgates" and had fully unprotected sex for the first time in the hope of welcoming a child into our world. She came on the first try. I believe it was our intentional love that *willed* a human to join us on this earth.

My final show in my rock band was at HEAVY T.O., a heavy-metal festival in Toronto in the summer of 2011. I was the only woman on the outdoor main stage alongside Mastodon, Rob Zombie, Slayer, Megadeth, Motörhead, and many more heavy-rock heroes. That hot summer day I was six months pregnant and showing. My bass was slung very low. Midset I dedicated the show to "all the women here today, and the women of the future!" and pointed to my belly. I got a good cheer and sent a psychic high five to my daughter inside me.

In October, River Eve Auf der Maur–Stone was born in water at home.

By that time, I had been on and off tour for a total of seventeen years and done five world tours. I'd certainly had my share of the decadent rock-dream life. I felt that motherhood was the only worthy way "out" *and* the only real opportunity for metamorphosis, the ultimate shape-shifting experience. Now, having lived in the same house with my little family for almost as long as I was a nomad on tour, my life story is balanced between two equally beautiful and challenging experiences: the road and the domestic. These spheres are the antithesis of each other, yet I have had both. I am both.

Like my sign of the zodiac: Pisces, *one fish going upstream, the other going down.*

I sit on a wonderful precipice of middle age now, my next big transformation. Since leaving music behind—in addition to the most honorable and timeless role of my life, being a mother—I have devoted the past decade to building a platform for independent and innovative voices in arts and culture. In 2010, Tony and I cofounded Basilica Hudson, a reclaimed 1880s solar-powered industrial factory turned environmental and alternative-arts hub in the Hudson Valley region of upstate New York. This blossoming region is a couple hours north up the Hudson River from New York City and overlooks the stunning Catskill Mountains.

When this Montrealer fell in love with a New Yorker, we found a special place to nest off the usual beaten path, geographically in between our two beloved home cities. We were seduced by a historic town surrounded by nature where we could engage deeply in the place where we live and raise our daughter. I wanted to be off the road to raise a child and was motivated by a deep desire to make a little corner of the universe into something I could believe in. It's been a true learning curve this past decade, being a mother to both a human and an art-factory dream. We host indie music shows, goth dance parties, farm and flea markets, indie-film screenings, art exhibits, and 24-HR DRONE: Experiments in Sound and Music, an immersive experience entirely inspired by my 3D sound dream. Created with our '90s DIY ethos, Tony and I built it hand to mouth and word of mouth.

As for my grunge parents . . . after almost two decades of barely any contact, in 2020 Courtney and I both agreed to play Hole songs for a Planned Parenthood benefit concert in New York. I had never considered a Hole reunion for twenty years but reconsidered when invited to do this. Courtney and I came back together casually and naturally to support women's right to choose—during a dubious federal administration that shockingly was threatening it.

The concert was to be produced by Hal Willner, our beloved *MTV Unplugged* producer. Then the unthinkable happened. Just a week before the concert, the world *really* changed with COVID-19. The concert was canceled, the world stopped, and Hal was taken down with it. He was the first person we knew to die from complications of the virus. He coincidentally died on the anniversary of my father's death, and with him the possibility of playing Hole songs again also seemed to slip through the cracks of time.

Courtney and I have not made music together since 1999, but being in touch again has been healing and fun. In the past few years, she has taken much better care of herself and has a good support team. She ejected herself entirely from the United States and now lives in the United Kingdom. They treat her like rock royalty there, as they should.

Courtney is, in many ways, an incredibly noble creature. Her intelligence and fortitude are always overlooked in the media caricature of her personality. When the world attacked her for being a difficult woman, even when it blamed her for things she did not do and tried to destroy her, she never played the victim. What I most admire about Courtney is that her dignity is so strong, perhaps even keeps her alive. With all the corrosion that happened in her life, both inside and out, she should've been dead dozens of times over. It's really beautiful to have witnessed her survival.

Her relationship with me today says a lot: She has never once tried to tear me down, and she could have after I left Hole. She never spoke poorly about me in public, other than that one time she told an interviewer that I'd gone on to become Billy Corgan's purse. (But that was okay because it was funny and true. I really was more of a bass accessory for the band.) She basically was saying to me, you're gonna be trapped. And she was right—I could've been.

I suspect I may be the only female on the planet who experienced Courtney in this way. Some kind of soul-constellation drama, lovers, or queen rivals in another life long ago? Whatever it is, I'll take it—and I'm excited about blowing people's minds with the moral excellence of Courtney Love.

In other great healing female news, I reconnected with Patty about a decade after she disappeared. She got clean, married, and had a daughter, Beatrice, who has grown up alongside River as a "cousin" in recognition of the "Rhythm-Section Sisters" that Patty and I will forever be.

Who knew that Hole, the band, would become my gateway to the underworld to find my larger purpose? That Hole would be my portal to becoming whole.

As for my "spiritual fucking cowboy," he more or less disappeared from my story but graciously made a little cameo during the writing sessions of my second solo album. Capitol Records wanted me to write songs with Billy (still looking for a man to save the day!). He accepted, and I went to Chicago for a weekend. In Electrical Audio, Steve Albini's studio, we shared a special moment recording a couple of songs we composed together in a stream-of-consciousness style. They sounded more like him than me, but I am grateful we tried, and one day maybe those songs will see the light of day. Most important, they live in our shared tale of two music-devoted humans who orbited around each other during the most thrilling decade of our lives.

My grunge parents were seminal figures in this little lifetime of mine. I love them, always.

My kettle whistles as I fill a tea ball with my favorite loose-leaf tea: *"Wild Woman": An organic high-grown Ceylon tea with wild blueberries, black currants, hibiscus, elderberries and corn flower petals. One heavenly sip of this organic tea is enough to make you go wild!*

My writing ritual is to steep a cup of this tea in my special oversize navy-blue ceramic mug. Shaped like a German beer goblet, it has a handwritten inscription: *"Auf der Maur—McGee—1958–59."*

My father's high school graduation mug is a prized possession, one of the few things from Nick's kitchen that I never packed after he died, just took with me. It has been my tea mug wherever I have lived for the past twenty-five years. Every writing day, I carry the steaming cup over to my slender rose-gold laptop and wait for Bubbles, my cat, to join me on my lap.

My parents were both masters of the word. I grew up listening to them talk eloquently and wildly, with the ability to sway anyone listening their way. I also watched them both work passionately at their typewriters at their desks and, in my father's case, also at the bar. The rhythmic clicking noises were seductive and comforting. As a child I didn't know these noises represented my parents' strong opinions and their nuanced understandings of politics, culture, and humanity. That clicking reflected the hard-earned identities and sculpted characters they both put so much care into creating and sharing with the world.

What they deemed worthy of their time and intellect was golden to them. I was taught, through their work with the word, to treasure that kind of inner gold. The best thing my parents did for me was never tell me who I am or what I should do with my life. They led by example and let me find my own way. The atheist saint and the single mother did a great job.

I love music.

I love my parents.

By now, you know I fucking do.

I also believe in something I have found no better word for than "magic."

My missionary-style zeal for magical realms is informed by my metaphysical dreams (plus a little Grandma Auf der Maur!). They are the spine of my life story. This is ridiculous, of course. But it is also true. And all these highly driven weirdos in my life—like Billy, Courtney, and Dave—were likely attracted to that side of me and wanted to interact with it, to collaborate with it, and even to possess it.

I know my metaphysical vision also can freak people out and puts people off. Many academic and intellectual types, including my own atheist parents, don't relate to it. Some think of it as self-aggrandizing, delusional escapism. Nevertheless, it has been the truth of my life. *These things happened to me.* They are inextricable parts of my story.

Today, in the real world, I hear the echoes of the sci-fi, postapocalyptic environments I saw in the hauntings of my teen dreams: Drought, dust, uninhabitable landscapes brought on by climate catastrophe. Alien machines that rewire brains to create a culture of mimicry that kills individuality and obliterates one-of-a-kind analog creations. Not to mention the rise of fascism, war, and political degradation of our once shiny democracies of the New World.

The demons of my dreams are real, and we are in danger of being overpowered by them.

How did they rise so high? Perhaps they were called by an "emptiness" that came with our disconnection from Mother Nature. The demons warned me: *Your Emptiness Is Calling Me.*

Our music scene was raped by the big-money fame factory. This was followed by the fear mongering of Y2K, the tragedy of 9/11, a creepy new digital reality, and even more dystopian rising concerns of planetary degradation.

This '90s analog dreamer wishes to tell you she is deeply concerned about our human connection to our planet and our future. Our world is on fire, and our minds are melting. Our addictions to fossil fuels and digital reality are intertwined with the demonic capitalistic industries I've whispered about in this book. Both addictions are the biggest threats to our physical and emotional existence. And I know a thing or two about addicts.

Even so, I have faith in the beauty humans can spin, with song, words, art, and love. That part seems quite simple to me now. Find your voice. Stay true to your own course, always with deep regard for the collective. Start a band, choose an instrument, take photos, write in your diary, listen to your dreams. Believe in something beyond yourself, do what you love, and take care of your friends and soulmates, even if you drive each other a little nuts.

Our future and future generations depend on our ability to look inside ourselves with love, in order to love others. Dig deep, dig in. For one and all.

If You're Listening, Come in
If There's a Fire, a Need, a Desire
Are You Willing and Able to Set the Stakes Higher?
This Time, Pass it On, Come Sit by My Fire

Travel Out of Our Minds, and Into Our Hearts, Standing by.
Our Hearts Have Been Standing by, For So Long

Yes, You're Listening
You're a Dreamer so Come In,
Cause We Have the Tiny Scales to Swim

Where Has the Love Gone in Our Behavior?
Where Has the Light Gone in Those Faces?

Travel Out of Our Minds, and Into Our Hearts, Standing by.
Our Hearts Have Been Standing by, For So Long

—"Out of Our Minds," by Melissa Auf der Maur (2010)

PHOTO CREDITS

Page ii	© Melissa Auf der Maur	Page 157	© Melissa Auf der Maur
Page 14	© Melissa Auf der Maur	Page 157	© Melissa Auf der Maur
Pages 16–17	© Melissa Auf der Maur	Page 161	© Melissa Auf der Maur
Page 19	© Archives Guy Borremans	Page 164	© Melissa Auf der Maur
Page 22	Family archive	Page 170	© Mark Seliger
Page 22	Family archive	Page 178	© Melissa Auf der Maur
Page 24	© Archives Guy Borremans	Page 178	© Melissa Auf der Maur
Page 29	Family archive	Page 187	© Melissa Auf der Maur
Page 32	Family archive	Page 207	© Melissa Auf der Maur
Page 37	Family archive	Page 211	© Melissa Auf der Maur
Page 39	Family archive	Page 212	© Melissa Auf der Maur
Page 41	© Melissa Auf der Maur	Page 213	© David Markey
Page 43	Family archive	Page 220	© Melissa Auf der Maur
Page 53	Family archive	Page 221	© Melissa Auf der Maur
Page 58	Family archive	Page 228	© Melissa Auf der Maur
Page 64	Family archive	Page 230	© Melissa Auf der Maur
Page 78	© Melissa Auf der Maur	Page 244	© Melissa Auf der Maur
Page 78	© Melissa Auf der Maur	Page 252	© Melissa Auf der Maur
Pages 84–85	© Melissa Auf der Maur	Page 276	© Melissa Auf der Maur
Page 89	© Melissa Auf der Maur	Page 285	© Melissa Auf der Maur
Page 102	© Melissa Auf der Maur	Page 310	Material republished with the express permission of *Montreal Gazette*, a division of Postmedia Network, Inc.
Page 103	© Melissa Auf der Maur		
Page 106	MAdM Archives		
Page 126	MAdM Archives	Page 313	Family archive
Page 137	© Melissa Auf der Maur	Pages 322–323	© Melissa Auf der Maur
Page 138	© Melissa Auf der Maur	Page 325	© Melissa Auf der Maur
Page 143	© Michael Lavine	Page 334	© Guzman

Page 338	MAdM Archives	Page 369	© Melissa Auf der Maur
Page 344	© Matthew Rolston	Page 380	© Anton Corbijn
Page 351	© Guitar World, Future Publishing	Page 387	MAdM Archives
		Page 396	© Melissa Auf der Maur
Page 357	© Ross Halfin	Page 402	© Melissa Auf der Maur
Page 369	© Melissa Auf der Maur	Page 411	© Melissa Auf der Maur

ACKNOWLEDGMENTS

Thank you, Merci...
MUSIC. You called, I answered.

The drive and desire to write my first book came from my unstoppable blazing muse: MUSIC.

I worship all who share this music journey with me: the band members (those I played with and those who came before and after me) in Tinker, Hole, and The Smashing Pumpkins, you are my destined music families in this lifetime.

My many Fender bass guitars and Ampeg amps, I could not follow the waves without you.

Grateful for every person who wrote songs with me, shared recording studio time, festival stages and tours with me. How lucky are we?

Beyond music, into my "real life", I want to thank:

My trailblazing mother and father, who showed me how to live by finding my own voice.

I love you. Embodied within me, I hear you loud and clear.

Without my city of Montreal, I would not be who I am. You remain the best city in the world to this well-travelled city lover.

My brilliant and loving husband, Tony Stone, you are the earth beneath my feet that makes me human. Our beloved daughter, River, you are my greatest teacher of the future. Babushka Bubbles and Bella Chai, our Siberian Feline Angels (and RIP Isis: Queen of the Feline Throne of My Heart), you are the connectors between my spirit and the cat creature realm that I dance between.

Big love to my bonus-track human family! My sweet baby (half) brother, Yves de Fontenay, and your gorgeous family of women—Irena, Sasha, and Alice (Oui! Je t'adore!)—you all grow towards the sun and show me how.

Hope Edelman, your twelve-month virtual handholding while we dove deep into my life as a writer was pure reflective, therapeutic bliss. Your care for the story of all women is selfless and true. You helped me grieve and let go, just where I needed to. Eternally grateful.

Wow, to the dedicated women in my MAdM Productions studio. Two women safeguarded me, my stories, my diaries, my faxes, and my photography archive for this ever-expanding multimedia memoir project. Photographer/Archivist Katherine Driscoll, and Photographer/Storyteller Jessica Chappe, thank you both for your *true* passion for photography, meticulous scanning, and categorizing work that has supported this telling of the story of a Gen X photo/music/magic lover. I trusted you with my most intimate parts, and you held them with the greatest care. (Thank you, sweet Sonia Ruscoe, for kicking off the project with your sweetest heart!)

Big thanks to my smarty-pants literary agents, David Kuhn and Nate Muscato, and the Aevitas Creative Management team (and Parker Posey for connecting us!), you made this happen.

Da Capo Publishing team found me thanks to Ben Schafer, a guardian of counterculture, bohemian punk stories. Thank you for helping us get our stories out there. It is essential to sustain these movements to make the future cool. And to the fabulous audiobook team, Ethan Donaldson, Sara Gordon, and Tom Mis: dogs, cats, magic, and existential thoughts forever.

My "Memoir in a Year" writers' cohort, with Chris Daley at the helm, to hold our feet to the fire to deliver our weekly "word counts!" Thank you for the companionship during the early days of this writing process. The nurturing feedback and care for one another sent me on my way, to here. May our varied personal journeys be shared with others, in the elegant power of the word.

Mike Renaud, your generosity and grace with the visual language makes you the best Creative "Spirit" Director a girl can hope for.

Thank you to John Pelosi: As an art lawyer, you supported both my Basilica Hudson art factory dream and this dream to tell my '90s story in words and photography. Legal protector of my soul.

Brian McCarter, your keen cosmic eye and mythological lens helped me keep balance in the potentially alienating but essential threads of this story: the "woo woo witchy poo" thread of my life and the reframing of the "demon warrior goddess". Soul Spine activated!

To all my friends, from Montreal, Hudson, LA, NYC, UK, and around the globe. You have listened to my dreamy, trippy, hippy, '90s ramblings for so long. To share this with you means I can sit back in quiet for a while and let the next chapter of life be born, with you at my side. Friends are everything. Walk. Talk. Tea. Museums. Travel. Infinity loop!

And, second to none, YOU, the music fan.

WE MAKE BIG MAGIC TOGETHER.

The *exchange* holds THE KEY.

In my heart are forever thoughts of healing: to all the victims and survivors of 9/11.

Finally, as always, my eternal pledge to you, the MUSIC: I need, I want, I will. Pass It On.

xMAdMx